Administration and Supervision of Music

SECOND EDITION

ROBERT L. COWDEN

ROBERT H. KLOTMAN

SCHIRMER BOOKS
A Division of Macmillan, Inc.
New York

Collier Macmillan Canada
Toronto

Maxwell Macmillan International
NEW YORK OXFORD SINGAPORE SYDNEY

For:

Corinne
Chris and Cheryl, Craig, Clark and Linda
Mallory, Ryan, Andrew, Justin (our future)

R. L. C.

For:

Paul Max, Alexander Isadore, and Samuel
Eric (our future)

R. H. K.

"The School Administrator's Dilemma" by Wallace B. Appelson is reprinted by permission of Phi Delta Kappa from Catcher in the Wrong, edited by Billy L. Turney. Published by F. E. Peacock Publishers, Inc., 1968.

Schirmer Books
A Division of Macmillan, Inc.
866 Third Avenue, New York, N.Y. 10022

Collier Macmillan Canada, Inc.
1200 Eglinton Avenue East, Suite 200
Don Mills, Ontario M3C 3N1

Library of Congress Catalog Card Number: 91-6885

Printed in the United States of America

printing number
1 2 3 4 5 6 7 8 9 10

Library of Congress Cataloging-in-Publication Data

Cowden, Robert L.
   Administration and supervision of music / Robert L. Cowden, Robert H. Klotman.—2nd ed.
     p. cm.
   Includes index.
   ISBN 0-02-871211-0
   1. School music supervision. 2. Music—Instruction and study—United States. I. Klotman, Robert H. II. Title.
MT3.U5C78 1991
780'.71—dc20   91-6885
                                            CIP
                                            MN

CONTENTS

12 SPECIAL TOPICS 215

Accreditation · Certification · Negotiation · Religious Music and the Schools · Constituent Groups · Sexual Harassment · Stress and Burnout

13 ISSUES AND CHALLENGES OF ADMINISTRATION 247

Issues in Music Education · Future Operational Patterns for Music Administration

PREFACE

Administration and Supervision of Music is a complete revision of the text *The School Music Administrator and Supervisor: Catalysts for Change*. Not only has this edition been brought up to date, but several new, significant topics have been added. In addition, the book has been expanded to include administrative concerns and procedures in higher education, so that it now covers the entire spectrum of an administrator's responsibilities both in the schools and in the colleges and universities.

This book is addressed to women and men alike. Initially, we wrote *he/she* and *himself/herself* before we reluctantly accepted the criticism that this procedure was both cumbersome and unreadable. Until a nongenderized pronoun comes into common usage we are using the generic *he* and *him* to include *all* people. More and more women are becoming active in all aspects of music administration, and we hope that the information contained within this book will encourage women to compete in this field.

> It must be remembered that there is nothing more difficult to plan, more doubtful of success, nor more difficult to manage than the creation of a new system. For the initiator has the enmity of all who would profit by the preservation of the old institutions and merely lukewarm defenders in those who would gain by by the new ones.
>
> Machiavelli, *The Prince*

INTRODUCTION

*E*ducation is a cooperative enterprise of the schools and the public, but it is axiomatic that when conflicts of interest arise, the ultimate decision rests with the public. In a democratic society, voters elect their representatives to boards of education, which are obligated to carry out the mandates of the public. The people's responsibility is to strive to obtain the best possible education for their children by supporting positive board of education action. If such action is not forthcoming, then the people should elect members to the board who are sympathetic to their views. This is the democratic process.

At the collegiate level, members of governing boards in private institutions are appointed in most cases by a board of trustees. They may represent certain prescribed constituencies, such as ministers in the case of church-related colleges. Such boards usually contain alumni as well, and some of those seats may be filled by election. Board members in public institutions are often appointed by the governor of the state, and here, too, certain constituencies, including geographical regions, may seek representation. It is common now for public institutions to have one student member on the board, often appointed by the governor to a two-year term.

The board of education and the board of trustees then select the proper administrators to implement the programs desired by the community and university, respectively. As the community and its aspirations change, so must the purposes and objectives for education be altered within the community. It is in this sense that the enlightened administrator becomes a catalyst for change.

A recognized principle of change is that "all change is not necessarily progress, but one cannot have progress without change." The administrator's function is to determine whether or not the proposed change is desirable—that is, whether or not it is in the best interest of the child and the community or whether it will impede learning rather than contribute to it. Education has long been accused of changing for the sake of change to create the impression of being "up to date." Too often educators have grasped at straws, eagerly adopting any gimmick or panacea, and some may have even listened to soothsayers. They have been accused, with some justification, of being reactors rather than visionaries and planners. This can no longer be tolerated. "Accountability" has become a part of educators' com-

1

mon parlance. Administrators must plan in such a way that their decisions and results may be judged and upheld in the court of public opinion. Change and progress are not accidental. They are the result of careful planning and systematic procedures designed to achieve recognized desirable goals.

It is essential that one understand this concept of administration if one is to assume the role of leadership that accompanies the responsibilities for administering and supervising the school or university music program. Music administrators must realize that their actions and judgments will affect the musical education of an entire unit, and therefore, they cannot ignore the need for appropriate decision making.

There are definite skills and techniques that are essential for a competent administrator. It is no longer sufficient that the individual be a faithful teacher who has put in the required years and is now ready for a special reward in terms of an administrative appointment. Competent administrative leadership is crucial to the survival of music education in our schools and universities; to develop individuals who are prepared to accept this responsibility requires special study and examination.

It is the purpose of this text to define those skills and techniques which are necessary for the development of a successful music administrator. Actually, one cannot isolate the responsibilities of music supervision and administration. They encompass every facet of the music program—testing, classroom teaching in all areas, human and community relations, psychology, budget and finance, and curriculum planning and evaluation for the improvement of instruction. They are complex assignments of overlapping, interwoven responsibilities that may require of the individual a quick value judgment when guidelines may or may not exist or infinite patience when time can be an asset rather than a detriment. A music administrator must keep abreast of curricular developments and innovations not only in the field of music but also in related areas if he is to be the leader of his department. He must be sensitive to current issues confronting the school and interpret the music program in light of these issues as demands arise. Moreover, the successful music administrator must be an effective, articulate, and persuasive spokesperson for the music unit, able to interpret goals, objectives, and dreams to the outside world as well as to the individual to whom he reports.

But even this aspect of the job is only a segment of the administrative responsibilities. Administrators must be able to exercise sound, economical judgment in preparing a budget or recommending expenditure of funds. They must work within the context of the school personnel practices when making or recommending assignments. Administrators and supervisors must be active in recruiting competent teachers. And if this is not sufficiently complicated, music supervisors and administrators must be expert in scheduling classes to protect the time allotments available for music in the schools and in dealing with personality conflicts between teachers, between teachers and administrators, and between administrators themselves. They are frequently called upon to interpret the music program in light of school policies and to maintain appropriate school-community relations. They are the educational leaders in music; they are the instructional leaders in music education; they must provide educational leadership in the curricular field of music.

One might construe this text as being only urban-oriented because of the authors' backgrounds. That is not the case. The basic principles apply whether in a rural area, a small community, or an urban area, whether in a large university or small college. Only the degree to which the ideas presented are utilized and the manner in which they are applied will vary. Small communities as well as large cities need guides and procedures for developing programs. Suburban areas are ultimately affected by city concerns, for though every situation is unique, each is part of the mosaic we euphemistically call national patterns.

Personnel problems exist in the rural areas as well as in big cities, in universities as well as colleges, and administrators need guiding principles to assist them in dealing with such concerns. In the current climate, ethnic studies, for example, have acquired as great a relevance in suburban areas as in the inner city, if not greater.

"Relevance" implies widespread applicability as it relates to the social-political realities of our times, and music education is not exempt from the responsibility of keeping music in the mainstream of contemporary life. This does not, however, imply merely doing certain music just to be "with it." Musical activities are governed by a school's philosophy, and its overall philosophical goal can be couched in terms of specific objectives. If the purpose of music education in a school or theory class is to teach students how to analyze, organize, and perform music, then activities will be directed toward analyzing, organizing, and performing. And if the music that is used has widespread applicability to the social-political realities, then and only then does it become relevant. Unless the music lends itself to the basic goals, it is irrelevant. The responsibility for directing, guiding, and educating the staff so that music education will be in the forefront of current thought rests with the administrators and in the music department.

As we become more computerized and better organized through systematic planning, it will be necessary to consolidate and combine efforts so that smaller communities or schools will offer the same opportunities provided by larger or more wealthy units. The challenge under these conditions is to retain the identity and unique qualities of the smaller units. It is only by knowing both the pitfalls and the advantages of modern planning that we can administrate for desirable change and progress, as well as efficiency, without undermining the unique characteristics of the school and community.

It is interesting to note that this concept of combining effort and exchanging ideas exists even among colleges and universities. For example, a midwestern collegiate conference has formed a consortium of its institutions to create an academic organization called the Committee on Institutional Cooperation. The music education faculties of each of these institutions meet annually, rotating among the campuses, to discuss pertinent topics of current concern and discuss ways to improve communication and cooperation among them.

In a society that places a high premium on function and materialistic gain, it might be tempting to imitate successful management procedures of business. In some school systems it has even been suggested that educators be replaced by successful business executives. This could well be a dangerous direction for education, particularly education in the arts and humanities. Such ideas often occur in transitional periods, but they do little to answer the needs of educating children. A better solution is better educators—that is, educators who understand what is needed, how to plan to accomplish their desired goals, and how to implement such programs. The organizational techniques of business and government can provide some answers, but not panaceas. In the final analysis, administrative judgment must prevail, and this is dependent on how one anticipates its effect on learning.

1

The Process and Purpose of Administration and Supervision

ACHER—COMMITTED TO GROWTH OF STUDENTS
—COMMITTED TO TEACHERS
DMINISTRATOR—COMMITTED TO GROWTH OF

*A*ll processes in administration and supervision, including decision making, are guided by an individual's basic philosophy. It is a philosophy that should have evolved out of many and varied experiences and be in keeping with the social and educational philosophy of the times. Inherent in this governing philosophy should be a dedication and commitment to progress and growth for students and teachers involved in today's music education. It must be survived the test of practice and time, and withstand examination in the arena of current public debate. To be functional, such a philosophy must be sufficiently flexible to adjust to changing times and maturing opinions. Just as times and situations change, certain characteristics of one's philosophical position will mature and adjust to these changes.

A philosophy for an administrator or supervisor is not acquired solely through academic investigation. It must be tempered in the crucible of time and developed through a series of classroom experiences as well as administrative opportunities. It evolves not in a sterile laboratory but in actual situations, thriving on mistakes as well as successes. In short, no matter how well one understands the process of administration and supervision or how much one reads the available material on the subject, one does not become an instructional leader in music—for that is the role of the music administrator—until one actually participates in the administrative process, whether in the classroom or behind a desk. In short, the process entails growing on the job. One does not "arrive" with the administrative or supervisory appointment. Rather, one merely passes into another phase of one's education.

5

Administering, directing, or supervising a music program is in a sense a clinical type of operation that will vary with each situation and each individual. There are those who may insist that every administrative decision can be reduced to some scientific principle. "If one can argue that science gives birth to application, so also can one argue that just as often it is art, practice, and technology which give birth to science."[1] Ideally, the decision-making role in administration should balance the application of scientific principles with human, artistic concerns.

As a physician diagnoses his patient's ailments, so must the music administrator diagnose and prescribe corrective measures for his music program, including preventive action that will keep his healthy, successful program from succumbing to inertia and complacency. In addition, the chief administrator in music and his supervisor or staff who implement the corrective measures must be able to communicate with those above and below the line and staff relationships, to plan programs, and to exercise foresight. They guide and direct the music program or department as its instructional leaders. Their central function is to coordinate the efforts of everyone involved.

Music administration and supervision is the art of dealing with people, both inside and outside the educational structure. Comparisons of administrators in education with those in industry are as useless as the proverbial comparison of apples with oranges. Education is not a product that can be counted or measured empirically. Music administrators and teachers are dealing with people and aesthetic values, and people need time to grow and mature. They present variables that cannot always be predicted. Behaviors can be identified and measured, but aesthetic quality and aesthetic judgment cannot. Music teachers should be able to account for behavioral learning, but not lose sight of ideals that are inherent in the art and cannot be measured immediately. There are aspects of music management—budget planning, scheduling, analyzing enrollments, and implementation of government projects, among others—that may utilize management techniques and systems planning. A sensitive administrator, however, will distinguish between those areas that rely on management techniques and those which do not.

[handwritten in left margin: NOT THE CURRENT FAD]

■

SCIENTIFIC APPROACH TO DECISION MAKING

Historically, one can trace the introduction of scientific management into educational philosophy to the turn of the twentieth century, when business and industry emerged as the most influential and prestigious forces in our society. In addition, with the rapid growth of urban areas that resulted from mass immigration from Western Europe, efficient tactics and procedures had to be developed to accommodate the rapid expansion of school systems, and the success of business and industry in their manipulation of human resources seemed to present a logical exemplar for educators.

In 1910, Frederick Taylor introduced a system of "scientific management" to the business world that resulted in a new executive concept for school administrators. It led to a "cult of efficiency," which emphasized scientific business skills in the operation of a school in a business-oriented society. This type of thought dominated educational administrative thinking until 1929, when the public became disenchanted with business and industrial practices as a result of the economic collapse of the nation.

During the period that followed, there occurred a revival of the concept that the administrator's major concerns were education and instruction rather than business. Daniel Griffiths suggests that this may have been a result of a reawakening of America's social conscience by the Great Depression.[2] It certainly must have influenced a concomitant trend—the utilization of human dynamics in school administration and school management.

In the 1950s, the human relations element continued to dominate administrative thought, but attempts were being made to develop a "scientific basis for school administration, under which theory served as a guide to administration action."[3] However, this still presented certain dilemmas. Theory varied considerably between individuals and communities, and so many human variables were constantly injected that it was almost impossible to formulate a consistent, definitive position in respect to any existing theory.

If properly understood and properly utilized, a systems approach for solving some problems can be implemented, but these problems must be tightly structured. Because of the nature of music and music teachers, this can present almost insurmountable obstacles and perhaps even an undesirable approach to problem solving. The nature of the art of music and music instruction is filled with variables designed to enhance the art form. Under certain conditions and in certain areas of music education, such as those dealing with the affective domain, a systems approach would be a futile and wasteful effort. However, a systems analysis works well with studies in the cognitive and psychomotor domains.

A competent music administrator will utilize systems planning where it is functional and desirable. There are areas where it can be useful and areas where it does not apply (see pages 14, 133, and 134). Since successful systems planning is dependent on careful structure, a consistent approach or methodology needs to be devised to bring structure to units that might be otherwise poorly structured. As guidelines for structuring such conditions, Optner suggests the following seven steps:[4]

1. The problem process must be flow-charted, showing at least the principal decision-making points.
2. Details of the principal decision process must be described.
3. The principal alternatives and how they were generated must be demonstrable.
4. The assumptions pertinent to each alternative must be clearly identified.
5. The criteria by which each alternative will be judged must be fully stated.
6. Detailed presentation of data, data relationships, and the procedural steps by which such data were evaluated must be a part of any solution.
7. The major alternative solutions and details to explain why other solutions were eliminated must be shown.

For example, if a concerted effort is being made to improve music instruction for the purpose of improving reading skill in an elementary school through a new approach, a systems concept might be instituted thus, following the steps outlined above:

1. See flow chart in Figure 1–1.
2. The asterisks mark principal decision points and would require detailed description and specification.
3. Should the new approach not achieve the desired results, then the department might consider utilizing a different approach, such as the Kodaly, Manhattanville, Orff, or other book series or a creative writing approach.
4. At this point, the architects of the system flow chart would require detailed information as to why the various alternatives are possible. This includes observable advantages and disadvantages.
5. Criteria should be specific and determined by those individuals responsible. For example, does the alternative achieve the goal of improving reading skill without destroying enjoyment and interest in music? Does it expand the repertory to include music from all periods as well as from a variety of cultures?

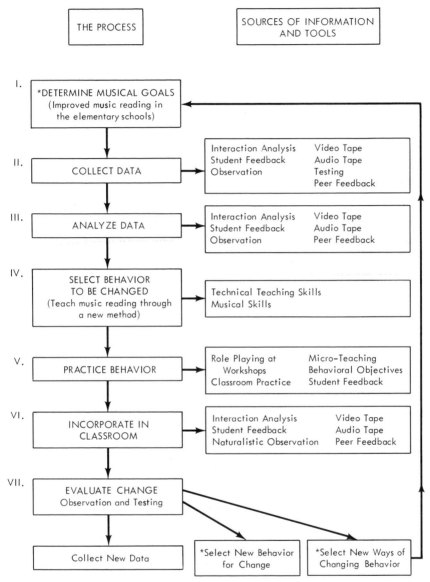

FIGURE 1–1

6. The sixth step would involve all of the items under the heading of "Sources of Information and Tools."

7. The last item in the system analysis would be in the form of a summary and report as to why one approach to teaching music reading was selected over another, noting such things as the advantages and disadvantages of a new approach as opposed to a strict traditional method. It is actually a review and evaluation of the entire "system," organized for the objective of improved reading skill in the elementary school.

A word of caution: readers should remember that under no circumstances should basic philosophical thinking be altered to adjust to systems analysis. Philosophical and musical positions dictate the direction of music and musical education. The basic philosophy governs the nature of the system structure. Systems analysis and operations research are merely tools to expedite planning and decision making. At no time should they be used to impede opportunities for better education for students. Systems approaches are not panaceas!

■

THE HUMAN APPROACH TO DECISION MAKING

One of the difficulties in administration and supervision is to develop the ability to perceive oneself as others do. Perception is a form of behavior, and if the administrator or supervisor cannot see himself as others do, then he may in turn misperceive a situation that requires decisions. So often individuals in roles of leadership are called upon to make quick decisions with little opportunity for lengthy research and investigation. They must then rely on their empirical observations and a prevailing philosophy to dictate a position. No one wants to make an incorrect decision or be accused of poor judgment. Logic may seem to be the proper process for such decisions, but unfortunately things are not always logical as *we* perceive them. Because of the many variables that exist in an administrative decision, directors and supervisors of programs in music education need to develop antennae that will assist them in recognizing these situations.

Many administrators, to avoid making an error, will avoid a decision. This, in a sense, is tantamount to a negative decision and represents a type of action. Deferment of action may be desirable under certain circumstances, but it must be based on careful thought and judgment. It is in essence a form of decision. There are, however, times when action is absolutely necessary and a measure of administrative risk is involved. A competent music administrator will assume this risk and make a necessary decision based on the facts that are available, including his understanding of the existing variables.

If persons read this book expecting solutions, they will be disappointed. There are no absolute solutions for all problems. No one can be a successful administrator by merely reading a book, any more than one can play the violin by reading a text on how to play. One can only measure administrative result in relation to the time and context. In a sense, each one's success will be measured by his ability to function in difficult circumstances. As Robert H. Roy said, "most decisions are easy and most results not critical. But, infrequent as they may be, there *are* difficult decisions to be made and critical results to evaluate, and it is here that the administrator and his supervisors stand or fall."[5]

Thus, administration and supervision entail acquiring basic knowledge and skills involving music and musical education, developing a guiding philosophy to provide direction for the individual, possessing the necessary ability to deal with people in a positive sense, knowing the technical information available to assist in arriving at decisions, and constantly testing and evaluating all of these areas in the clinic of the classroom and the total school musical environment.

The ideal music administrator is one who views himself not merely as a "manager" but as one who is involved in *creative decision making*. He should envision himself as one whose major function is to alter the course and direction of future music programs. His decision will be based on scientific, humanistic, and artistic experiences of the past as well as those being developed for the future.

THE FUNCTION OF MUSIC ADMINISTRATION

The singular purpose of music administration and supervision is to provide musical and educational leadership. This aim should govern virtually every action taken by the individuals involved. Indeed, one cannot separate the terms *music* and *education* as though they were two clearly independent functions. All teachers of music, whether in a concert, a studio, a rehearsal, or a classroom, are responsible in varying degrees for both functions as they affect their students. The music administrator and his staff are concerned about the dual concept "music education" as it affects the total school and university population. The terms are interdependent and interrelated. In this sense, decisions referred to as "solely educational" will have a corollary or related effect on music, and vice versa. Therefore, decisions should be made, and courses of action pursued, in light of this dual concern, and the administrators will have to assume responsibility for the weight or emphasis given at a particular time to a specific choice.

The university music leader is concerned equally with all facets of the school or department's programs—musicology, theory, performance, music education—as they contribute to the development of an educated musician. To isolate any of the pertinent aspects would fragment the student's education. Incidentally, it was precisely this concern that led to the creation of the Comprehensive Musicianship

Project, sponsored by the Music Educators National Conference and the Ford Foundation in the 1960s.

The term *leadership* conveys different meanings to different people and is affected by different circumstances. The dictionary defines the word *lead* as "to guide by example; induce to a course of action, persuasion or thought; direct by influence." *Leadership* is defined as "the ability to lead." Underlying these definitions is the idea of movement. Thus, *leadership* in this context means providing the necessary action or catalyst to move individuals or a group in the direction of problem solving and achieving mutually acceptable goals. To accomplish this action, the concepts listed below need to be considered.

1. *Change Occurs Through Changing the Behavior of People*. Changes manifest themselves in a variety of ways. It may be in the actual conduct of a teacher's daily instruction, changing their values, perceptions, understandings, or even skills. By altering one of more of these factors, the music administrator is effecting change. It may occur in the behavior of an outstanding teacher with years of service or with a neophyte struggling to succeed. An example of this kind of change occurred in Detroit through the use of a Music Educators National Conference (MENC)–Ford Foundation composer-in-residence. A teacher in an "advantaged" suburban area of the city had rejected a composition by the composer as being too difficult for his students. A teacher in an inner-city school who was close to retirement was then approached and offered the music with the challenge that it was described as being too difficult for the advantaged school. This teacher was selected because she was an outstanding musician who had always done excellent work but had been quite conservative and traditional in her programming. She accepted the challenge and gave a beautiful performance of the composer's music. She later confessed privately that she had agreed to do the composition because she felt so inadequate when dealing with contemporary music and did not wish to admit to this weakness. She also felt that working with the composer would be of a tremendous value for her students and that she did not want her "inability" to deprive them of this opportunity. The significance of this incident was that in the few years that remained prior to her retirement, the teacher who performed the work included a contemporary piece on each of her remaining concerts—a significant change in her behavior. Similar examples have occurred in other communities where Contemporary Music Project (CMP) composers were placed.

2. *Leadership Is Not Always Observed or Measured by Overt Behavior or Manner*. It is far more important that leadership be measured by the quality of ideas rather than the quantity of programs. As much leadership may emanate from behind a desk as from a speaker's platform or a podium. An administrator's decisions carried out successfully by others—who receive appropriate credit—is evidence of good leadership. After all, one of the major functions of administration is the coordination of the ideas and efforts of members of the staff toward the achievement of their goals.

3. *Leadership Is Dependent Upon Value Judgment in Establishing Priorities.* It involves decisions that affect programming, organizing, and shifting responsibilities. One could devote one's entire time to "housekeeping" chores without being confronted with any decision making that would effect change in the music program. (That is about as effective as the steward rearranging the deck chairs on the sinking Titanic.) A good music administrator must learn to choose what needs to be set aside as well as what should be pursued. These decisions will be based on how the music administrator envisions his role as the music leader in the community or university.

4. *The Music Administrator Should Serve As a Catalyst to Stimulate Rather Than Inhibit the Activities of All of Those Who Are a Part of the Music Scene.* In this sense, leadership provides the necessary interaction to promote change. Within departments there are too many rules that prohibit action rather than encourage initiative. Often teachers hesitate to suggest imaginative innovations for fear of ridicule or disapproval from superiors. It is better to be critical of things not attempted than to be overly concerned about unsuccessful experiments.

5. *Change Does Not Occur Unless There Is a Disturbance or Imbalance Within the Group.* Complacency is not conducive to change. Leadership requires that the music administrator or his assistants shift the balance in such a way that a weakness in the program becomes a matter of concern or a source of disturbance to those involved. Those affected may then interact to restore the balance within the group and remove the cause of irritation.

For example, string programs have generally suffered in most communities. Where an active, interested school administrator has expressed a concern and a desire to ameliorate this situation, positive action has been taken. In most of these cases, strings were able to survive and even stronger programs were developed. In some instances, it might be the personality of the teacher that is the catalyst, but someone has to express concern and provoke the necessary imbalance in the existing structure if the program is to improve.

6. *Music Leaders Should Evaluate Their Own Effectiveness.* This must be done in terms of how well they have achieved the established goals of the community, school, and staff while maintaining rapport and group support in relation to item 5. It is even conceivable that periodically the department might distribute to its staff a questionnaire that would enable teachers to react without recrimination to current practices and services emanating from the central music office or the school's. Unless there are avenues of interaction, the music administration is not always aware of the true impact of its programs in the classroom.

In any music department, it is difficult for the level of performance to rise higher than the capacity of the individual in that department who is carrying the greatest authority, prestige, and influence. Competent individuals are seemingly unable to function at their best when, over long periods of time, they are frustrated and held down by weak leadership. It is for this reason that competent leadership is so crucial to the success of a music department.

■

THE NATURE OF MUSIC ADMINISTRATION

The nature and function of music administration and supervision will vary according to the size of the community and its goals and aspirations. It will also vary according to the place assigned to it by the current educational leadership. None of these items remains fixed. The times and a changing society will alter them. Their position will be adjusted periodically according to the effectiveness of the music program.

If one has a president, a superintendent, or a chief administrator who feels that the entire focus of a particular program needs to be "basic skills," then to maintain an acceptable music program, the aims and objectives established for music will emphasize basic-skill learning, expressed in behavioral terms. In one junior high school, electronic pianos were installed in a general music class to improve reading skills in music because the administration had made a commitment to raise the general reading level of its student body under a government-funded program. Coordination of the eye and ear with tactile response contributes to better reading habits. By emphasizing this aspect of the use of the electronic piano, a valuable musical instrument was made available to those students. There evolved from this class numerous creative projects and musical learning experiments that went far beyond the basic reading emphasized in the proposal.

Most communities, both large and small, are quite heterogeneous but have pockets of homogeneity. A large heterogeneous community may thus be described as the outer city, and a homogeneous enclave as the inner city. In rural areas there will be consolidated school districts and county systems. The function of the music program will differ even within these communities. At the university level, its function will differ according to its perceived mission. This does not imply that one program is better than another because its function under certain circumstances may be different. In a school system the music administration must respect and consider differences, whether they be ethnic, racial, or socioeconomic. It must maintain a sufficiently flexible structure that will permit the music program in all parts of the community to grow and flourish under these diverse conditions rather than inhibit one area by imposing the attitudes of another upon them, unless they be beneficial to that area.

An inner-city area populated by blacks or Latinos may be more preoccupied with the "black image" or the "Latino image" in music than a predominantly white segment of the community. This need should be supported and given the strongest possible assistance. Although the degree of emphasis may differ, it does not exclude the predominantly white area's responsibility to educate itself regarding the contribution made by blacks and Latinos to the total music scene. Here one must make a judgment as to the degree of involvement. In Appalachia there exists a rich folk culture that should be explored in a similar manner. Virtually every section of our country and every segment of our community could be given as a similar example. Our universities should offer courses that accommodate these concerns.

There is also a direct relationship between the effectiveness of the music program in the classroom and its relevance to the music that the students hear outside the school environment, whether rock, soul, electronic, aleatoric, jazz, or any other style. Sensitive music administrators must help teachers devise ways and programs for relating this music to the classroom experience if the schools are ultimately to achieve the stated aim—to include the 80 percent of the student body that rejects "music education" in today's schools. Too few higher-education offerings provide for this concern.

In their positions of leadership, the administrators and directors must implement and facilitate the work carried on by the entire school program—the activities that contribute to the actual learning that occurs in the classroom. They must provide the necessary articulation between levels of instruction, across disciplines, between community and staff, and between staff and school administration. (When a social studies department in one community prepared a brochure commemorating Martin Luther King Day, the music department provided a section in the publication devoted to significant music in this man's life.) In many school systems, the related-arts and humanities programs were instituted because of impetus created by music departments.

The school music administrator and his supervisors represent music education as it is envisioned by the school administration, the professional staff, and the community; that is, they are employed or promoted on the basis of how they appear to these people and they are responsible to them. The music administrator becomes a unifying force for school music in his school system. Through proper processes, he gives the music program the unity of purpose that is essential for growth and development within the schools.

To improve the instructional program, music administrators will conduct or assist supervisors in organizing in-service programs, meetings, clinics, and workshops. Their major effort will be directed toward developing a better climate for music learning.

They will help formulate and set up procedures to review general policies and procedures relating to the music department and the total staff and community. Working closely with the personnel department, the school music directors and their supervisors will assist in staffing the schools with competent personnel, who will in turn carry out the objectives of the school music program in the classroom.

Do only what only you can do.

◼ DELEGATING AUTHORITY

Too often music administrators find it convenient to devote much of their time of fulfilling perfunctory, routine duties. As indicated earlier, these matters may be handled by a competent individual who has had some experience in the mechanics of office and music department management. The chief music administrator must do much more. He must assume the responsibility for developing leadership and introducing innovations within the department. To do this, he must indulge in creative, visionary thinking and be able to delegate to others responsibilities commensurate with their abilities and available time. Much of the process of administration is based on the premise of delegated authority and responsibility. Assignments should not be confined to routine clerical tasks, but should offer opportunities to delve into creative, expressive activities as well. This is one of the best means for developing leadership within a department.

Music leaders need to devote most of their energies, efforts, and time to working in the field or, in the case of higher education, in the classroom. They should work directly with teachers and students to facilitate learning and improve instruction. However, to be truly effective, they must also learn to delegate responsibility and authority in certain areas of planning instruction. When teachers are permitted to make decisions or share with administrators in planning and organizing activities, they, too, grow and develop leadership capabilities.

To be effective, delegated responsibility must be clearly defined and be accompanied with the necessary authority and support to carry out the assigned tasks. When the authority is granted, however, the music administrator must not be punitive in reprisal for error. If this occurs, it will inhibit future decision making. When an error in judgment occurs, correction should be treated as a matter of education rather than something requiring penalty. So often administrators are reluctant to delegate authority for fear that it will undermine their own position or reflect incompetency. This is an immature posture and reflects certain basic insecurities. The moment more than one person is involved in an activity, it is imperative that the others know their duties and responsibilities. Administrators must make it clear to supervisors and administrative staff what is expected of them and how they have been empowered with decision making. They, in turn, must delegate similar responsibilities to their teachers. Some of these questions may be answered by previous behavior or custom. On the other hand, it may be necessary for the music administrator to clearly delineate these responsibilities. In any case, it should be primarily based on departmental needs and potential for growth and development. Delegation of authority and work not only releases valuable energy within the department but also raises the esteem of those in responsible positions in the eyes of their colleagues and staff.

On the other hand, insufficient delegation retards growth within the music department. By retaining all power and responsibility in his hands, the administrator will cause the supervisors and members of the administrative staff to feel neglected. No individual, regardless of his position, should strive to make the music department completely dependent upon him.

To assign tasks without providing the necessary authority is to remove the force that makes it possible to fulfill the responsibility. This is a serious error most often typical of administrators in high positions of authority who are fearful of diluting their own power. On occasion, no suitable person is available to assume a particular task. In such an instance, it is incumbent on the individual in charge to develop the personnel necessary to implement such a responsibility.

NOTES

1. Robert H. Roy, *The Administrative Process* (Baltimore: Johns Hopkins Press, 1965), p. 2.
2. Raymond E. Callahan, *The Education and the Cult of Efficiency: A Study of the Social Forces That Have Shaped the Administration of the Public Schools* (Chicago: University of Chicago Press, 1962), p. 2.
3. H. W. Handy and K. J. Hussain, *Network Analysis for Educational Management* (Englewood Cliffs, N.J.: Prentice-Hall, 1969), p. 2.
4. Stanley Optner, *Systems Analysis for Business and Industrial Problem Solving* (Englewood Cliffs, NJ: Prentice-Hall, 1965), p. 21.
5. Roy, p. 2

SUPPLEMENTARY READINGS

Abeles, Harold F.; Hoffer, Charles R.; and Klotman, Robert H. *Foundations of Music Education.* New York: Schirmer Books, 1984, pp. 81–97.
Dressel, Paul Leroy. *Administrative Leadership.* San Francisco: Jossey-Bass, 1981.
Eble, Kenneth E. *The Art of Administration.* San Francisco: Jossey-Bass, 1979.
House, Robert. *Administration in Music Education.* Englewood Cliffs, N.J.: Prentice-Hall, 1973.
Mannis, Daniel B. "What Kind of Music Educator Are You?" *Music Educators Journal* 57, no. 7 (March 1971), p. 32.
Walker, Donald E. *The Effective Administrator.* San Francisco: Jossey-Bass, 1979.

STUDY QUESTIONS

1. What is the guiding principle for music administrators in the decision-making process? How does one arrive at it?
2. What is a "scientific" approach to decision making? How would you describe and structure such an approach?
3. How would you proceed to select a musical goal, develop a flow chart, and proceed through a set of logical steps to arrive at a decision?
4. How would you define and describe the "human" approach to decision making?
5. What is the singular function of music administration? Explain its meaning to you.
6. What are the characteristics in a situation that identify change?
7. What are the implications of, and parameters for, delegating authority?

2

Organizational Structure

The music administrator may hold a variety of titles, but regardless of the official one given to that individual by a school system, if he is held responsible for the final decision from the music unit, then he is its chief administrator. Titles are mainly for identification purposes and will vary according to community size, institutional character, and the salary schedule, which is constructed on work loads. In some instances, the official title will reflect the emphasis and significance that a particular community or institution may hold for its music program.

Director of Music

In large school systems or even small communities where the music program is held in high regad, the title *director of music* is often utilized. It conveys the image of full responsibility for the school music program. There may be supervisors on the staff, depending upon the size and scope of the music program. However, whether it be a large staff or a single individual, the director is responsible for directing curriculum planning and all tasks expected of the titular head of the school's music program. (See Appendix C.)

Supervisor of Music

This title implies direct contact with teachers and the class-room. In many cases, it is directed to a special curricular area or a particular level of instruction—vocal supervisor, elementary string

19

supervisor, or the like. In such cases, there is usually a director to coordinate the activities of the supervisors, and the role of the supervisor is of a different nature. However, there are many communities that use the title *supervisor of music* to identify their chief administrator in music. Here he is considered the *director*. (See Appendix C.)

Coordinator of Music

This individual may have the responsibilities of a supervisor or a director but, as a coordinator, may lack the authority for implementing his decisions. Under these conditions, his role is more that of a resource person or merely an adviser. He assists in coordinating music activities throughout the school system as well as coordinating music with other areas of instruction.

Consultant

This individual is similar to a coordinator of music in that he has little authority and functions primarily as an adviser. This individual's expertise is brought to bear when specific services are requested. He may prepare directives or bulletins, but lacks the authority to enforce what is recommended.

Department Chair or Supervisory Teacher

Within a building, it is sometimes necessary to coordinate and administer the music responsibilities of the staff members. Where this occurs, a department head or senior teacher may be designated as the individual responsible for administering the music curriculum within the specific building. He may be an expert teacher with the personal qualifications necessary for administrative leadership, and in a small school system he may be the sole spokesperson or administrator for music education in that community.

PERSONAL CHARACTERISTICS

In our current atmosphere, it is essential that school music administrators take a look at themselves as human beings. Since they are responsible figures representing the board of education's public image in music, they must be concerned about personal traits and attitudes. If they are to be effective in changing curricula and improving instruction, they must be able to work with people. In fact, their effectiveness is directly related to their ability to communicate with staff, administration, and the public. They must be as effective in human relations as they are in music. No longer can music educators dismiss as inconsequential, incompetence and ignorance in other, pertinent fields. By the same token, they cannot appropriately make decisions affecting music if they are not musical persons—that is, people who think as musicians.

Enthusiasm for the task and its inherent responsibilities is of utmost importance if administrators and supervisors are to provide the leadership necessary for success. This is a contagious trait that can infect an entire staff. Other essential elements for effective music administration are sincerity and integrity. The nature of the job requires that the individuals in charge be dependable and responsible. Staff and public must have confidence in their judgment and reliability. In addition, they must possess the energy, vitality, and stamina necessary to pursue their objectives and overcome obstacles that normally exist in all climates. They should be able to remain calm under pressure and recognize the impersonal nature of attacks that may be leveled at schools during periods of stress.

Music administrators should be friendly and enjoy working with people—all people. There is no place for prejudice or discriminatory practices in a school or university program. As a matter of attitude, music administrators should convey a feeling of accessibility for the benefit of the community, school, teachers, and students by maintaining an open-door policy.

Music administrators need to possess a measure of empathy sufficient to enable them to see beyond the superficial emotional responses that cause so many personal and personnel problems. They should never be in competition with their staff members and should be more than willing to share the limelight with them whenever possible. Too many deans, directors, and supervisors feel that unless they appear on every program, their image will suffer. There are appropriate times to do this, but if the opportunity is better suited for someone else, then the music administrator should be wise enough to step aside and permit the appropriate person or situation to take precedence.

No one administrator can possess all of the qualifications and all of the skills identified in a text. Administrators are human beings with human frailties. It is the purpose of this portion of the book merely to identify some of these skills, in the hope that the conscientious individual will constantly strive to improve himself.

As musicians, music administrators should have exhibited a degree of competency in a single area of instruction or on an instrument. As individuals who are responsible for general planning and for interpreting the total music education program to professional educators as well as the general public, they should be articulate and skilled as public speakers. They should be informed about current educational practices and techniques.

They need to be well organized and able to organize the work of others. They should exhibit those qualities which command respect; equally important is their respect for the dignity inherent in all people—other administrators, students, teachers, parents, and so on. One cannot command respect by virtue of a title or through the authority vested in a position. It is a quality that is earned through proper processes and through individual behavior. Enlightened administrators in today's schools and universities must possess greater executive skills in coordination, delegation, planning, and communication. They must possess the essential knowledge of the administrative process.

COMMUNITIES AND ADMINISTRATION IN SCHOOLS

The role of the music administrator will vary with the community the scope and size of his music staff, and the nature of the school music program (self-contained or departmentalized). It would be unusual for any two situations to be alike. No formula or panacea can be offered to apply to every situation. Potential music administrators must be flexible and be able to adapt according to the community and the school situation.

All communities have aspirations for their schools, and each envisions a particular music program for its school population. This is actually the point of departure. This is where the work of the enlightened music administrator begins. It is not his responsibility to reject these aspirations but to accept them and, through educative processes, effect desirable change. This introduces one of the major dichotomies in education. It is an acknowledged principle that no program remains stationary. The status quo is impossible and undesirable, and yet, one builds on it. If community objectives for music are undesirable in the eyes of competent leaders, then they must educate for change, so that ultimately the community rejects undesirable goals and selects aims more appropriate for improved education.

Music administrators must therefore continually evaluate objectives and quality in a program to determine whether the school music program is actually fulfilling the needs of the students. They must constantly strive to develop programs that will bring greater literacy and understanding of all music as a communicating art form; they must facilitate the exposure to music necessary to guide students to the enjoyment of, and love for, the aesthetics of music. But above all, the music administrator must be devoted to music as an art form and devoted to teaching as a profession.

TRADITIONAL PATTERNS OF ORGANIZATIONAL STRUCTURE AND BEHAVIORS

Line and Staff

In the United States the basic structure of school operation is fairly uniform throughout all communities. This may seem a surprising statement, since there seem to be so many variants. However, one should not confuse structure with specific instances of delegating responsibility or vesting authority in different offices. Variations in the size of the school system and the attitudes of its administrators do not alter the major premise of this structure.

"Line" personnel are those individuals who have the responsibility for decision making. They have the authority and the obligation to see that the objectives of the organization are implemented. Their names or offices appear on the vertical line.

"Staff" personnel are responsible for advising and keeping line personnel informed as to what progress is being made in achieving the organization's goals. In addition, staff personnel carry out assigned tasks under an overall line director, and their names or offices appear on the horizontal line.

The structure is based on the concept that *the local community is responsible for the education of its inhabitants.* There are a series of checks and balances to see that this is properly done. To educate its young, the citizenry elects a board of education, which may bear other titles in other communities but still has the responsibility for carrying out the education of the children according to the ideals and mandates of that community. The board in turn selects a superintendent, who, as a professional educator, is responsible for carrying out and enforcing the board's objectives and programs. He also serves as an adviser to the board and assumes the role of educational leader of the community.

The entire structure functions as a series of line and staff relationships designed to expedite learning and implement instruction in the classroom in accordance with the superintendent's and the board's mandates. The larger and more complex the system, the greater the number of individuals involved in these line and staff relationships and responsibilities. Inflexible adherence to this structure may in turn contribute to a more bureaucratic type of operation, which can on occasion inhibit instruction and learning.

It is important that a creative, sensitive music administrator understand this structure so that he does not allow it to frustrate his efforts and those of the teachers. Instead, the music administrator should work within the structure to revise and change it when possible so that it does not impede education and learning. The line and staff relationships are arteries of communication, and administrators must be careful to see that these arteries do not harden or become inflexible. They will recognize it as a complex social system that is to be analyzed and studied in order to understand the behaviors that occur.

This does not imply that protocol is not observed or that it is ignored. It *must* be observed. What is implied is that a successful music administrator must assess the nature of the structure and determine its strengths and weaknesses. There are advantages and disadvantages to the line-and-staff organization. Such an organization indicates where responsibility and authority lie. It shows at which level one is responsible for consultant status and to whom, and at which point the administrator has the authority for decision making. Needless to say, these decisions are always subject to review by the line and staff above.

It is generally accepted in principle that staff members should possess expertise in special areas to assist and advise those in the line organization. A staff member's assignment is generally based on his expertise. Such staff members are the instructional leaders. Whereas individuals in the line structure are empowered with varying degrees of decision making, they are dependent on staff individuals to assist in these decisions and to supply them with appropriate know-how and information.

On paper, the line-and-staff type of organization appears to be rather rigid and fairly set in its structure. One must remember that within each of its components there are subsystems of human beings and that when dealing with this structure, one is involved not only with the behavior of groups but with the behavior of individuals. With the stress on rapid change and technological advancement, it is of utmost importance that an environment be created within the system that will enable the participants to grow according to their own unique capabilities and capacities and to prevent their feeling like pawns or numbers on a computer card.

Unless this opportunity for growth exists within the organization or music department, the organization itself cannot grow and deal effectively with the unpredictable, changing environment outside it—that is, the community. It is equally important that optimum cooperative relationships be developed between line and staff as well as between the various subgroups that form within the individual departments. If a department of music or a total organization is to be effective, it is essential that competition between groups be converted to cooperation and collaboration. "Unfortunately, instead of seeing universities as pluralistic democracies, administrators frequently turn to other models in the society to make conscious or unconscious comparisons. Using these models, administrators regard universities variously as being similar to business organizations, to industrial enterprises, to the military, to churches, or even to families. In all cases, a hierarchical structure is implied. But in the real world, universities do not operate much like these other organizations. They operate like pluralistic democracies."[1]

On occasion change may be initiated by revising the line and staff relationships under the euphemism "reorganization." However, merely rearranging the boxes is meaningless unless responsibilities and roles are actually altered. Reorganization should mean utilizing an individual's competencies to better advantage or even reeducating him for another task for which he may have a better potential for success.

Beyond line and staff relationships, Robert Roy identifies a third organizational component, "the functional executive."[2] This individual is similar to a staff member in that he possesses special expertise but also functions as a line individual in his particular domain; for example, an assistant superintendent in charge of curriculum presides over all of the various subject areas, which in turn function in a staff relationship with him.

Most competent educators are sensitive to the needs of their school system. They will assist, when properly approached, in bending the structure where obstacles impede instruction and progress. For this reason, music administrators must be aware of the nature of the organization structure and its function. Like all elements in education, this method of operation must be constantly evaluated and subject to reorganization wherever it is in the interest of better education.

Today strict line-and-staff organization is being abandoned. Means are being devised to create much more participation by those outside of the line-and-staff structure. Programs of activity are being organized around those directly concerned with the activity. These include parents, pupils, and community and civic agencies. Figures 2–1 and 2–2 represent the traditional table of organization. To further illustrate the hierarchy, the figures break down the significant offices that affect music education.

In smaller communities, responsibilities will be combined and placed under the aegis of a single office. There may be fewer individ-

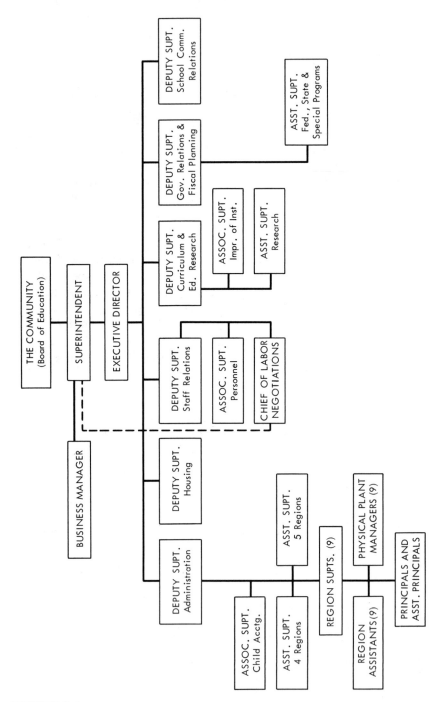

FIGURE 2–1

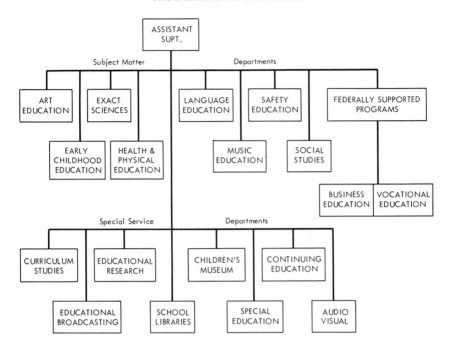

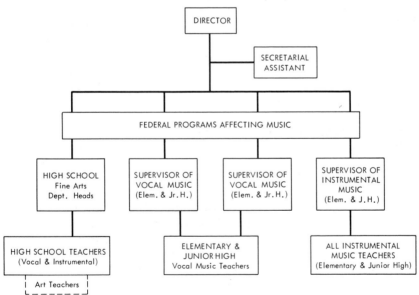

THE DEPARTMENT OF MUSIC EDUCATION

FIGURE 2–2

uals involved, thus reducing the line-and-staff operation. However, someone must assume or be assigned the authority for each of the areas designated on the charts. They may be combined into departments or assigned to other areas of the operation, but the need for assuming responsibility for these duties exists in every school system. Figure 2–3 represents a typical small community, where the superintendent might even serve as a principal or be responsible for innumerable tasks that would be assigned to another individual in a large system.

In a school of music or even a department of music, one can find any number of functioning committees depending on the philosophy or attitude of the chief music administrator. For example, at Indiana University in addition to the administrative committee and the School of Music Council there are twenty-eight different appointed committees: Graduate Curriculum Committee, Ensemble Policy Committee, Undergraduate Curriculum Committee, Instrumental/Choral Operational Committee, Opera/Ballet Operational Committee, Chamber Music Committee, Equipment Committee, Distinguished Ranks Committee, Music Library Advisory Committee, Lecture Committee, Casting Committee, Artist Diploma Advisory Committee, Promotion and Tenure Committee, Scholarship Committee, Music Resources Committee, Academic Computing Committee, Advisory Committee to the Affirmative Action Office of the School of Music, Performer's Certificate Hearing Committee, Teaching Awards Committee, Technology Programs Advisory Committee, Recording Policy Committee, Musical Attractions/Special Committee, Administrative Computing Committee, Research Topic Proposal Committee, Public Broadcasting Committee, Academic Fairness Committee, Undergraduate Honors Committee, Doctoral Styles Committee.

Identifying the Responsibilities of the Chief Music Administrator

The specific duties that a music administrator may assume will vary according to community and the significance it attaches to the music program. However, if music administrators are to assume a position of leadership and be effective in bringing about necessary changes to improve instruction, they will wish to assume responsibility for as many items listed as possible. Their effectiveness may then be determined by the manner in which they arrive at their decisions as well as the degree of progress that they are able to attain in these areas:

1. Providing leadership and advice to the school system or university regarding the organization and content of the course offerings in music.

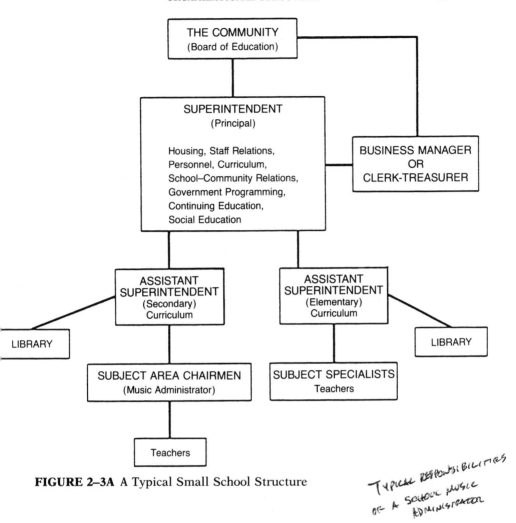

FIGURE 2–3A A Typical Small School Structure

Typical responsibilities of a school music administrator

2. Developing and coordinating a program of instruction designed to carry out the aims and objectives of the music curriculum.
3. Advising and assisting in the selection and placement of teachers of music.
4. Providing leadership in organizing and carrying out in-service training programs for the professional staff.
5. Recommending an appropriate budget for the total music program—equipment, supplies, instruments, books, audiovisual materials, music, maintenance, and the like.
6. Establishing the necessary liaison between the schools, professional organizations, and cultural agencies in the community.
7. Maintaining proper evaluating procedures, with the aim of improving instruction and refining the school music program.

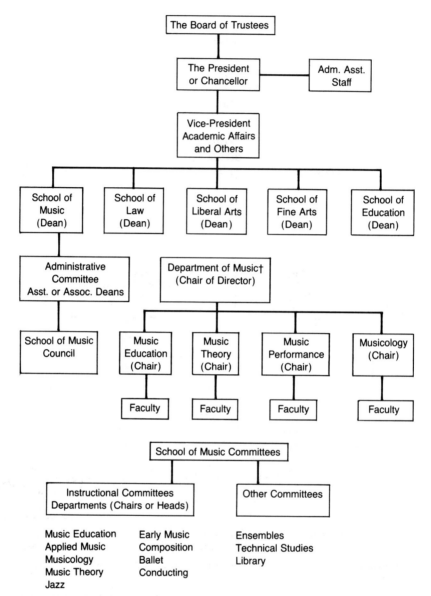

FIGURE 2–3B A College or University Structure*

*This structure varies with all colleges and universities and merely serves as an example of the nature of the structure.

†Where music is taught in institutions of higher education that do not have schools of music, the music instruction usually resides in a department that is found either in a liberal arts or fine arts unit. In many institutions music education is found in the School of Education.

8. Serving as a clearinghouse for concert dates, arrange schedule for in-school and out-of-school programs, community engagements, and the like.
9. Assisting in planning for new buildings and future programs.
10. Organizing citywide or countywide programs and festivals.
11. Producing media programs for television and radio.

The manner in which a music administrator pursues these responsibilities may have considerable bearing on how successful he is in accomplishing his goals. Success cannot be measured by how fast reforms are instituted, but rather by how long they remain in practice. Thus, if changes are to have a significant effect in school music programs, the process is as important as the idea itself.

The Responsibilities of a Dean or Director in a University

The primary responsibility of any chief executive in music is to enhance the quality of instruction in his department or school. This may be achieved in several basic areas:

1. Making faculty appointments and overseeing search, screening and recruiting procedures to find the best available candidates for faculty.
2. Providing appropriate facilities and equipment to implement instruction.
3. Providing the leadership necessary to ensure the development of an outstanding library.
4. Supervising curriculum development for the benefit of students in all areas of music instruction and performance.
5. Conducting an active student recruitment program to ensure a balanced enrollment.
6. Raising resources (e.g., funds, equipment) so that programs can function at an excellent level.
7. Evaluating faculty fairly both to improve instruction and to reward quality.
8. Making provision for faculty development opportunities so that persons can grow and improve as professionals.

The dean or director should strive to provide the best possible environment for the faculty so that he can bring out the best in each individual. To do this, the music executive must recognize that the individual needs of faculty will be different (e.g., size of studio).

Identifying the Responsibilities of the School Music Supervisor

As curriculum specialists, supervisors usually work in direct contact with teachers and students. The effectiveness of supervisors, like that of directors, is determined by their ability to work with people and instill confidence in their ability to assist. Although they function in a staff relationship with the director, they assume a line position with respect to the teachers under their guidance and service.

Supervisors have the following responsibilities:

1. To assist the director in his role as an instructional leader by serving as a consultant to him and providing the necessary advice and guidance in their specific area of competence.
2. To provide leadership for teachers in curricular matters.
3. To implement and improve instruction in the classroom.
4. To assume responsibility for coordinating specific areas of instruction, such as elementary instrumental music or general music in the middle/junior high school.
5. To assume leadership roles in developing guides for instruction and special programs under their jurisdiction.
6. To assume specific responsibilities identified by the director.
7. To assist in developing and maintaining an educational philosophy based on sound principles of involving all segments of the community—teachers, pupils, parents, and school administrators.

Types of Administrators

Administrators, including deans, chairs, directors, and supervisors, function in many ways to achieve their aims and goals. There is no one approach to all problems. There are so many different ways to deal with problems as there are individuals. Approaches will of necessity vary with the personality of the individuals and the situations with which they are confronted. However, it is obvious that one cannot teach democratic attitudes with undemocratic procedures. On the other hand, music, by the very nature of the art form, is not always democratic. In musical structure and ensemble performances, someone has to determine musical interpretation and musical values. A conductor makes autocratic decisions on the podium, but matters change when he exchanges his baton for an administrator's pen. This is the dilemma of music and ensemble performance. It often leads to misinterpretation on the part of music educators. However, one must not confuse lasting changes that affect long-range attitudes with those activities that demand immediate musical judgment. Change can only be realized through careful planning and by involving many people, even those with conflicting ideas.

Music administrators may be divided into four categories. First, there is the authoritarian, who relies on personal power and position. He justifies his actions by the speed with which decisions are implemented and programs instituted. It matters not whether these ideas are generally accepted and will be continued after "the authority" is gone. At the other extreme is the administrator who is completely "permissive" in his approach to problem solving. Rather than make a decision for which he may be held responsible, he will form a committee. (This was the attitude that prevailed in the 1950s and is still evident today.) Committees that are properly constituted with purposeful objectives are useful, but they cannot always replace real decision making.

The third type of administrator is the one who is complacent and happy, "having arrived." This administrator may best be described as one who subscribes to a laissez-faire policy. It is not that he objects to change, but having achieved success in past programs, he says, "Why change?" This kind of administrator is impervious to the changing character of society and the world around him.

The fourth type of administrator is the democratic administrator, who consults and confers but is willing to accept responsibility for decisions. This individual believes in the democratic process and pursues it. He is one who is able to interpret and assess group response and is able to act accordingly. When change is necessary, such a person is willing to educate staff and citizenry, so that there is a better climate for effective change with a measure of stability. He attempts to bring expertise, wherever it may be, to bear on the making of decisions that are critical to the greatest number of people or the most needy.

The higher one rises in the administrative hierarchy, the more exposed one becomes to criticism. This may be a problem, depending on the individual. This condition is presented in the following humorous series of axioms:

THE SCHOOL ADMINISTRATOR'S DILEMMA

If he's friendly with the clerical staff, he's a politician.
If he keeps to himself, he's a snob.

If he makes decisions quickly, he's arbitrary.
If he doesn't have an immediate answer, he can't make up his mind.

If he works on a day-to-day basis, he lacks foresight.
If he has long-range plans, he's a daydreamer.

If his name appears in the newspapers, he's a publicity hound.
If no one has ever heard of him, he's a nonentity.

If he requests a large budget, he is against economy.
If he doesn't ask for more money, he's a timid soul (or stark mad).

If he tries to eliminate red tape, he has no regard for the system.
If he insists on going through channels, he's a bureaucrat.

If he speaks the language of education, he's a cliché expert.
If he doesn't use the jargon, he's illiterate.

If he's late for work in the morning, he's taking advantage of his position.
If he gets to the office on time, he's an eager beaver.

If the office is running smoothly, he is a dictator.
If the office is a mess, he's a poor administrator.

If he holds weekly staff meetings, he's in desperate need of ideas.
If he doesn't hold staff meetings, he doesn't appreciate the value of teamwork.

If he spends a lot of time with the board, he's a backslapper.
If he's never with the board, he's on his way out.

If he goes to conventions, he's on the gravy train.
If he never makes a trip, he's not important.

If he tries to do all the work himself, he doesn't trust anybody.
If he delegates as much as possible, he's lazy.

If he tries to get additional personnel, he's an empire builder.
If he doesn't want more assistants, he's a slave driver.

If he takes his briefcase home, he's trying to impress the board.
If he leaves the office without any homework, he has a sinecure.

If he enjoys reading this description, he's facetious.
If he doesn't think it's clever, well, he's entitled to his own opinion.

NOTES

1. Donald E. Walker, *The Effective Administrator* (San Francisco: Jossey-Bass, 1979).
2. Robert H. Roy, *The Administrative Process* (Baltimore: Johns Hopkins Press, 1965).

SUPPLEMENTARY READINGS

Briggs, Paul. "Arts Can Shatter Urban Isolation." *Music Educators Journal* 56, no. 5 (January 1970), pp. 56–57.

House, Robert. *Administration in Music Education*. Englewood Cliffs, N.J.: Prentice-Hall, 1973.

Kaplan, Max. "Music in American Society, Introduction to Issues." *Music Educators Journal* 53, no. 8 (April 1967), p. 43.

MENC-NEA. "Music in the School Curriculum." *Music Educators Journal* 52, no. 2 (November–December 1965), p. 37.

Weerts, Richard. "The Role of the Music Supervisor." *Music Educators Journal* 53, no. 7 (March 1967), p. 49.

White, Howard G. "The Professional Role and Status of Music Educators in the United States." *Journal of Research in Music Education* 1 (Spring 1967), p. 3.

STUDY QUESTIONS

1. By what titles are music administrators known? How do the titles reflect duties and responsibilities?
2. What personal characteristics does the successful music administrator possess?

3. What is the meaning of line-and-staff organization? Describe and discuss.
4. Diagram the organizational structure of the school system in the community where you attended secondary school.
5. What are the responsibilities of the chief music administrator in a school system? In a college/university?

3

Leadership

The topic of leadership is one about which much has been written. Researchers in the business, political, and military worlds have been particularly interested in suggesting definitions, in establishing lists of characteristics, and in developing profiles. Students of human behavior, too, have studied the characteristics of those who seem to manage to accomplish a great deal and seem to develop a cadre of "followers," persons eager to do their bidding or attach their wagon to the same star.

Leadership is vital in the enterprise of music education. Without it, programs languish and lack focus. If leadership is absent, there is no single direction, but a myriad of directions as defined by the interests and proclivities of individual faculty members. It is the first and perhaps most important responsibility of the music administrator, whether in the public school setting or on the campus, to exert leadership—that is, to challenge faculty members to think about goals and objectives and to chart a course for their programs.

If one is to lead, the implication is that there are those who will follow. Just as there is "leadership," so there will be "followership." The music administrator exerts leadership by example. He inspires faculty to follow because of knowledge possessed, professional reputation, character, and musical accomplishment. In addition, the leader is able to articulate statements and action, inducing faculty to want to be a part of the enterprise and a member of the team.

■

DEFINITIONS

The myth that leaders are born and not made is just that—a myth. The military structures a great deal of its education and training around the concept that people can learn to become leaders. Through the courses they take, the experiences they have, and the models they study, young persons learn to become officer-leaders. This is not to say that some persons are not more "natural" leaders than others. Nor is it to say that some persons do not gravitate to leadership roles while others become followers. Nor is it to say that there are not an infinite variety of leaders with an infinite variety of leadership styles. A leader may be remarkably successful in one setting but a dismal failure in another.

John W. Gardner defines leadership as the "process of persuasion and example by which an individual (or leadership team) induces a group to take action that is in accord with the leader's purposes or the shared purposes of all."[1] A leader must sense—must know—who the followers are and what it is that they want and need. Knowing that, the leader plots a course of action that will fulfill the want and need. James MacGregor Burns defines leadership as "inducing followers to act for certain goals that represent the values and the motivation—the wants and needs, the aspirations and expectations—of both leaders and followers."[2]

Burns states that a major task of leadership is to bring to the consciousness of followers a sense of their own needs, values, and purposes. "Leadership over human beings," he says, "is exercised when persons with certain motives and purposes mobilize, in competition or conflict with others, institutional, political, psychological, and other resources so as to arouse, engage, and satisfy the motives of followers."[3]

There is an assumption that *direction*—movement toward a goal—is involved in leadership. One thinks in terms of upward movement—of moving in the direction of higher values, greater security, or more self-fulfillment for both leader and followers.

There is also an assumption that with leadership, things get done: organization is imposed, and a focus of activity is provided.

It is true that some groups of people may not need leadership. Or they may not need it all the time or in the same doses. But just get a group of any size together for any purpose and pretty soon the need for leadership emerges. Someone has to control the discussion, call on people, take notes, make assignments. Leadership is one of the things that you may not realize you need until you do not have it. When the time comes to make a decision, solve a problem, call for a vote, or provide alternatives, then leadership must be there. Can you think of any community of people that has been in existence for any period of time (e.g., church, school, community, military, union) that does not have leadership? The leadership may be informal, but it is *there*. It may even rotate, but it is still *there*.

One doesn't have to look far to see music programs in school districts that suffer from a lack of leadership. When a vacuum exists, someone will rush in to fill it; someone will take over and *do* things, whether or not they are in the best interests of children or the entire music program. Pockets of excellence will exist around the efforts of a superior teacher, but without strong central musical leadership in a school district, those pods of excellence will be scattered and haphazard. Likewise, one can see on college campuses elements of excellence in the music department. But in those instances where the entire department—or most of it—is respected for the way it prepares musicians and teachers, the explanation is usually that there has been competent, challenging, caring leadership for a substantial period of time.

■

STYLES

There are many kinds of leaders and styles of leadership. Leaders are successful if they can adjust their behavior to time and place and can respond to issues and events in an appropriate way as they arise. The key in determining the success of leadership is the leader-follower (or leader-constituent, as Gardner prefers to call it) relationship. As long as that is working, all is well. When the trust and confidence are eroded and the parties become estranged, then the board fires the chief executive officer, the faculty votes the chairman out, the dean is asked to return to teaching, the supervisor is asked to become a teacher again, and the politician is retired from office.

Tucker describes leadership styles as being directive-supportive or autocratic-democratic.[4] The directive leader engages in one-way communication. He does a lot of telling, but rarely listens. The nondirective leader provides ideas but very little guidance as to how the ideas are to be implemented and practically no monitoring of progress toward the goal. Supportive leaders engage in two-way communication; provide personal or psychological support; and encourage, praise, and express concern for the follower. The autocratic leader sets a course and charts the direction. He may consult with followers or colleagues from time to time, but his attitude is "I'm the boss and I'm in charge." The democratic leader consults with people—to a fault perhaps. He seeks input into nearly everything and believes wholeheartedly in participatory governance.

Michael Maccoby describes four types of corporation executives: the spectator, the technician, the jungle fighter, and the gamesman.[5] The spectator is passive and acquiescent and may flourish in mature organizations. He leaves people alone. The hierarchy is well developed and functions effectively. The attitude is "Let's keep the peace and not ruffle feathers." The technician is a superb bureaucrat. Rules and regulations are followed to the letter, and deadlines are always met. This person is aware of, and has read, the literature on management techniques and follows the best advice he has read. Imagination and vision are in short supply. The jungle fighter is ambitious and sees his present position as but a stepping-stone to something more prestigious. Life will never be dull around this person, as there is always action, if not just the perception of action. This person may be a brilliant leader but may also be dangerous. There may be some human sacrifices along the way. The jungle fighter is a forceful advocate for the group, but one becomes suspicious that the advocacy is more for the person than for the group. This leader is not likely to remain for a significant period of time. The gamesman takes a leadership position to improve the organization. Life is a game, this person believes, and strategy and tactics are appealing. This person likes to win, but remains a sportsman and knows how to accept defeat. This leader is strong but flexible, a leader who is sometimes led, a manager who is sometimes managed. He is intelligent and courageous and has a sense of humor.

Kenneth Eble speaks of serving and leading—of the leader in the role of serving the followers he seeks to lead.[6] This person does not abuse the power he possesses. More than that, he shares that power with associates. Authority will not be shunned. Rather, it will be delegated insofar as possible. Such a leader believes that delegating authority is the same as exercising that authority himself. This person is psychologically whole and seeks to surround himself with other "together" persons.

Charismatic leadership is yet another style. The most prominent examples are probably found in religion, although they exist also in politics and the arts. The charismatic leader may reject the mundane and the routine, and place great stock in the extraordinary, even the miraculous. There is drama, even high drama, attached to the way this leader operates, and the stirring of emotions among followers is important to this person's success and the movement or organization he represents.

Music administrators must think about their style from the standpoint of what they are comfortable with and what is appropriate at the moment. Consider the question of hiring a faculty member. The music administrator who is eager to bring the best possible person to the faculty, who *knows* just who that person is because of contacts in the profession, is in for a rude awakening. That kind of "solo" operation will not work in today's world, where positions must be advertised, candidates must be screened, and applicants (plural) must be interviewed.

The administrator who has a working style that is very much "hands-on" may succeed in a music operation that is small and uncomplicated. That same individual could be a dismal failure in a situation where there is a sizable faculty, several programs, and many persons who are affected by what the music department does. The ability and willingness to delegate is a must in such an operation. Questions of style as they relate to a particular position are of critical importance in the selection of a person for an administrative post in music and should be pursued vigorously.

CHARACTERISTICS

The effective leader has good interpersonal skills, enabling him to work easily with followers and those for whom he may be responsible. The effective leader has good listening habits and perceives not only what is being said but also how the speaker feels about an issue. A sense of respect for coworkers is exuded by the leader in all dealings.

Analytical skills are crucial, and dispassionate analysis is much to be prized. In the field of music, emotions often run high. One's leadership is diminished by the inability to step back and view a problem from afar.

Communication skills (both speaking and writing) are essential for the effective leader. Music administrators who are inept in matters of communication are constantly saying, "But this is what I meant to say." One can communicate carefully ninety-nine times out of a hundred with those with a need to know, but that one time when a person was not properly consulted or informed about an issue will be long remembered by the disgruntled individual.

The effective leader conveys a consistently positive attitude and an enthusiasm that is contagious. He is passionate about music, about teaching, about projects.

The ability to plan strategically is an important quality for the leader. The music administrator, when wishing to advance a new programmatic idea, considers not only how to proceed but also the likely sources of opposition and an approach that will account for those elements. Political astuteness and awareness is essential.

The effective leader has the will to make unpopular decisions. When an issue is potentially explosive and persons hold strong views on different sides, the leader consults and listens, but then makes a decision based on what is in the best interests of the students and the department or school. Criticism may come and must be dealt with in a nonpersonal way.

The effective leader surrounds himself with quality people—people with perhaps even greater abilities than the leader of the unit. He realizes that success for the music unit comes through the deeds of others; the leader is the one who sets the stage, directs the players, provides the resources, calls out encouragement, and applauds the results.

One observes an effective leader in music administration as having a sense of humor, high standards for performance, the ability to mediate disputes, and a curiosity that identifies him as a student as well as a teacher. He has an uncanny sense of timing—of knowing when to lay back and when to act, when to keep silent and when to speak out.

Perhaps most important of all for the effective leader is the quality of integrity. The music administrator who tells different things to different people and who breaks confidences is doomed to failure. The first-rate leader not only is honest in his dealings with people but is *perceived* as being honest and trustworthy.

■

TASKS

John W. Gardner suggests nine tasks that are significant in the life of the leader:[7]

1. Envisioning goals: "Leaders point us in the right direction and tell us to get moving," opined one high school senior. Possible goals emerge from many sources, but it's the leader's continuing task to sort them out, to prioritize them, and to declare some to be short-range and others long-range.

2. Affirming values: In any community there are shared values and beliefs. They may relate to tradition, to custom, to long-held assumptions. These values embody that which is worth living for and striving for. The successful leader affirms those values by word and deed.

3. Motivating: Leaders must help their constituents develop positive attitudes toward the future and a healthy balance between optimism and realism. Circumstances that create negativism or frustration need to be altered or ameliorated. Followers need to have a

sense that "I'm really motivated to take this particular action and I want to do it as well as I possibly can."

4. Managing: While many view leading and managing as separate functions most leaders find themselves managing on occasion. They have to plan, set priorities, organize, set agendas, and coordinate numerous activities and events, many of which occur simultaneously.

5. Achieving workable unity: Trust is an important element—perhaps indispensable—for a leader who wishes to keep conflict at a minimum.

6. Explaining: People want to know what the problem is, why they are being asked to do certain things, how they relate to the larger picture. All leaders find themselves explaining to constituents at several levels. Failure to accept this responsibility may result in unhappy, disgruntled followers.

7. Serving as a symbol: When a person moves from labor to management—enlisted man to officer, or faculty to administration—he suddenly becomes a symbol of leadership. Old alliances may be impossible to keep. And the speech and action of the new leader are suddenly looked at with more care, even suspicion.

8. Representing the group: The leader, whether he likes it or not, is the group's representative. What he says or does is interpreted by outside forces as representing the group. Job announcements for administrators in higher education will often state "serve as spokesperson for _____ unit."

9. Reviewing: Leaders must be aware of what and where the action is, must know the forces that impinge on his organization and its constituents. When that is known, the leader determines which of several alternatives for leadership is to be used. Some old paths may be perfectly correct; others may not be. At that point, a new tack must be taken to achieve the desired goal.

THE SUCCESSFUL MUSIC EXECUTIVE

A study entitled "Music Executive Success" was conducted by Robert L. Cowden in 1983 to determine the rate of turnover among music executives in higher-education music units belonging to the National Association of Schools of Music and the success qualities that enabled music-unit heads to retain their positions for longer than five years.[8] Findings of that study include the facts that the turnover rate among music-unit heads was highest among institutions with the smallest music-major population, both public and private. Of the twenty-five success factors listed, both groups' (music executives and chief academic officers) first choice was "honesty"; the second was "willing

and capable of working with superiors for the benefit of the unit."
These responses were from institutions where the music executive
had been in place for at least five years, and the qualities felt to be of
greatest importance to longevity in an administrative post were good
working relationships with people, a cooperative spirit, fairness, honesty, the ability to set and maintain high professional standards, and
leadership.

Other factors that contributed to the success of the music administrator as identified by the chief academic officer and the music
executive himself were that he sets a good example for faculty, has
flexibility to meet changing situations, considers all sides of an issue,
solves problems well within the unit, demonstrates high professional
standards, makes decisions that are to the overall advantage of the
entire unit, exerts leadership for achieving departmental objectives,
communicates well verbally and in writing, and acts deliberately
rather than precipitately or out of anger.

In asking chief academic officers about leadership style in personal interviews at fourteen institutions where the music executive
was presumably successful the comments heard were that "he works
for consensus," "he is aggressive without being confrontational," "he
is democratic rather than autocratic," and "he's really adept at pick-
ing the right issues to fight about." "He uses friendly persuasion" was
a comment frequently heard. Yet another way of looking at the factors that make for a successful music administrator is to examine the
responses to Cowden's questions of chief academic officers and the
ways they evaluate the person who heads the music unit:

- Does he push me to find resources for the music unit?
- Is he willing and able to live within the constraints imposed
  and yet make the unit the *best* it can be?
- Do grievances get to me very often?
- Are the wheels running smoothly?
- Is he able to identify goals and objectives and then accomplish
  them?

Cowden interviewed faculty members on these fourteen campuses as well. In responding to a question about leadership in its
ideal form, faculty members said, "What we need is a leader with
vision, someone who can see into and project the future; we need to
know where we are going and how we are going to get there."

At a workshop for music administrators in public schools and
colleges held at Eastern Illinois University, Rhoderick Key, then
chairperson of the Department of Music, distributed a dozen suggestions for the person who wishes to be a successful leader:

If You Would Be a Leader

1. ESTABLISH HIGH STANDARDS. If you are satisfied with mediocre work, you are never going to get more than mediocre work from many of your associates—except maybe from your successor.

2. CONTROL YOURSELF. Do not lose your temper when things begin to go wrong. Anger warps judgement; warped judgement leads to poor decisions. Things said in anger can undo in thirty seconds all the good will and high morale you have worked hard to build up. If you want to control others, learn first to control yourself.

3. RESPECT THE IDEAS OF OTHERS. When you make a decision not in accord with the ideas or point of view of an associate, do not belittle him or his opinions. Let him know that you respect his ideas and are appreciative of having had the opportunity to learn his views. If you treat him that way, his reaction will be good and he will always feel free to express himself honestly to you. The next time he may be right.

4. LEARN THE VALUE OF TIMING. Many difficult things can be accomplished easily if done at the right time. If you time your efforts correctly, people will say: "Things certainly go smoothly around here." Wrong timing leads people to say: "What is he trying to do now?"

5. WELCOME RESPONSIBILITY. Leadership and responsibility go hand in hand. Once you refuse responsibility, you have reached your ceiling.

6. DEVELOP AND SUPPORT YOUR ASSISTANTS. Outstanding leaders in the business and industrial world habitually surround themselves with good men. Where do they come from? Most of them are developed through example and proper handling. Good leadership develops the full potential of subordinates by giving them opportunities to demonstrate their ability.

7. LEARN HOW AND WHEN TO DELEGATE. The bigger the job, the greater the need for delegation, or you become the deluxe bottleneck of the organization, and progress stops.

8. GENERATE LOYALTY. Do not expect your people to be loyal to you if you are not loyal to the enterprise and to your associates. You also must be loyal to your immediate staff. One of the best ways to demonstrate loyalty to your associates is to learn to take blame and give credit. *Even when you think it belongs elsewhere?*

9. BALANCE IS NECESSARY. Balance means having a "feel" for things that will instinctively lead you to devote your personal attention to the appropriate subject at the proper time and not overemphasize one subject at the expense of another. How many times have you heard it said of a man: "He is smart all right, but he goes off on a tangent"?

10. BE YOUR BEST SELF. Never try to act the role that you think an important person should play. If you do, your insincerity is evident, you are spotted as a phony and you lose the confidence of both subordinates and superiors. Trying to by-pass or undercut your associates is a dangerous and dishonest procedure—hardly your best self at work.

11. WHEN YOU TAKE OVER A NEW JOB, DO NOT CHANGE EVERYTHING. Sit back a little while and try to find out some of the reasons why things are done as they are done. Evaluate these reasons against your experience and judgement and make changes. This does not mean that you should hesitate to clean house when you find a mess.

12. MAKE DECISIONS PROMPTLY. Get all the facts you can in the time available. Evaluate them, make up your mind, and then go ahead. Never make quick decisions just in order to appear decisive, but make them as quickly as possible after you get the appropriate facts.

Leaders come in all shapes and sizes, are male and female, are from a variety of races, and embrace many creeds. They may be highly educated or perhaps even illiterate. What they have in common is that a group of people is willing to follow each of them. These leaders recognize that their power, their authority, their ability to reach goals comes directly from their constituent group. They *know* their constituents and have a sense of what they need and/or want; the leader then sets about meeting those needs/wants. The leader makes it possible for followers somehow to be successful—to achieve goals that are important to them.

Styles of leadership are as varied as the numbers of leaders themselves. Further, leadership style will be altered by a single leader according to the demands of the moment.

Robert Tannenbaum and Warren H. Schmidt write:

> The successful leader is one who is keenly aware of those forces which are most relevant to his behavior at any given time. He accurately understands himself, the individuals and group he is dealing with, and the company and broader social environment in which he operates. And certainly he is able to assess the present readiness for growth of his subordinates. But this sensitivity or understanding is not enough, which brings us to the second implication. The successful leader is one who is able to behave appropriately in the light of these perceptions. If direction is in order, he is able to direct; if considerable participative freedom is called for, he is able to provide such freedom.
>
> Thus, the successful manager of men can be primarily characterized neither as a strong leader nor as a permissive one. Rather, he is one who maintains a high batting average in accurately assessing the forces that determine what his most appropriate behavior at any given time should

be and in actually being able to behave accordingly. Being both insightful and flexible, he is less likely to see the problem of leadership as a dilemma.[9]

And so it is with leaders in the field of music. The music supervisor in the schools or the music executive on a university campus assesses his constituents, plots his course, sets goals, gets others to buy into those goals, and sets about achieving them with the cooperation of others. At times, he will be a cheerleader; at other times, a supportive colleague. At certain times, there will be need for firm exhortations to the troops; at other times, quiet one-on-one talks will achieve the necessary and desired results. But the effective leader will know how to behave, depending upon the prevailing climate and the prevailing attitudes of the constituent group(s) with whom he deals.

NOTES

1. John W. Gardner, *The Tasks of Leadership* (Washington, D.C.: Independent Sector, 1986), p. 6.
2. James MacGregor Burns, *Leadership* (New York: Harper and Row, 1978), p. 19.
3. *Ibid.*, p. 18.
4. Allan Tucker, *Chairing the Academic Department* (New York: Macmillan, 1984), pp. 41–55.
5. Michael Maccoby, *The Gamesman* (New York: Simon and Schuster, 1977).
6. Kenneth Eble, *The Art of Administrating* (San Francisco: Jossey-Bass, 1978).
7. Gardner, *The Tasks of Leadership*, 1986, p. 6.
8. Robert L. Cowden, "Music Executive Success," *Proceedings of the 59th Annual Meeting*, Reston, Va.: National Association of Schools of Music, 1984, pp. 75–97.
9. Robert Tannenbaum and Warren H. Schmidt, "How to Choose a Leadership Pattern," *Harvard Education Review* 27 (March–April 1957), pp. 95–101.

SUPPLEMENTARY READINGS

Bennis, Warren. *Why Leaders Can't Lead*. San Francisco: Jossey-Bass, 1989.
Berg, Kenneth A. "Educational Leadership." *Clearing House* 50, no. 5 (January 1977), pp. 212–214.
Brann, J., and Emmet, T. A., eds. *The Academic Department and Division Chairman: A Complex Role*. Detroit: Balamp, 1971.

Brown, David G. *Leadership Vitality: A Workbook for Academic Administrators*. Washington, D.C.: American Council on Education, 1980.

Brown, M.A. "What Kind of Leadership Do Faculty Members Want?" *College Management* 8, no. 1 (January 1973), pp. 25–26.

Cohen, M. D., and March, J. G. *Leadership and Ambiguity: The American College President*. New York: McGraw-Hill, 1973.

Conger, Joy A. *The Charismatic Leader*. San Francisco: Jossey-Bass, 1989.

Gibb, C. A., ed. *Leadership: Selected Readings*. New York: Penguin Books, 1969.

Gouldner, A., ed. *Studies in Leadership*. New York: Harper and Row, 1950.

Hersey, Paul, and Blanchard, Kenneth H. "So You Want to Know Your Leadership Style." *Training and Development Journal* 28, no.2 (February 1974) pp. 22–37.

Newmann, Yoram, and Boris, Steven B. "Paradigm Development and Leadership Style of University Department Chairpersons." *Research in Higher Education* (1978) 9, p. 4.

Palmer, Rupert E., Jr. "The Chairman as Servant: Or, How to Lead a Department from a Position of Weakness." *ADE Bulletin* no. 61 (May 1979), pp. 38–40.

Selzrich, P. *Leadership in Administration*. New York: Harper and Row, 1957.

Stogdill, R. M. *Handbook of Leadership*. New York: Free Press, 1974.

Tead, O. *The Art of Leadership*. New York: McGraw-Hill, 1935.

STUDY QUESTIONS

1. What is leadership?
2. What are the characteristics of an effective leader?
3. What leadership styles can you identify? Name specific persons who exemplify those styles.
4. What makes a leader successful or unsuccessful?
5. If you were interviewing a person for a position of leadership in music, what questions would you ask? What would you want to know about how that person operates?

4

Management

Concepts discussed in this chapter include the management of people, things, resources, and time—all of them important for the music administrator. Also discussed will be skills that the managers of music units need to have at their command in order to be successful.

Management is a process that guides and directs the operations of an organization in the realization of established goals. Paul Hersey and Ken Blanchard state that management is "working with and through individuals and groups to accomplish organizational goals ... it is a special kind of leadership in which the achievement of organizational goals is paramount."[1] Peter F. Drucker states simply that management is "organizing people and processes to get things done."[2]

While various writers have characterized management as a science, an art, or public relations, Dabney Park opines that "management is not just a science, not just human relations, not just an art. It is all three and more."[3]

Common to all the several definitions of management are the notions that both "people" and "things" are involved and that "direction" is presumed. Effective managers must be able to deal with people. They must guide, lead, and help them be as productive as they can be. Further, managers must be able to handle resources (money, equipment, supplies) in an efficient manner so that the organization receives the largest possible benefit. Resources, whatever they are, never go far enough. There is always a greater demand than supply. If large numbers of people are using resources, there is apt to be waste and redundant effort—both of which must be controlled by the alert manager.

The notion of "direction" implies that goals are important. The manager of an organization must be aware of the goals of that organization, must help shape them, and must move the organization toward their realization. While in the ideal sense it would be nice to believe that *all* the members of an organization help to determine its goals, embrace those goals, and then work to achieve them, the real world reveals that that is rarely the case.

A music staff may, for example, go on a retreat, work hard at coming to grips with goals and objectives for the music unit, and return enthusiastic about moving toward the accomplishment of those goals. They return to their teaching assignments, and the fire burns brightly for a while as they undertake their responsibilities with renewed enthusiasm. However, as time passes, the enthusiasm dims—partly because the individual music teacher is responsible for only a small part of the overall picture. That teacher may see himself as contributing to only partial realization of one or more goals.

The role of the effective manager is to keep looking at the large picture. He must keep reminding colleagues of the goals toward which they are all working. He must see to it that resources are placed where they will do the most good and certainly must be channeled in the direction that moves the organization toward its stated goals. The manager is the only one in the organizational scheme who has the control of resources and people, who has the vision of the whole, and who can keep all facets of the organization in perspective.

And what of the factor of time? What does an effective manager need to know about the use of time? Alan Lakein says that "people waste 80% of their time, even when they appear to be perpetually busy."[4] He says that the 80–20 rule is operative when it comes to managers—that is, 80 percent of the interruptions will be caused by 20 percent of the people in the organization or will be created by 20 percent of the activities.

Lakein suggests that one should analyze time carefully, should delegate whenever possible, and should organize the unavoidable. The effective manager will analyze how he spends time as well as how colleague's lives are organized. This has an implication for the music supervisor who is planning the schedules for an instrumental music teacher who teaches in four or five schools. Travel can be arranged efficiently or not. While there are many factors to consider (building schedules, time of day, academic course offerings, availability of facilities), one does not want a large amount of time to be spent in a car. Nor does one want to create a situation where no lunchtime is provided and a sandwich has to be consumed while rushing to the next school. Time is important to us all, whether a teacher, a supervisor, a director, or a dean.

Meetings are a fact of life in the world of music administration.

In higher education, many see meetings as a plague on our lives, but they need not be if they are well organized and purposeful. The well-organized manager will see to it that a meeting has an agenda. It will have a purpose to be addressed to make it worthwhile for people to attend. If no purpose can be articulated, then the meeting should not occur. The only people he will call to the meeting are those who ought to be there, who have something to contribute, who have a stake in the outcome. In the public school sector, where faculty are governed by a union contract, there is often a provision that limits the number of staff meetings per year, that prescribes their length, and that even specifies the time when they will occur. Often there is the provision that faculty will be compensated a stated sum for even attending such meetings. In those instances, the meetings had *better* be worthwhile, purposeful, and productive. Such agreements give life to the cliché "Time is money."

The concept of delegating suggests that such a tactic has the catalytic ability to stimulate both personal and organizational growth. The manager may—indeed, should—delegate tasks to those with whom he works, but the corresponding obligation is then to follow up—to check that there is progress and to call to account those who have received delegated tasks.

Lakein offers managers some suggestions on how to conduct the affairs of their organizations: handle a piece of paper only once; divide correspondence into high, medium, and low priority; keep the door closed; protect some creative time; write things down; and start with difficult jobs. Successful managers of music units will probably agree that these are excellent suggestions. Many music managers are successful because they follow one or more of these suggestions. But such things are not easy to do. It is difficult to look at a piece of paper and make an instant decision about it. Do I send it on to someone else? Do I act on it now? Do I throw it away? Do I send it to my secretary for filing? Do I need to think about it for a while before deciding what to do? Is there a deadline attached to it? The successful manager is able to minimize the time required to deal with each piece of paper and can make accurate and speedy decisions about its disposition—even if it is to place it in a folder for consideration later. The successful manager *does* protect time for himself each week. Some managers write terms such as *library, research, travel,* or *X* on their calendars and absent themselves from the office (the best choice) or close the door (the next best choice) in order to accomplish something of importance.

Making lists, prioritizing lists, and beginning the workday with difficult or complex jobs are all ways to help managers be more productive and move forward the organizations they serve.

Questions that the manager should ask as he is trying to make the best use of time are these:

1. What am I doing that really doesn't need to be done at all?
2. Which of my duties could be handled by someone else equally well?
3. What do I do that wastes the time of others?

In addition to these questions, Eble posits several axioms that relate to time management:

1. Sorting out what there is to do is the first step toward getting it done.
2. Dealing with people is more taxing and time-consuming than dealing with things.
3. Doing the things you don't want to do first can save the day for things you can do with enthusiasm and satisfaction.
4. There is never enough time. The able administrator makes the available time fit.[6]

The manager of music units will hear over and over again about how busy people are, how many commitments they have, how swamped they are, how thinly they are spread, and how harried they feel. It is true that musicians are often overextended, that they want to do lots of things but often do not have sufficient control of their lives to do them successfully. There is a built-in resentment—and rightfully so—for things that intrude on practice time or reflection. The music manager is sensitive to all this and works with and around it.

Thankfully, the academic year has its breaks. It may be nonstop from the beginning of the semester to the end, with some wild times around holidays or tours, but at least there are some built-in deviations when "school is out" and a new tempo can be established. Management of time is not an easy exercise for a faculty member; it is a *must* for the successful manager of music units.

EFFECTIVE MANAGEMENT

Effective management of a music unit occurs because there is communication, teamwork, participation in decision making, because there is the encouragement for persons to take initiative, because there is mutual support. Effective management is characterized by careful and fair performance evaluation and by a high level of motivation to do an excellent job.

Communication

In a music unit, communication is critical. Since a heavy schedule of recitals, concerts, athletic events, and ceremonies involve music teachers and students, it is *assumed* that the participants need to know when and where they occur, when and where they are to report, and the extent of their obligations. Others also need to be informed—administrators, custodians, secretaries who respond to phone calls, the attending public, parents. Faculty need to *know* about deadlines for budget requests, bus requests, and textbook orders. Good communication with all constituencies is essential. It is an expectation. Each year one highly successful music supervisor sends a detailed summary of results (including excerpted adjudicator comments) of solo, small-ensemble, and large-group contests to principals, superintendents, and board members in the school district. It is a piece of communication, he believes, that provides the music program with more benefits than any other activity. Many college music chairs send frequent memos of information about the accomplishments of the department to deans and vice-presidents and newsletters to alumni that accomplish the same purpose. You can have ninety-nine examples of excellent communication in your organization and only one miscue and your world will come tumbling down. You will get an angry call from a parent, a faculty member will storm into your office, or the first oboe player will arrive an hour late. The successful manager is constantly asking, Have I informed everyone who needs to know? Is there anyone I've forgotten? What more do I need to do?

Teamwork

An important concept of music making is teamwork. Musicians learn this from the beginning as they fit what they do into the band, orchestra, or chorus. When you have a solo to perform, it must be heard, and it is the conductor's job to provide the proper level of accompaniment so that it *can* be heard. Most of the time, however, we are part of the group. Whatever we do must blend and balance with the section of which we are a part. We may be a designated—or undesignated—leader for the section, but we learn first and foremost that we are a part of a whole that is greater than the sum of the parts. In other words, we are "team members." The same thing applies at the management level. "Management team" is an important concept that should include not only persons with titles such as *dean, director, head, supervisor,* or *chair* but also those designated *teacher, conductor,* or *instructor.* The successful music-unit manager causes the persons with whom he works to feel as if they are part of the team, as if they are colleagues, as if they are a part of the action in *real* ways—not only in lip service.

Decision Making

If an individual is really a member of a team, he participates in not only the establishment of the goals and objectives for the organization but also the decisions that are required to achieve those goals. Allowing colleagues to make decisions and be held accountable for them is a way the successful manager empowers the people with whom he works. This delegation of decision-making authority carries with it the view that persons should be allowed to make occasional mistakes. And one should learn that one matures from these mistakes. Another way of thinking about decision making is to relate it to the manager himself. If decisions—even trivial ones—are difficult, labored, and protracted, the manager loses face with colleagues and thus their confidence. If decisions seem never to be made or cannot be made without *extensive* consultation and agony, then the vacuum will be filled by others who *will* make the decision. There is the difficulty that every manager faces about whether a certain decision can and should be made quickly or whether it should be made deliberately. This is a judgment call in many instances, but the successful manager will be correct most of the time. It goes without saying that there will always be those critics who complain either that "decisions are too precipitate" or that "decisions take far too long around here."

Initiative

When one works in a collegial atmosphere—characteristic of most music units—the manager should encourage the members of the unit to make many of their own decisions, to think up new ideas, to view their own contributions critically. In short, members should be encouraged to take the initiative. It may be a revised schedule, a new course, an innovative or experimental teaching tactic, a new ensemble, a new performance opportunity, a fund-raising idea, or a reorganization plan. Whatever the case, faculty should be *rewarded* for displaying initiative. Reward may come in the form of public recognition, money, a revised schedule, promotion, or other creative ways devised by the manager.

Mutual Support

The musical art depends upon a piece of music, a medium to convey that music, and a human being to hear the product. There is no better way to support a musician than to hear what he sings or plays. The effective manager, knowing this, attends as many performances as possible all across the curriculum. Moreover, he encourages the attendance of others. Since support should be mutual, it should follow that support will be extended to the manager in the job he is attempting to do on behalf of students and faculty. Support is more than personal, of course, and extends to moral, financial, and programmatic matters as well. A successful manager is known as one who supports the colleagues and program for which he is responsible.

Performance Evaluation

Since the topic of evaluation is to be dealt with later, it is sufficient to say at this point that the successful manager is concerned with performance evaluation. We live in a world where nearly everyone in the work force is subject to evaluation. The problem then is to develop a system of evaluation that is as fair and impersonal as possible. The manager should be certain that any plan provides for all possible inputs; that is, those affected by the teaching or other activity of a music teacher should be asked to render judgment as to how that person is doing his job. Opinions or evaluative judgments may be sought from students (probably *not* at the elementary or junior high level), colleagues, parents, other administrators (e.g., director of athletics, principal), or anyone else with whom the teacher interacts. It should be noted that two distinct purposes exist for faculty evaluation: the improvement of instruction and the establishment of a rationale to reward (or not reward) someone for the job he has (or has not) been doing. It is not easy to isolate and separate these purposes, yet the effective manager of people can, and does, do so.

Motivation

Effective managers utilize a variety of motivational devices to produce the best performances from their people. Sometimes motivation takes the form of a reward, but sometimes, the form of a penalty. It may be the providing of a compliment for a job well done or suggestions for improvement where the result was less than optimal. It may be a significant presence—an MBWA (management by walking around) philosophy. It may be words, gestures, body language, public recognition, merit raises, or other things. It may be responding positively to an urgent plea for a piece of equipment, for relief from an early morning class, or for removal from a committee. It may be a birthday greeting or a sympathy card at a time of bereavement. It may be help in solving a professional problem or a personal crisis. It may be the hope of holding a position of high visibility in the community or profession. An elementary general music teacher was heard to say, "I am motivated to do the very best job

I can, not only because that's what I want, but also I know that that is what my boss expects. Furthermore, she always takes pains to praise me when I've done well and, among other things, that helps to make it all worthwhile." That's motivation!

■

TOOLS OF MANAGEMENT

In seminars for music administrators in higher education and public schools over several years, Ray Robinson, the former president of Westminster Choir College, identified the tools of management as being planning, organizing, directing, coordinating, and controlling. Following is a look at each of these tools and its implications for music-unit leadership.

Planning

The element of planning has different dimensions. There is the long-range plan, which may well cover a five-year period for the music unit. It may include enrollment projections, funding expectations, capital projects, equipment acquisitions, curricular change, and repair and replacement expectations. Medium- and short-range plans may cover everything from five years down to a plan for today as conceived by the manager. The effective manager brings together the resources (people and money) and develops a plan for the organization that makes maximal use of each to reach the goals that have been established. Without adequate planning, there will be no guide to the goals—or as Alice observed in *Alice in Wonderland*, "If you don't know where you are going, any road will take you there." It is not easy to look ahead when you are enmeshed with today's or this week's problems. Yet, if a goal is to be reached, there must be planning as to ways and means of getting there. Planning takes some skill, and as with other skills, the more you practice, the better you become. The more extensively planning occurs in an organization, the easier it becomes for everyone to plan and the more assurance there will be how others will operate and function in the organization.

Organization

Tables of organization often employ such concepts as unity of command, span of control, delegation of responsibility and authority, and homogeneity of assignments. The unity notion suggests that a person has one boss and that no one but the boss gives him directions concerning what to do. Music teachers, unfortunately, often have more than one boss: it may be a supervisor *and* a principal, or a division coordinator *and* a chairman. With this kind of built-in confusion, it is incumbent on the manager to be sure that conflicting signals are not being sent, that diverse or contradictory expectations are not being created. The span of control refers to the number of people that each supervisor can effectively control. The question for each manager is how many people he can manage effectively or how many people his assistant managers can manage. Factors to consider would include geography, discipline, numbers, and complexity of the organization. Can one music director manage a city school system that covers two hundred square miles with eighty thousand students, one hundred school buildings, and three hundred teachers? Probably not. Can one head manage a university department of music with more than four hundred majors, fifty-five faculty members, and graduate programs, including a doctorate? Probably not. In both situations a sensible, workable span of control *can* be established that will *extend* responsibility and authority to assistant managers who may be called assistant directors, administrative assistants, supervisors, or coordinators. Thus, the actual span of control is manageable and people are not expected to do that which is humanly impossible. Part of extending the span of control to others is the delegation of responsibility and authority. It is extremely important to delegate authority *with* responsibility so that the individual will feel empowered to carry out a task and be accountable for the results.

"Homogeneity of assignments" assumes that the manager asks people to perform tasks that are similar. If there is one secretary, that individual will do everything. If there are two or three, it is wise to divide the responsibilities so that they function more as specialists. One may have responsibilities for budget and travel, another for calendar and schedules, and another for summer programs and graduate assistants, with all of them helping with correspondence but perhaps even having that divided by divisions in the department. Positions should be described in terms of what is to be accomplished, the skills necessary, and the amount of responsibility and authority attached.

Direction

Simply stated, this management tool is giving a person a specific job. The effective manager, in describing job duties to an individual, will be careful to include the why-it-is-to-be-done part so that the person carrying out the directive will know how to proceed when the first obstacle is reached. The manager of a music unit may be in the position of actually providing direction for colleagues, secretaries, custodians, students, and others. The amount and kind of direction will vary widely, according to the person involved, the skill level and education of the person, and the responsibility and authority associated with the task.

Coordinating

The manager of a music unit must at some point put all of the pieces together, be sure that all elements are working harmoniously (certainly not at cross-purposes), and be assured that everyone is moving toward a common goal. This assumes, of course, that a goal (or goals) has been set, that adequate planning has occurred, and that people are doing their assigned jobs.

The manager, as the only one who knows what *everyone* is doing, must coordinate in both a horizontal sense (e.g., between five high schools in a school district) and a vertical sense (e.g., between elementary, middle, and high schools).

Controlling

Simply put, this is checking up on what is happening. It is follow-up and follow-through. Managers do *not* assume that just because they have assigned a job to an individual or established a deadline that those assignments can now be ignored or forgotten. There must be monitoring of the entire operation on a regular basis. As you work with certain people more and more, you come to trust and depend on some but realize that others require constant supervision. The latter group will forget deadlines, misunderstand instructions, do the job incorrectly, pass on incorrect information, and in other ways perform unsatisfactorily. The alert manager will be sensitive to such situations and will be ready with corrective action as needed.

A citywide music festival involving dozens of schools and teachers, hundreds of students and pieces of equipment, and thousands of sheets of music is an excellent example of the use of tools of management we have been discussing. Some one person must be in charge; that individual must plan, organize, delegate, direct, coordinate, and control the event. The event could not take place without the help and cooperation of many people, to be sure, and is ultimately a team effort, but all of the tools of management are evident in its successful conclusion.

The Skills Combined

Mr. Clef, the head of a college music department, is interested in considering the establishment of a new program in music/business. He brings up the subject in a faculty meeting and states that it is one of the goals for this year to consider the ramifications of instituting such a program—to consider whether such a program is desirable, whether there is a demand for it, who else is offering such a program, what resources would be required, and so on.

A committee is appointed and properly charged by Mr. Clef and the research begins. One person seeks information about which colleges and universities offer courses or programs in music/business within a 150-mile radius. Information about the character and emphasis of those programs is assembled, along with course titles, numbers of majors, and length of time to complete the program.

Mr. Clef contacts people in the music industry to ascertain their perception of the need for such a program at this institution and in this geographic location. He inquires about internships (cooperative professional practice programs) and the companies' interest in participating in such programs. Clef also engages in considerable dialogue with the business department of the college to discuss the courses in that area that would be appropriate for music students to take who were aiming for careers in music/business.

Contacts with professional associations are made by another person with questions about the need for a program of this type, job opportunities, the availability of faculty with the necessary expertise, and the role the associations might play in assisting the institution in establishing such a program, if the decision to proceed is made.

Still another person is assigned the task of determining the resources needed for such a program. These would include materials for the library, equipment, budget for promotional materials, travel money, and a faculty line (or partial line), among other things.

After four months Mr. Clef meets with the committee, and each member reports on what he learned. A decision is made to proceed, so the committee formulates a proposal for the department curricular committee. This group raises questions not previously considered. When these are satisfied, the curricular committee makes its presentation to the faculty. Still more questions are raised in this setting. Fears are expressed about what would happen to students majoring in performance or music education. After two meetings of the faculty and considerable debate the proposal is adopted.

Mr. Clef then guides the proposal through the remaining levels of required approvals in the college, which involves faculty across the entire college, a dean, and an academic vice-president. Finally, all approvals are secured. The program is put into place, and promotional materials are developed.

The process has taken a year and a half from start to finish. All the tools of management previously mentioned have been required. Mr. Clef, the head of the music department, has had to plan carefully, to organize at each step of the process, to assign tasks to others because there were far too many for him to do himself, to coordinate the efforts of those to whom he had assigned specific jobs, and to control the process with calls and meetings with his colleagues to be sure they were carrying out their assignments.

The result of this exhibition of management skills by a music administrator has been the adoption of a new program in music/business, which includes course work in both music and business, as well as a six-month internship experience. The music department in this college now experiences a dramatic increase in enrollment because of the new program. Important liaisons have been established with the music businesses, manufacturers, and agencies that are to provide the students with paid internships. And nearly all (94 percent) of the students who graduate from the program during its first five years will be offered employment in the music industry—58 percent of them in the very companies where they have served their internships.

DUTIES OF THE ACADEMIC MANAGER

Drucker suggests that a manager has several responsibilities, many of them applicable to the academic manager:[7]

1. To solve problems: While it is true that some problems solve themselves over time, the rule is that if a problem is *not* solved, the organization may be compromised or even endangered. A problem that festers or remains unsolved usually gets worse. As time goes on, more and more people are affected.

2. To be an entrepreneur: The manager of a music unit is constantly trying to promote, enhance, and redirect resources to place the organization in the best possible light. "If we position ourselves in this manner, we will be able to take advantage of this end-of-the-year windfall, or this redistricting, or the visit to the city of this artist," he reasons. The effective music administrator will take advantage of opportunities or openings to advance the cause of music and the position of the department in the institution, the community, the state, or the nation. This entrepreneur will be willing to take risks, to seek out faculty and students in unusual places, and to consider offbeat or unusual credentials.

3. To be efficient: There are never enough resources to do all that one

wants to do or to do all that one's bosses expect one to do. There are demands from all constituent groups, not the least of which are the teachers for whom one is responsible. So the effective manager must optimize resources, get the greatest return for the dollar, do the most with the least. "Efficiency" is doing things right and may be distinct from "effectiveness"—doing the right things.

4. To define the business: This involves setting goals and detailing objectives in the simplest terms. "Our business is the education of students first and foremost. Our business is *not* to interfere in the territory of the professional musician. Therefore, we will not play for the opening of a new store, or play at a professional basketball game, or hire our group out to play for dances. Nor will we have combos available for wedding receptions and bar mitzvahs." Such a definition establishes some parameters for activity. The effective manager and his colleagues will have to be both general and specific, both philosophical and practical, in defining the business.

5. To motivate: The manager must be a good person to work for. That does not necessarily imply that he is "liked"; it does imply that he is respected. There must be a payoff for doing a good job. The effective manager knows that rewards must go to those who produce. It may be time off, a salary boost, merit pay, equipment money, approval for a trip, support for a research project, or the time and expenses to attend a professional meeting. The wise manager asks advice from colleagues not only because he respects their opinion and judgment but also because he knows that this procedure reflects "I respect you and your views"—a motivation to the person being asked to maintain such a relationship and to continue to be worthy of such trust. On occasion, the manager may have to criticize a person for whom he is responsible. That, too, is motivation to do a good job—or certainly to do better next time. Like a parent, the manager can mete out discipline with respect, love, and the understanding that "I'm sure this was a mistake, an error on your part, and that it won't happen again. Maybe it was my fault for not letting you know clearly enough of *my* expectations."

6. To communicate: Hardly anything is more important for the effective manager. You can hardly communicate too much. It is better to send too many memos than not enough, to make too many phone calls to the studio of a busy teacher than none at all. The failures of communication may be remembered for weeks, months, or even forever. The effective manager expresses thanks to those who have performed well—in person and in writing. Such expressions pay off when next you need to ask such a person to write some letters, make some calls, serve on a committee, or organize a festival. If that person knows that the efforts will be appreciated, it will be much easier to say yes.

7. To be fair: The effective manager is fair in dealing with everyone. He is honest, objective, and consistent—one of the hardest qualities. The manager not only *is* fair but is *perceived* to be fair by those

with whom he works. There are no "pets"—teachers who seem to get all the goodies, the choice assignments, the most recognition. In being fair, the manager considers only *what* is right, not *who* is right. In a meeting where divergent views are expressed, the manager forges a compromise, if that is appropriate, or comes down on the side of what is best for the organization or what is "fair" for the students and/or the faculty.

8. To be decisive: This does not mean that the manager makes an immediate decision on *all* issues. It does mean that the manager knows when to make an instant decision, when to think about a matter for a day or two, when to consult with others, and when to ruminate for a longer period of time because tempers need to cool or the political waters need to be allowed to calm. To the person who is pushing for a decision that the manager is not prepared to make, he might say, "I've been thinking about this issue, and here are the options I see. Do you see any others? The consequences of deciding A, B, or C are such and such. Do you think that I have analyzed the situation correctly?" This approach says that a decision is in the process of being made and even gives the questioner an opportunity for providing input and advice. It helps to defuse the critic. But the manager is in trouble if he is perceived by colleagues as being indecisive. One might then overhear in the hallway, "There is no point in bringing this matter to the attention of the director of music. He won't make a decision anyway." The vacuum will be filled by someone else—in a manner, perhaps, that is not in the best interest of the department.

■

CHARACTERISTICS OF THE
EDUCATIONAL MANAGER

Terry O'Bannion, in speaking to a group of higher-education managers, likened the academic enterprise to a circus.[8] A circus demands *expertise*, it boasts *variety*, and it celebrates great *performance*. Elements common to higher education and the circus include tradition, continuity, control, rebellion, and an enormous complexity of relationships.

If circus performers and academic managers are to survive, they must possess concentration, muscle tone, and flexibility. They must *practice* their skill endless hours and *discipline* themselves to the rigors of performance. And they enjoy—even revel in—the recognition they receive, no matter how small.

Some academic managers are lion tamers, others are clowns, still others are highwire artists. The lion tamer is always in charge, is totally involved, is single-minded. He succeeds with his animals because he trains them from the time they are cubs; he feeds them; he practices with them daily; he keeps them on a regular schedule; he carries a gun, but he never uses it. And he bears the scars of having made some mistakes of trusting where he should not have. The rules of empowering are the same—no surprises, constant vigilance, commitment to quality of performance, love of task, respect for the players.

The clowns bind the circus together. They make us laugh by reminding us of our humanity. They help us realize that one can laugh—indeed, *should* laugh—at our own mistakes and ineptitude, and admit that we are human. There is relief in humor; it defuses tense situations and provides relaxation in times of stress.

Then there is that highwire artist—the person who performs forty feet above the ground some incredible trick at the right split second. The audience gasps audibly at such a moment, and a few may even have a snatch of desire to see him fall. The comparisons with the academic manager are several—balancing while performing difficult tasks, balancing between faculty and administration, between quality and limited resources, between building a professional community and demanding professional accountability, and between staff development and staff evaluation programs. One needs a strong net—a good support system. You need the equilibrium to stay on the wire most of the time. The highwire artist falls from time to time, but there is usually a net to catch him, a support system that is forgiving. And, as with falling off a horse, the best thing to do is get right back on again.

O'Bannion, in speaking of academic managers said, "Each time you take the risk, each time you return safely to the wire, even when you muff the trick, you remind us of the possibility inherent in our mission. . . . As academic managers you are the artists in our institutions, controlling the savage beast, taking a fall and laughing about it, walking a thin wire—teaching us by your example to be more of an artist."[9]

A MANAGERIAL GRID IN MUSIC ADMINISTRATION

Both industry and government, as a result of their involvement in the technique of "organizational development," have utilized "managerial grids." Although the grid has not appeared to any great extent in the field of education, its application to programs and teachers has become inevitable. By substituting the words *programs* for *produc-*

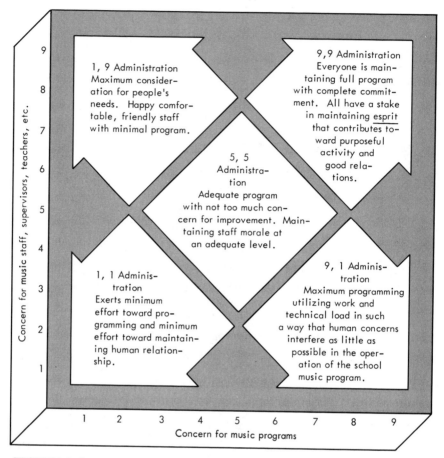

FIGURE 4–1

tion or *output*; *staff and teachers* for *employees*; and *administrative* for *managerial,* a grid would function in a school music department as shown in Figure 4–1. There are two key variables shown in every music department—existing programs and members of the staff. An administrative grid concerns itself with the relationship between these programs and its concern for people. In this particular case the word *concern* is not used in terms of results but rather as a measurable degree of concern. This is not to be construed as meaning merely the meeting of human needs or the devising of programs as such; it actually refers to measuring how program development and meeting human needs influence and interact with each other.

The various combinations are shown in Figure 4–1. The horizontal line represents programs, and the vertical line measures the concern for individuals. The scale runs from 1 to 9, with 1 being the lowest concern and 9 being the highest.

The 1,1 in the lower left-hand corner indicates a minimal interest in members of the staff and a minimal music program. The upper left corner, which reads 1,9, indicates the maximum concern for total staff but a minimal concern for music experience and programming. The 9,1 reading in the lower right-hand part of the grid exhibits the maximum concern for programs with little concern for human relationships and staff needs. The ideal, of course, is the 9,9 in the upper right-hand corner, which reveals concern for optional programs with maximum concern for staff. In the center of the diagram we find the middle of the road, which indicates a 50 percent concern in both areas.

Once the music administrator and/or his supervisor-colleagues have studied and reviewed the grid, they may wish to revise priorities and practices. The grid should force them to assess their procedures and adjust them as they work toward the 9,9 goal on the grid.

Steps taken in the process are as follows:

1. Each administrator and/or supervisor examines his own style or approach utilizing administrative-grid procedures. Such examination should include a self-analysis instrument, self-administered testing based on current practices in behavioral objectives, and other pertinent evaluative educational devices.
2. The members of the staff then involve themselves in a group evaluation in order to determine the "team" effectiveness.
3. The entire staff of music administrators, supervisors, department heads, or whoever else is included in the administrative design for music then reviews, diagnoses, and determines the major areas needed for improvement.

The entire approach is self-administered by the administration. A consultant may be involved, however, only at the instigation of the group doing the self-evaluation. Once all factors have been determined, then a program of in-service education may be instituted to improve the weak areas so that the ultimate 9,9 on the grid may be achieved.

Actually, both organizational development and administrative or managerial grids are based on commonsense procedures. But, unless a definite program is designed or structured, they, like so many obvious commonsense procedures, may be overlooked or never used.

■

CONCLUDING OBSERVATIONS

The successful music administrator is aware of the principles, techniques and qualities mentioned in this chapter. Few have studied them in a formal sense, but the effective ones have instincts that help them or have observed other managers (successful and not so successful) in a critical way. Still others have had mentors who have provided both advice and opportunity.

Unfortunately, there are few opportunities to learn to become an effective manager of a music unit. There are individual graduate courses in universities, individual sessions that deal with management techniques at meetings of professional associations, and even week-long seminar workshops conducted on a very few college campuses. In higher education, the American Council of Education has sponsored internship experiences for several years. A few music administrators have pursued doctoral programs in administration of one kind or another.

The typical music administrator comes to the position from the teaching ranks. He is usually perceived as a successful teacher and is well organized, energetic, and able to get along well with people. From there on, it is an on-the-job learning experience. In many colleges there is a rotating-chair concept, whereby one person may serve one three-year term (and possibly another), then another person, and so on. There is little incentive to stay in such a position, because the release time is too small, the secretarial help is inadequate, and the person must teach and maintain academic credentials while running the department—more like two full-time jobs. There is practically *no* incentive to plan very far into the future.

Yet when music managerial positions open in the public schools or at colleges and universities, there are plenty of applicants. People are attracted to administration for a variety of reasons: they want to help make a difference, to contribute to the improvement of musical education, or to deal with ideas, plans, and programs. There is excitement in music administration, in addition to frustration and discouragement.

In the next few years we will see more-organized attempts to educate music managers. Professional bodies and officials at major colleges and universities will offer more courses, more seminars, more workshops, perhaps even concentrations within graduate degrees that pertain to the management of music units. It is long overdue.

NOTES

1. Paul Hersey and Ken Blanchard, *Management of Organizational Behavior*, 4th ed. (Englewood Cliffs, N.J.: Prentice-Hall, 1982), p. 3.
2. Peter F. Drucker, *Management: Tasks, Responsibilities, and Practices* (New York: Harper and Row, 1974), pp. 45–47.
3. Dabney Park, Jr., "What Management Is and Isn't," *Educational Record* 61, no. 4 (Fall 1980), p. 74.

4. Alan Lakein, *How to Get Control of Your Time and Your Life* (New York: Peter H. Wyden, 1973).

5. Kenneth E. Eble, *The Art of Administration* (San Francisco: Jossey-Bass Publishers, 1978), p. 13.

6. *Ibid.*, pp. 14–22.

7. Peter F. Drucker, *Management* (New York: Harper and Row, 1973).

8. Terry O'Bannion, "Liontamers, Clowns, and Highwire Artists: A Profile of the Academic Manager," Proceedings of Academic Chairpersons: Administrative Responsibilities, conference sponsored by Kansas State University, Orlando, Florida 1984 (Manhattan, Kansas: Kansas State University, "Issues in Higher Education" series).

9. *Ibid.*, p. 9.

SUPPLEMENTARY READINGS

Balderston, F. E. *Managing Today's University*. San Francisco: Jossey-Bass, 1974.

Basil, D. C. *Women in Management*. New York: Dornellen, 1972.

Byars, Lloyd L., and Rue, Leslie W. *Personnel Management: Concepts and Applications*. New York: Holt, 1980.

Drucker, P. "How to Manage Your Time: Everybody's No. 1 Problem." *Harper's*, December 1966, pp. 56–60.

Ewing, D. W., ed. *Long-Range Planning for Management*. New York: Harper and Row, 1972.

Gordon, F. E., and Strober, M. *Bringing Women into Management*. New York: McGraw-Hill, 1975.

Henderson, A. D. "Finding and Training Academic Administrators." *Public Administration Review* 20 (1960), pp. 17–22.

Herzberg, F. *The Managerial Choice: To Be Efficient and to Be Human*. Homewood, Ill.: Dow Jones-Irwin, 1976.

Hungate, Thad L. *Management in Higher Education*. New York: Teachers College, Columbia University, 1964.

Jellema, William W., ed. *Efficient College Management*. San Francisco: Jossey-Bass, 1972.

Lahti, R. *Innovative College Management*. San Francisco: Jossey-Bass, 1973.

McGregor, D. *The Professional Manager*. New York: McGraw-Hill, 1967.

Vaill, Peter B. *Managing as a Performing Art*. San Francisco: Jossey-Bass, 1989.

STUDY QUESTIONS

1. How is management different from leadership?
2. What is management?
3. How does one go about setting goals for a music unit?
4. How does one organize time for maximum efficiency?
5. What is there about music administration that is inherently inefficient?
6. What are the tools of management? To what extent should a manager have command of those tools? How should they be used?
7. How does one learn to become an effective manager of a music unit?

5

Personnel Practices

*A*mong the major concerns for the chief executive officer of a music unit in a university or a public school are those pertaining to personnel matters: recruiting; selecting; evaluating; and providing opportunities for growth and development of faculty. In seeking faculty for a music department, the music administrator should identify specific competencies as well as personal qualifications that will fulfill the desired need. This does not negate the possibility of selecting an outstanding individual whose competencies may differ from those necessary for a specific vacancy, as when a shift of present assignments will allow the utilization of the talents of the desired individual. Specifying the competencies being sought does, however, provide direction in the selection process and guidelines in selecting music personnel.

After a person has been hired, the music administrator has the immediate responsibility of providing guidance to that person by evaluating his work and identifying areas of strength and weakness. Data must be accumulated so that a recommendation can be made concerning the continued employment of the individual in the music unit.

The selection and evaluation of personnel in the public schools, while different in process, is no less important than similar functions in colleges and universities. The object here, too, is to seek out and select the most qualified candidates, to provide support and assistance for faculty members, to identify strengths and weaknesses, and to suggest ways and means to improve performance.

Rarely are students involved in the assessment of teachers in the public schools. Nor, as a rule, are there peer committees to sift through evidence and render a judgment about a colleague's effectiveness. Sometimes, however, there are parents and members of the community who become involved in the evaluation of a faculty member. Normally the evaluation responsibility rests with a building principal, a supervisor, or a city director of music.

This chapter will discuss ways and means of selecting and screening possible candidates for employment in the music unit and methods of evaluating the contributions of music faculty members. Sections on the hiring and evaluating of music faculty members in higher education and public schools are included to show the differences that exist.

■ HIGHER EDUCATION

The Vacancy

Vacancies in the field of music in higher education occur for a variety of reasons. Faculty members retire or leave for personal, professional, or family reasons. Others are on temporary tracks and are in and out annually. A few—but *very* few—move to positions in other colleges and universities (see Appendix D for position notices).

With the increase in retirement age from sixty-eight to seventy, some faculty members are remaining in positions for a longer period of time than was previously the case. In part because of this, an increasing number of institutions are offering early-retirement inducements, which make it extremely attractive to retire early.

Once a vacancy in the music unit has been determined, for whatever reason, a decision must be made as to where the position should be allocated. The department is faced with a decision as to whether the allocation should be made to the area in which the vacancy was created, split between two areas where need exists, or allocated to a new area within the department. Ross suggests that consideration be given to several questions in coming to grips with this problem:

1. What have been the enrollment patterns in the areas to be considered over the past 3–5 years?
2. What is your best guess as to enrollment predictions in these areas for the next 3–5 years?
3. How reliable are your enrollment data?
4. How do these areas relate to the general program needs of the total music unit?
5. Is the funding for the position and its support services sufficient to carry out the goals you have set for the area?
6. Would the assignment of the position to a particular area reflect your unit's general mission?[1]

Careful consideration must be given to the allocation of positions. If a new program, such as one in music/business, is to be created, a line to support that program must be found somewhere. The likelihood of receiving a new faculty line is bleak in today's world. Thus, a line—or a partial line—from an area within the department will have to be secured. Some hard choices have to be made following internal study and perhaps much negotiating (see Appendix C).

A key question—made popular by Peter Drucker—is, What is our business?[2] Is our business music performance, music education, music theater? Is it opera, music combined with some outside field? Is it a combination of the foregoing? Who are our constituents? What "business" can we conduct in a quality manner, given our resources, our market position, our location, our history and reputation.

Answers to these and other questions about mission, goals, and purpose need to be addressed before a determination is made about filling a vacancy. Once a determination has been made about the area in which the position is placed, we are set to accomplish the search.

The Search Committee

The identification of a search committee chair is a crucial first step. At some institutions the department chair, director, or dean chairs search committees. It is more common, however, for other faculty to serve in such roles, and quite often an area coordinator (such as the head of the keyboard division) serves as chair of a search committee to seek a colleague in the particular area. There should be a mixture of gender on search committees, as well as a person of minority status, where possible.

In the instance where a committee is chosen to select a new keyboard faculty member, it is wise to include a person on the committee with disciplinary interests in an area different from that in which the selection is being made. A theory person on a keyboard committee, for example, can be looking for different things, can be asking different questions, can be making observations different from those of other committee members. He can be assessing how this candidate will fit in with the remainder of the faculty, the level of "complete" musicianship, and the breadth of interests outside the keyboard area. Experience has shown that such persons can be a leavening influence on search committees.

To avoid tie votes, search committees should have an uneven number of members. Should they be three, five or seven? Experience indicates that in instances where searches have to be carried out quickly or at odd times, such as in the summer, a three-person committee can be satisfactory. Under normal circumstances, however, three people usually do not represent enough points of view.

A seven-person committee is cumbersome in many ways, not the least of which is finding agreeable meeting times. A five-person search committee seems to be ideal and is recommended for most searches. Yet another consideration in search committee size is the number of job applicants in the pool. If the position is in the area of piano, where the applicant pool is apt to number more than a hundred, a five-person committee is needed to handle the work load and to conduct the follow-up of the most promising candidates.

The Job Description and the Screening Process

A vacancy announcement should contain the <u>title</u> of the position, the <u>date the appointment</u> is effective, <u>qualifications</u>, <u>responsibilities</u>, expected <u>rank and salary</u>, <u>materials to be submitted</u>—by when and to whom—and the <u>deadline</u> for submitting materials. Most institutions also include a descriptive paragraph about the institution, department or school, and region in the announcement of the position. Search committees often take the position that they will not begin an evaluation of materials unless, and until, the file is complete (see Appendix D for a sample job description).

The object of position announcements is to attract a highly qualified pool of candidates. Descriptions should be complete but terse— telling enough but not everything—and be both specific and general. It may be that as an administrator you know *exactly* what this person will be doing for every portion of his assignment. But, if any latitude is possible in a position, it is best to leave the full breadth of the job undescribed. This allows room for negotiation—for tailoring to some extent the position to the person. It may well be that the very best candidate for the position can handle 80 percent of the assignment with ease but is less qualified for that final fifth. If there is some latitude possible, it works to everyone's advantage. The use of "general" language in the description will add to the number of interested candidates.

Materials to be submitted with applications often include a letter of application, transcripts, curriculum vitae, current (within two years) letters of reference, programs, reviews, and offprints. In the case of performance faculty, tapes are a part of the process. When there is a reasonable period of time for the search, there may be a cutoff of candidates based on the quality of the credentials. A final group, or short list, of candidates is then asked to submit audio and/ or video tapes for consideration. Some search committees wish to approach this phase of their evaluation "blind" (i.e., with the names of candidates obscured on the tapes). A tape is numbered by a neutral person (e.g., the music librarian) and is then listened to and rated by each member of the search committee. After all tapes have been evaluated, there is a meeting at which the anonymous ratings of the tapes are compared to the ratings of the candidates according to their credentials. Such a system allows for objectivity and fairness, both important principles in the selection of a faculty member. It provides also for a "star" performer (i.e., one whose credentials might not have been as strong as others) to have renewed life in the pool of candidates.

The Pool of Candidates

The object of any faculty position search is to bring together an institution with a need and the best possible person to fill that need. In order to do that, there must be a pool of candidates that is of a size sufficient that a quality selection can be made. A sizable pool of qualified candidates needs to be developed through broadly based advertising. Notices of the opening should be sent to the College Music Society,[3] to the *Chronicle of Higher Education*,[4] and to Luttons Music Personnel Service.[5]

In addition, notices should be sent to members of the National Association of Schools of Music (NASM).[6] Many NASM institutions have placement agencies (especially those offering the doctorate), and others have faculty who are interested in making a move. It is also helpful to seek out contacts that would be helpful in attracting candidates from protected classes. Certain specialized journals can be helpful in reaching certain populations (e.g., the National Association of College Wind and Percussion Instructors)[7] of musicians/teachers. And finally, there are the letters and phone calls to persons known by members of the faculty who can help by providing names of persons to contact or the names of candidates "who would be just right for your job."

The Interview/Audition

After the candidate pool has been reduced to the number to be interviewed in person (three is common), the interview/audition must be arranged. Interviews for most faculty positions can be conducted in one day; some cannot because of personal schedules, class or rehearsal times, or the need to touch base with a large number of people on the campus.

If the position is one involving classroom instruction, clearly the committee must see and hear the candidate teach a class or deliver a lecture. If the position is in performance, an audition is essential. It is also helpful in such cases to ask the candidate to teach a lesson or to conduct a master class with students. If conducting is involved, the candidate needs to have a group with which to work, in order to observe the person's priorities—his ability to detect errors and to make suggestions that produce a positive musical difference.

There need to be personal interviews with the head of the music unit and with someone from the dean's or vice-president's office. Conversations also need to be arranged with students, who can ask questions in a setting where they feel free to cover matters of concern to them.

Obviously the interviews (it may be a good idea to bookend the day with two of these) with the search committee are of critical importance. These are the people who know the candidate best—who have identified him as the cream of the crop of candidates and have said in effect, "This person is worth the college's money and our time to bring to our campus for this interview/audition." Does he live up to expectations? Is this individual the dynamite person we were led to believe he was?

The interview/audition process must be thorough and tough. It must include an examination of everything about the candidate *that is relevant to the job.* Questions must be probing. You must find out what a candidate believes, how a candidate thinks. The committee must develop a perception of a candidate's attitude toward learning. You must probe the depth of musicianship. There is a need to know of commitment to the profession and something of the individual's short- and long-range goals. A key question to ask is, Will this individual complement the other members of the faculty; does he/she have something *different* to offer—perhaps even something unique? Too many music faculties in higher education are uniform in character, with one faculty member being a near copy of the other. Students are not well served by such homogeneity.

A packet of materials should be assembled for candidates. Such things as descriptions of fringe benefits, evaluation procedures, departmental or school structure, catalogs, curriculum sheets, promotional materials, scholarship information, campus maps, and information about the community are helpful.

Integrating the Information

The process of establishing a vacancy, securing approval to search for someone to fill the vacancy, and conducting the search can take several months (even years on occasion). There is nothing more important in the life of a music department than the selection of quality faculty. It follows that the process of selecting its members must be fair, rigorous, open, and related directly to the job for which the vacancy exists.

All persons who participate in the interview/audition process should be asked their opinion of the candidate. Students observe things that faculty do not. The accompanist at an audition brings a unique perspective to the process. The dean's or vice-president's office can offer a perspective based on hundreds of interviews across many disciplines. It goes without saying that the persons closest to the process, the search committee and the head of the music unit, will have more experiences with the candidate upon which to draw in arriving at a recommendation.

The sum of the impressions of all of the candidates should result in a highly informed recommendation. It could be that all are acceptable in a certain priority order. It may be that only one is acceptable or that none is, in which case it will be back to the pool for the search committee unless it has developed an alternate list to fall back upon.

The goal of appointing the best possible person to the position is one that should be foremost in the mind of everyone involved in the search process. When that person has been determined, it is up to the head of the music unit to sell his superiors on the qualities of the candidate so that an attractive offer can be made. Further conversation may be necessary to convince the candidate of the merits of the department, the college, and the community. Interview/auditions are two-way streets where each side is seeking answers to questions—as well as to impress the other. Some searches have come to unhappy conclusions because of an institutional attitude that every candidate in the world can hardly wait to join the faculty. As a result, the interview process may have been unfriendly, perhaps even confrontational, and may have left a bad taste in the candidate's mouth. When the offer actually is extended, the candidate who already has a job may respond, "No, thanks."

Assuming that the search committee and the music-unit head are in agreement about the particular candidate and that other necessary officials have given their approval, an offer is extended. This is commonly done by phone and in an "unofficial" manner to be certain that the candidate is still interested and that the terms are acceptable. If they are not, then some negotiations may take place. When the parties are in agreement, there is usually a final series of forms that must work their way through the system (including a sign-off by the affirmative-action officer) to the person who writes the official letter of appointment (usually the chief academic officer). When the candidate returns a signed document signifying acceptance of the offer, the search may be considered closed. Then, and only then, should all candidates in the search receive a formal notification of the appointment. While this may lengthen the process, it represents a much better alternative than having to say, "We closed the search, but now are having to reopen it; I know I told you once that you were no longer being considered but we've changed our minds and the situation has changed." The wise music administrator does not burn bridges in matters of faculty searches.

It is an exhilarating experience to bring to the faculty an outstanding person. The enthusiasm of a new faculty member is energizing to colleagues. Such a success justifies the time and care involved in bringing such a person on board.

■

PUBLIC SCHOOLS

Recruiting

Since a music department is no better than the teacher in the classroom, everyone on the faculty should be involved in securing competent personnel. The music administrator should be especially concerned that all individuals involved in the music program pursue every avenue and source for both experienced and inexperienced personnel with the desired potential to become members of the music faculty. Some of the most competent teachers have come directly from completion of their bachelor's degrees, so one should maintain an active recruiting program on campuses as well as in other locations.

Visits to select higher-education institutions to seek out potential music teachers should be conducted on a regularly scheduled basis. If a music supervisor or director conducts the interview, then the interview/audition may be handled on the scene, with advance notification. This would save everyone considerable time and expense, and indicates an interest on the part of a school system in the university's graduates. This interest builds rapport with the institution and aids in procuring the better graduates. Notices of vacancies that exist should appear in appropriate journals and professional newspapers so that all interested parties have an opportunity to apply and be considered.

The Selection Process

The quality of experiences offered in a school classroom is directly related to the quality of a teacher in that particular situation. There may be other factors involving personnel that impinge upon these learning experiences, such as conflicts within a school, but essentially a competent, creative teacher will manage almost any situation with varying degrees of success. It is therefore incumbent on a music administrator to pursue every possible means to secure the most able teachers for the music program. Many school systems have prepared printed materials describing and publicizing the advantages of teaching in their school system.

Procedures for selecting teachers will differ. In larger, urban communities the personnel office may be the sole agency for selecting, appointing, and assigning staff. It selects a teacher and then notifies the director of music or the music department of the appointment. It is then the administration's responsibility to assimilate the individual into the practices and curricular concepts of the school system. Incidentally, regardless of the size of the community, it is desirable, if possible, that the building principal meet the new teacher before the assignment is finalized. Unfortunately, leaving the sole responsibility for selection to a personnel office has too many negative aspects for music teaching. Rather than emphasizing the quality of teacher secured, such a plan operates on the basis that once a so-called qualified person is found, the system will educate and develop him. In some cases, this practice was established to eliminate the abuses of prejudice and discrimination in selection procedures. In some instances, it was a more expeditious way of dealing with the problems of school staffing and may be quite adequate in certain areas of instruction.

The Interview/Audition

Music is an art form that deals with organized sound involving aesthetic judgment and musical communication, and as such, it must be taught by teachers who possess, in addition to educational skills, certain artistic skills that can be measured only by an audition. Arguments by school officials against the use of the audition are based on the idea that by virtue of a certificate and a college degree, candidates have exhibited sufficient training to merit at least an opportunity to prove themselves in a classroom. Intellectually this may be true, but what a transcript primarily reveals is the number of courses taken and the academic success in those courses. It does not measure musicality. It is true that a skilled administrator can find subtleties in a transcript that are clues in these areas. However, in such cases it is even more to the advantage of the candidate to be auditioned. Any misconceptions regarding his musicality may then be dispelled. The audition should not be just a performance test per se. It should consist of both an interview and a performance, including some conducting. Teachers cannot be expected to maintain the same proficiency on their performing instrument as can a professional. They should, however, by rhythmically accurate in performance and be able to distinguish intervals prop-

[handwritten marginal notes: WHAT SHOULD BE INCLUDED IN THE INTERVIEW/AUDITION ARE: A) ELEM, GEN. MUS B) CHORAL c) (INSTRUM. etc...)]

erly. They should also be able to hear discrepancies in intonation and detect errors in a rehearsal. Regardless of the level of technical accomplishment, the performance should be musical. Candidates should be able to discuss their philosophy of music education and its application in a classroom situation.

Elementary general music teachers should be able to read at sight from the average fourth- or fifth-grade series book. They should be able to improvise and perform simple accompaniments to the songs in the book. (This might be on the piano or a guitar.) The degree of piano skill expected will vary according to the attitude of the music administrator and the curricular objectives for music in that school system. Musical examinations need not be complex or technically demanding to be revealing.

The interview should be conducted in such a manner that the candidate is comfortable and reassured that the director is genuinely interested in his ability and potential. There should be ample preparation before the candidate arrives. The transcript and credentials, including recommendations, should be fully examined so that when the candidate appears, the interviewer will be aware of his background and be able to direct the interview accordingly. It is important that the applicant be given every opportunity to express himself rather than be the object of an administrator's frustration in monologue. Specific answers are not nearly so important as thought processes, and questions should be couched in a manner to reveal those processes. It is far more important that the potential teacher be able to explain *why* he prefers a particular text than to explain the text itself. Opinions may change and one's ability to think and communicate is far more significant for growth and development than precise, expected responses. A teacher's potential is as important as his present knowledge, and that can best be revealed by the candidate's expressing himself at length.

Candidates should be provided with information regarding the nature of the community, especially the cultural and economic advantages. (The Detroit school system distributes brochures to prospective teachers.) Candidates should also be apprised of the nature of the position (see Appendix D), the fringe benefits, and the manner in which salary and tenure are determined. When the vacancy has been filled, all applicants should be notified of the outcome as quickly as possible.

It is important to remember that interviews and auditions, by their very nature, are periods of stress and anxiety for the applicant. Empathy and sympathy are important. A sensitive interviewer does not allow the pressure of the moment to influence his judgment. And under no circumstances should bias based on race or creed be a factor. If a rejected candidate wishes to reapply, he should be given every opportunity to do so. Every effort should be made to guarantee the applicant a fair and equitable hearing. Otherwise, the entire audition privilege of the department may be revoked.

In the Detroit public schools, for example, the director or his designated supervisor conducts the audition to determine the candidate's musicality and interviews the prospective teacher to ascertain his knowledge of materials, technique, and procedures. If there are any questions relating to other factors, the candidate is then referred to a representative committee made up of administrators, teachers, and personnel. It makes the final decision regarding the candidate's desirability. This procedure eliminates most prejudicial practices.

Finally, one of the most important services that the interview/audition renders is diagnostic. It not only gives the candidate an opportunity to analyze his own capabilities under pressure but may also serve as the initial step toward in-service education for a probationary teacher. New teachers become aware of weaknesses and strengths even before entering the classroom. The supervisor assigned to that teacher anticipates some of the problems and obviates difficulties with preliminary assistance and training.

Under no circumstances should the interview/audition be regarded as a means of eliminating candidates. It should be regarded only as a means of finding desirable, knowledgeable, even exciting teachers. Successful interviewing is a matter of attitude.

EVALUATING FACULTY MEMBERS

Higher Education

Teaching, and especially music teaching, is always being evaluated. Students evaluating their experiences in the studio, the ensemble, the laboratory, and the classroom are implicitly evaluating their teachers. The audience in the recital or concert hall is evaluating the teacher's handiwork, and while a performer's family may think the performance sheer perfection, faculty members will function as supportive or disgruntled critics, eager to look behind what they are hearing to determine whether the teaching-learning process has really occurred. The chairman or dean is evaluating every meeting or exposure with faculty to assess competence, sincerity, musicianship, scholarship, and whether the faculty member's chief concern is indeed with the student and his musical education.

Evaluation is of great importance in higher education—indeed, all education today—and is likely to become more so. To repeat a much overworked truism, we live in an era of accountability, and in order to be fully accountable, we must become skilled in evaluating people and programs (see Appendix A for evaluation forms).

The purposes of evaluation most frequently mentioned are the improvement of instruction and the contribution to a fairer personnel reward system. Researchers in the field term evaluation "formative" (evaluation used to provide feedback to the individual about his effectiveness) or "summative" (evaluation used to assign a rating of worth or merit).

Who should be involved in the evaluation of faculty members? Popular responses to this question include students, colleagues, and department chairs. Less frequently mentioned by faculty themselves are deans and alumni.

Student Ratings

Here are three common stated concerns about student ratings of faculty:

1. Students cannot really evaluate a teacher until they have left college and gotten some perspective on what was really valuable to them. Some of us may look back on our own undergraduate experience and say, "I disliked Professor X while I was in school, but now I realize what he did for me." Such changes of opinion are the exception rather than the rule, say A. J. Drucker and H. H. Remmers.[8] Their study showed that student ratings of instructors correlate positively with ratings of the same instructors ten years later (.40 to .49).

2. A second concern expressed is that the characteristics of students affect their ratings of instructors. On the contrary, the characteristics of age, sex, course grade, and class year make little difference in ratings of teaching. Graduate students, however, rate teachers higher than do undergraduates.[8]

3. The characteristics of instructors are said to be related to student ratings of teaching effectiveness. *Not so!* The sex of the teacher makes no difference. Researchers have found that instructors with a bachelor's degree are rated lower than those with a master's or a doctorate, and while teaching assistants are rated lower than regular faculty, there is no significant difference in scores among the four academic ranks.

One might expect that faculty members with the heaviest teaching loads would receive lower student ratings because of less time for preparation and other teaching-related activities, but the opposite is true. Analysis of ratings for eight thousand teachers by Centra and Creech[9] indicates that teachers carrying loads of thirteen or more credit hours were given the highest ratings.

Research and writing certainly help to keep a faculty member current, so one might suspect a positive correlation between scholarly productivity and teaching effectiveness. A few studies support this expectation, but several others report no association between research productivity as reflected in the numbers of books and articles published and students' ratings of teaching effectiveness. Publications apparently are not essential for good teaching; therefore, the use of publication counts will not reflect teaching performance as judged by students.

If one is seeking a rating scale, such scales can be found at numerous institutions across the country. The Educational Testing Service publishes the Student Information Report (SIR), which can be computer tabulated.[10] There are thirty-nine items on that form, with an additional ten items that can be added by the instructor. In the use of student evaluations of teaching, one should take steps to preserve the anonymity of the respondent. In order to secure the most honest and helpful responses, one should provide a neutral atmosphere (i.e., with the instructor out of the room). In the case of performance instruction, the student might return the form directly to the department chairman. More effective is the suggestion that faculty members hold a studio class or recital sometime during the evaluation period and pass out the forms to everyone at once, absent themselves from the room, and have the forms delivered to the office, as is done with other classes. Studies have shown that students are intimidated by the instructor being in the room at the time the evaluation form is being completed and that ratings are significantly higher when the instructor is present. Student rating forms should be able to be completed in ten or fifteen minutes; anything longer strains student interest and tolerance and diminishes the quality of responses, especially if evaluation forms have been completed in several courses.

In summary, the research about student ratings of teachers reveals the following:

1. There is general agreement among students and between students and faculty on the effectiveness of teachers.
2. The judgments that students make about their teachers on the spot and while they are still very close to the learning process persist and are replicated years after they graduate.
3. Student ratings are relatively independent of student characteristics that are commonly thought of as sources of bias (grade point average, grade expected in course, class level).
4. Student ratings are positively correlated with the amount of student learning.

Kenneth Eble states, "Student evaluations wisely-formulated, wisely-administered, and wisely-used are useful in improving teaching. It is also clear that student evaluations are not the sole measure of a faculty member's competence."[11]

In spite of the growing but still somewhat spotty evidence on the validity of student evaluations of teaching, their use is increasing.

Objectives

At some point the objectives of the institution or department and the priorities it holds may—or perhaps must—come into play.

In evaluating a faculty member in music, one must be careful to account for the factors that make him unique. There are people in theory, history, literature, and music education who teach in formal classroom settings with large lecture groupings, small drill classes, and even smaller seminars. There are those who spend their entire day in a studio in a one-on-one encounter. Others ply their trade on the cork end of the baton. Many faculty members, especially in smaller departments, engage in several of these teaching activities in a given week. It is doubtful if one kind of evaluation procedure or instrument, whether by student, peer, chairman, or dean, will suffice for all of these instructional settings.

Nor does any such procedure account for other elements to be evaluated—namely, service to the department, service to the university, service to the community, professional involvement and research, creativity and publication. One can easily enumerate the committees on which one has served, the offices one has held, the meetings one has attended, and the performances of the past year, but where does the assessment of quality come in? This is troublesome, to be sure, and is something with which the person responsible for the evaluation of faculty must wrestle. How does one say to a colleague, "Yes, I am aware you are on six committees, but your service on those committees is hardly distinguished." In matters such as this, it is the responsibility of peer committees and chairmen to come to grips with the matter of "quality." Just what is excellence in service? What is excellence in research? What is an excellent performance? These questions are difficult to answer and harder to objectify, but they are crucial to the growth and development of departments or schools of music and to those who populate them.

No HELP HERE...

Current Policies and Practices

In a *1975* study entitled *How Colleges Evaluate Professors,* Peter Seldin surveyed policies and practices in evaluating classroom teaching performance in 491 liberal arts colleges in the United States.[12] Another study by Seldin, conducted in 1983, surveyed all accredited four-year undergraduate liberal arts colleges listed in the U.S. Department of Education's *Educational Directory*.[13] Responses to this second survey were received from 616 deans, a response rate of 80 percent. Researchers (Seldin among them) have consistently found that academic deans identified classroom teaching as the most important factor in the evaluation of faculty performance.

Several methods emerge as "most popular" when it comes to evaluating faculty, as shown in Table 5–1. Current practices include self-evaluation, colleague evaluation through classroom visits, and student evaluation.

Self-evaluation. Many critics doubt the accuracy and reliability of self-evaluation. One researcher found that while most college teachers believe they can evaluate their own performance, few actu-

TABLE 5–1

Factors	Private Colleges (N = 515)		Public Colleges (N = 96)	
	Major factor %	Not a factor %	Major factor %	Not a factor %
Classroom teaching	98.8	0.4	99.0	0.0
Supervision of graduate study	3.1	7.8	7.4	5.2
Supervision of honors program	1.9	17.1	7.3	22.9
Research	31.3	7.0	45.8	2.1
Publication	27.0	6.6	40.6	3.1
Public Service	13.8	10.9	35.4	1.0
Consultation (govt., business)	1.9	36.1	5.2	26.0
Activity in professional societies	22.3	5.4	34.4	2.1
Student advising	64.9	1.4	43.8	6.3
Campus committee work	52.2	1.2	54.2	2.1
Length of service in rank	48.3	10.1	37.5	15.6
Competing job offers	1.7	64.7	2.1	59.4
Personal attributes	30.7	13.8	15.6	25.0

Source: Peter Seldin, *Changing Practices in Faculty Evaluation* (San Francisco: Jossey-Bass, 1984), 36.

ally do it. As a matter of fact, few college or university evaluation systems include self-evaluation. A 1977 survey by Centra found that self-evaluation ranked ninth among fifteen criteria in importance.[14] The goal of self-analysis is to encourage the teacher to examine what he is doing by answering a series of questions. A 1973 study by Centra revealed that 30 percent of the teachers rated themselves better than did their students; 6 percent gave themselves considerably poorer ratings.[15]

Colleague Evaluation Through Classroom Visits. This process can be particularly helpful if the visitor has advance information about material to be covered or a course outline, says one researcher. Jerry Gaff and Robert Wilson state that colleagues can provide information and criticism and can reinforce a teacher for his efforts and accomplishments, but N.L. Gage states that "when a teacher knows he is being watched by someone whose opinion will determine his promotion or salary, his performance may depend more on his nerve than on his teaching skill."[16]

[handwritten margin note: EVALUATION BY: ——— MUSIC ADMIN. PEER ELECTED COMMITTEE (OR: TENURE)]

This procedure obviously calls for a lot of trust—and perhaps a generous supply of faith as well. Many music-unit heads visit classes, lessons, and rehearsals of faculty members who are being considered for promotion. Such visits can form the basis for a firsthand statement in the recommendation concerning the promotion.

Evaluation by peers provides a perspective that differs from that of supervisors and students, and it is a fact of life at most institutions that personnel or promotion-tenure committees are elected to fulfill this function. Studies completed on 1956 (Maslow and Zimmerman)[17] and 1972 (Murray)[18] found that correlations between student and peer evaluations were .69 and .87, respectively. Highly respectable numbers, to be sure.

Institutions differ; departments differ. In department A there will be a heavy emphasis on performance ability, highly refined specialization, and the development of regional, national, or perhaps international reputation. Department B will serve its constituents best if faculty members are versatile and function effectively while wearing different hats. In Department C there may be a middle ground or even the situation in which many kinds of faculty exist together—that is, the full-time narrow specialist and the generalist who can pick up all the extra pieces and handle diverse assignments effectively. Thus, it becomes exceedingly important for each department, school, and college to work out its own procedures and standards for what will be assessed and how colleagues are to be utilized in this process.

Much has already been said about student evaluation. There is little doubt that it is here to stay. Positive student evaluations may generally be summarized as follows:

1. The instructor is well versed in his subject, organizes it well, and presents it interestingly.
2. The instructor is dynamic, enthusiastic, and stimulating as a person.
3. The instructor understands and sincerely likes students.
4. The instructor practices what he preaches; he sets a good example.
5. The instructor uses various instructional methods.
6. The instructor has a sense of humor.

Pos.

Negative student reactions are generally clustered around the following points:

1. The course is poorly organized, lacks substance, and is repetitious.
2. The instructor makes unclear or unreasonable assignments.
3. The instructor engages in improper or unfair evaluation.
4. Class time is wasted on irrelevant or unimportant matters.

Neg.

At least one large university has now mandated student evaluations in matters of faculty appointment or promotion. Centra found that the number of students rating each course and the number of courses per faculty members are critical items if one is making a decision concerning promotion.[19] Ratings from eight or ten students may provide *some* useful information for the instructor but little or no evidence for a promotion or tenure decision. Five or more courses in which fifteen students respond will yield a "dependable" assessment of teaching effectiveness.

The proportion of a class that rates an instructor is as important as the number of raters. If only twenty out of sixty students in a class respond to a rating form, it is possible they do not represent the reactions of the entire class.

It should be recognized that small classes (fewer than fifteen students) are most highly rated. Next come those with sixteen to thirty-five students. Classes with thirty-five to a hundred students receive the lowest ratings. Classes with more than a hundred students receive higher ratings, probably because colleges and departments assign their best teachers and resources to large classes.

The critical question is not *whether* student evaluations should be a part of the process but *what leverage* they should exert. How should they be incorporated into the process along with peer and chairman review?

Criteria for Evaluation

Seldin's 1983 analysis of the levels of importance of criteria used in the overall evaluation of faculty performance indicated the following:

1. Classroom teaching was a major factor for 99 percent of the deans.

PERSONNEL PRACTICES

2. Receiving responses of 50 percent or more as "major factors" were student advising, length of service in rank, personal attributes, and committee work.
3. Rated as "minor factors" by 50 percent of the deans were professional societies, public service, publication, and research.

Table 5–2 shows the ranking of thirteen factors considered in evaluating faculty performance as revealed in the data Seldin gathered in his 1983 study. The table shows the following:

TABLE 5–2

Factors	Private colleges (N = 515)		Public Colleges (N = 96)		Total (N = 616)[a]	
	Mean	Rank	Mean	Rank	Mean	Rank
Classroom teaching	1.02	1	1.00	1	1.01	1
Supervision of graduate study	2.23	10	1.96	9	2.14	10
Supervision of honors program	2.36	11	2.36	12	2.36	11
Research	1.75	5	1.53	3	1.71	5
Publication	1.79	6	1.63	5	1.76	6
Public service	1.97	9	1.65	6	1.92	9
Consultation (govt., business)	2.39	12	2.23	11	2.36	11
Activity in professional societies	1.83	8	1.67	7	1.80	7
Student advising	1.36	2	1.62	4	1.40	2
Campus committee work	1.49	3	1.47	2	1.49	3
Length of service in rank	1.61	4	1.77	8	1.63	4
Competing job offers	2.73	13	2.66	13	2.72	13
Personal attributes	1.82	7	2.11	10	1.86	8

[a]Includes five colleges not specified as private or public.

Source: Peter Seldin, *Changing Practices in Faculty Evaluation* (San Francisco: Jossey-Bass, 1984), 37.

1. The academic deans almost unanimously chose classroom performance as the most important index of overall faculty performance.
2. Private colleges gave greater importance than in the past to research, publication, public service and activity in professional societies. Public colleges continued to venerate these factors.
3. Personal attributes, length of service in rank, and competing job offers were less widely cited than before as important factors in promotion and tenure decisions.
4. Student advising was still widely cited by the private colleges deans as a major factor, although less frequently than in the past.
5. On balance, greater importance was given than before to a wider range of factors in an attempt to achieve wider reliability and scope in assessing overall faculty performance.

Sources of Information

What are the sources of information used to evaluate faculty? The primary source in 1978 and again in 1983 was evaluation by the chair. This was followed in both instances by dean evaluation and the use of systematic student ratings. In the study of Alexander Astin and Calvin B.T. Lee in 1966—after which Seldin patterned his work—it was found that only 23 percent of liberal arts colleges used rating forms filled out by students for evaluating teaching performance.[20] In 1973, Seldin found that *54 percent of a similar group* used specific forms to evaluate teaching. Ten years later two-thirds (67 percent) of the respondents reported "always using" student ratings.

Table 5–3 shows the order of the first three sources of information to be the same in 1978 and 1983, although the percentages are different. The next three sources are likewise in the same order: committee evaluation, colleagues' opinions and self-evaluation.

To summarize this information, six items should be noted:

1. The department chair and the dean were still the predominant information sources on teaching performance.
2. Information on research and publication record had become more widely used.
3. The evidence is compelling that administrators had come to rely on student ratings, whose use jumped dramatically, to help shape their own judgments of teaching competence.
4. Classroom visits, course syllabi and examinations, and faculty self-evaluation gained in popularity.
5. Faculty committees continued to play important roles in evaluating teaching performance.
6. Reliance on informal student opinions, enrollment in elective courses, and alumni opinions were losing importance.

TABLE 5–3

Sources of Information	1978 (N = 680) Always used %	1983 (N = 616) Always used %
Systematic student ratings	54.8	67.5
Informal student opinions	15.2	11.5
Classroom visits	14.3	19.8
Colleagues' opinions	42.7	43.3
Scholarly research and publication	19.9	27.3
Student examination performance	2.7	3.6
Chair evaluation	80.3	81.3
Dean evaluation	76.9	75.0
Course syllabi and examinations	13.9	20.1
Long-term follow-up of students	2.2	3.4
Enrollment in elective courses	2.7	1.1
Alumni opinions	3.4	3.9
Committee evaluation	46.6	46.1
Grade distributions	2.1	4.5
Self-evaluation or report	36.6	41.9

Source: Peter Seldin, *Changing Practices in Faculty Evaluation* (San Francisco: Jossey-Bass, 1984), 45.

(1979)

In a study to determine the practices employed in the evaluation of music faculty in NASM-affiliated colleges and universities, William Hipp surveyed 463 postsecondary member institutions on questions of procedures, criteria, sources of evidence, and formal participants in decisions concerning promotion, tenure, and merit salary increases.[21] Findings from this study revealed among other things the following:

1. More than 80 percent of music units used student evaluations in assessing faculty.
2. From 78 percent to 91 percent of institutions in the four categories of the study (public, private, baccalaureate only, and graduate) required faculty to submit periodic reports of their professional activities.
3. More than 50 percent of music executives reported the use of as-

sessments of the progress of a faculty member's students as a component of faculty evaluation.

4. Assessments of the achievements of a faculty member's former students are not widely used as a source of evidence in the faculty evaluation process.

5. Participants in the decision-making process as it relates to promotion, tenure, and merit salary increases in rank order of importance are as follows: music executive, special faculty committee, tenured music faculty, all music faculty, and students.

6. The single most important purpose of faculty evaluation was the improvement of teaching effectiveness.

Supporting Letters

Let us suppose for a moment that you are one of five members of a committee with the responsibility of voting for or against the promotion of Associate Professor Curtis. After considerable discussion, it is the consensus that Dr. Curtis's teaching is crucial in deciding for or against promotion. The chairman's letter—specifically the statement on teaching that follows—is the evidence on which a decision rests (literary license has been taken with Hildebrand's article):[22]

1. *Teaching.* It is clear that Professor Curtis is a dedicated teacher; he devotes much time to background reading for his course. He starts class promptly and takes time to talk with students before and after class. His exams are difficult and grading is objective and rigorous, though fair. In the past year he was asked to teach two extension courses and was invited to speak to two student organizations. He has guest conducted two high school festivals. At present he is working on a textbook in instrumental methods.

2. Students report that Professor Curtis stresses the intellectual aspects of his subjects, is well prepared, and presents points of view other than his own. He does not have distracting mannerisms. He is willing to meet with students outside class.

3. All members of the department concur that Professor Curtis is a fine teacher and musician. Unquestionably, he is an able, conscientious, and worthy instructor.

What is your conclusion? Should he or should he not be promoted? Actually the evidence presented in the chairman's letter does not help you determine whether he is relatively effective or ineffective.

Paragraph 1 merely describes what Professor Curtis does. The implication is that these things (reading, starting class on time, teaching extension classes, guest conducting, etc.) are good things to do. However, at no point does the chairman commit himself as to the quality of any of these endeavors, except to say that exam grading is fair. For all we know, he *must* do a lot of background reading to stay with the students. His extension course may have been his first and last. This may have been his first speech to student groups, and they may have been bored to tears. His guest conducting may have bombed. The mere performance of activities associated with teaching does not assure that the quality of instruction is adequate, let alone meritorious. The chairman is free with his opinions, but never indicates that any of them are based on firsthand observation.

In paragraph 2 it is not mentioned how many students were consulted or whether any formal device was used to assess student opinion. Students (plural) could be two or eighty-five. The student sample could be 1 percent or 99 percent of all students with whom Professor Curtis works. But the problem for the committee is that they simply *do not know.*

Here is another promotion letter written by a chairman on behalf of Associate Professor West. The section on teaching follows:

1. *Teaching.* A record of the courses taught by Professor West is attached. He teachers lower-division, upper-division, and graduate levels and enrollments range from 10 to 65 students. He conducts one ensemble which performs three concerts per year in addition to a one-week tour. His teaching load is two units above the average for the department.
2. The department recently adopted a form for student evaluation of teaching suggested by Hildebrand and Wilson in 1970; in addition a modification of the Abeles form for ensemble conductors is also used. Returns have been secured from 135 (86%) of the students in Professor West's classes. It will be noted in the summary that Professor West's scores are higher than the departmental mean on 88% of all items.
3. The promotions and tenure committee (five members) feel that these scores are representative of his teaching. As chairman, I have attended his classes and seminars. All members of the Promotion and Tenure Committee and myself have attended his concerts.
4. I consider Professor West to be an exceptional conductor, teacher, and musician. His work is of high quality. He is a credit to the institution and the profession. I recommend his promotion without reservation.

As we examine this letter, we see that paragraph 1 says nothing about the quality of teaching, but does establish that Professor West has a full—or perhaps overfull—teaching load. It also establishes the fact that he deals with a large variety of students and functions both as teacher and conductor.

Paragraph 2 cites the means for securing student reaction. It is neither casual nor capricious. A large percentage of Professor West's students had their say, and the results were highly supportive. The fact that he scored higher than colleagues on 88 percent of the items evaluated is probably good, but if the department is not noted for particularly good teaching, could be a left-handed compliment. Being better than mediocre may not be too convincing a recommendation. But at least the attempt to state comparative statistics was made.

It is worth commenting that the college instructor in his studio or classroom is perhaps the only professional whose métier is performed in the total absence of other professionals. Doctors and nurses see other doctors and nurses at work; lawyers observe lawyers; architects see the work of other architects; accountants see, and check, the work of peers.

Paragraph 3 establishes that this recommendation comes from firsthand observation by more than just the chairman. It is once a curse and a blessing that musicians deal in an art form that is so "public." In those cases where faculty are on display, they reaffirm or deny their claim to quality every time they enter the stage.

The chairman makes his big pitch in paragraph 4. It establishes beyond all doubt *his* recommendation on behalf of the candidate.

It is one thing to make a promotion decision at the department level, but it is something else to get a recommendation accepted at the college or university level. In conversations with departmental promotion and tenure committees and with the candidates themselves, chairmen are urged to stress the need for hard evidence and firsthand observation. If there is someone really worthy of promotion or retention, the departmental objective should be to present the strongest possible case to the committees and administrators at higher levels who must confirm or deny the departmental decision.

A procedure that many have found effective, especially for promotion to associate or full professor, is the outside letter of support. Sometimes the candidate solicits those letters; sometimes it is done by the chairman, and the decision about who solicits the letters is made on the basis of what is most comfortable for the faculty member. This documentation, if it is positive (and when isn't it?), helps college and university committee, deans, and vice-presidents say yes when they know little or nothing about the particular discipline of music. An outsider's opinion adds both respectability and credence to an application for promotion.

Some Rating Ideas

Tucker comments that when handled improperly, evaluation can destroy morale, decrease the chances for the department to meet its objectives, and place the chairman on the receiving end of a long series of grievances.[23] Not every faculty member is outstanding—

their self-evaluations notwithstanding—and the difficult task for the chairman is to differentiate among the members, most of whom perform at least satisfactorily. Tables 5–4–5–6 illustrate some of Tucker's concepts of evaluation. Based on a performance scale rating of 4 as outstanding, 3 as very good, 2 as satisfactory, and 1 as weak, Table 5–4 illustrates this rating system for Professors Jones, Smith, and Brown in the categories of teaching, creative activity (research), and service. The implication of this system is that all factors are of equal weight. In this comparison, Professor Jones emerges as the most effective faculty member, with a 3.33 rating out of a possible 4.0.

Another approach to rating faculty members is to have rating points be the product of the performance rating (4, 3, 2, or 1) times the percentage of load devoted to each area. Thus, if teaching represents 60 percent of the load; creative activity, 30 percent; service 5 percent and the miscellaneous category, 5 percent, then the performance rating of 4, 3, 2, or 1 would be multiplied by 60, 30, 5, and 5, respectively. Table 5–5 illustrates this treatment for faculty members X, Y, and Z. In these examples, faculty member X, with a 3.6 overall rating, is superior.

Supposing a department or school of music wished to apply more weight to one category, such as creative activity. One would then introduce a priority factor to be used as a multiplier of the percentage of load figure. If, for example, creative activity were a 1.5 priority instead of a 1.0, then the 40 percent of load in that category would be 60 (40 percent multiplied by 1.5). Table 5–6 illustrates this concept applied to faculty member Y, who, you may recall, had a rating point average of 2.9. After applying the increased priority figure for creative activity (faculty member Y is a pianist on the faculty), his adjusted rating point average jumps to 3.08 (370 divided by 120). If one were to apply an identical treatment to faculty members

TABLE 5–4

Area	Jones	Smith	Brown
Teaching	4	2	2
Creative activity	3	4	1
Service	3	3	3
Total	10	9	6
Average	3.33	3.0	2.0

The above could be done by a committee and/or by the chairman.

Assumption: areas are of equal weight.

Source: Allan Tucker, *Chairing the Academic Department: Leadership Among Peers,* 2nd ed. (New York: Macmillan, 1984), 155.

TABLE 5–5
Faculty Member X

Area	I Performance Rating	II Percentage of Load	Rating Points
Teaching	4	60	240
Creative activity	3	30	90
Service	3	5	15
Other	3	5	15
Total	13	100	360

Rating point average 3.6 (360 divided by 100)

Faculty Member Y

Area	Performance Rating	Percentage of Load	Rating Points
Teaching	2	40	80
Creative activity	4	40	160
Service	3	10	30
Other	2	10	20
Total	11	100	290

Rating point average 2.9 (290 divided by 100)

Faculty Member Z

Area	Performance Rating	Percentage of Load	Rating Points
Teaching	1	65	65
Creative activity	1	20	20
Service	4	10	40
Other	3	5	15
Total	9	100	140

Rating point average 1.4 (140 divided by 100)

Source: Allan Tucker, *Chairing the Academic Department: Leadership Among Peers,* 2nd ed. (New York: Macmillan, 1984), 157–158.

X and Z, their rating point averages would be 3.5 (down from 3.6) and 1.36 (down from 1.4), respectively.

Suppose the department wishes to establish a more complex system of weighted categories. Let us say that on a ten-point scale teaching is an 8; creative activity, a 10; service and other areas, a 5. In such a system, these priority numbers would be introduced after

TABLE 5–6
Faculty member Y

Area	Performance Rating	Percentage of Load	Priority	Adjusted Percentage	Adjusted Rating Points
Teaching	2	40	1.0	40	80
Creative activity	4	40	1.5	60	240
Service	3	10	1.0	10	30
Other	2	10	1.0	10	20
Total	11	100	N/A	120	370

Adjusted rating point average 3.08 (370 divided by 120)

Source: Allan Tucker, *Chairing the Academic Department: Leadership Among Peers,* 2nd ed. (New York: Macmillan, 1984), 160.

percentage of load as a multiplier to arrive at an adjusted percentage figure. If we take faculty member Y once again, we see a final adjusted rating point average of 3.09, a change from 2.9 in the first example and 3.08 in the second. Faculty member X would be at 3.58 and Z at 1.25. Table 5–7 illustrates this concept.

The system is flexible. It can, and should, be designed to fit each school or college within a university, each department and perhaps even each division within a department. It is conceivable that the priority decisions among the faculty would be different in departments where persons function totally in performance, in music history/literature, or in music education. In small departments where

TABLE 5–7
Faculty Member Y

Area	I Performance Rating	II Percentage of Load	III Priority	IV Adjusted Percentage	Adjusted Rating Points (I × IV)
Teaching	2	40	8	320	640
Creative activity	4	40	10	400	1,600
Service	3	10	5	50	150
Other	2	10	5	50	100
Total	11	100	N/A	820	2,490

Adjusted rating point average 3.09 (2490 divided by 820)

Source: Allan Tucker, *Chairing the Academic Department: Leadership Among Peers,* 2nd ed. (New York: Macmillan, 1984), 162.

faculty members have responsibilities in many areas, a departmental decision about priorities might be made.

The assumptions in the foregoing example are "summative"; that is, the object is to arrive at numbers that will enable administrators to make decisions about rewards—salary, merit pay, or promotion. Further, it is helpful to be able to compare one faculty member to another.

How one arrives at the critical numbers to which one would apply multiplication, addition, division, and then reach that magical adjusted rating point average is another set of questions. These suggestions are presented as food for thought, as ways of thinking about the evaluation process.

Post-Tenure Evaluation

Christine Licata makes the following observations about post-tenure faculty evaluation:[24]

1. Of full-time faculty, 85 percent teach in institutions where a tenure system operates.
2. By the late 1990s, approximately 80 percent of faculty will be tenured at such institutions.
3. A decline of college enrollments of between 5 percent and 15 percent is expected over the next twenty years.
4. The modal age today of tenured faculty is forty-six; by the year 2000 it will be between fifty-five and sixty-five.
5. Net faculty additions nationwide hover at about 0 percent.
6. Faculty movement from one institution to another has dropped from 8 percent in the mid-1960s to about 1 percent currently.
7. A faculty member who is tenured at age thirty-five and retires at seventy costs an institution approximately $800,000 over the life of his tenure.

Some believe that faculty performance diminishes after tenure or promotion to the rank of full professor. Yet the research related to the effect of tenure and age on teaching effectiveness and productivity does not support this belief. However, the seven statements made above suggest that evaluation systems for those fully tenured and promoted ought to be in place, as should programs of professional development to assist these people to continue to grow and contribute.

Licata makes six recommendations based on her study of post-tenure evaluations:

1. The *purpose* of the evaluation should drive all other aspects of the evaluation plan. Will it be formative or summative?
2. Faculty must be involved in the design of the plan.

3. Faculty and administration must agree on the specifics of the plan.
4. The need for flexibility and individualization should not be over-looked.
5. Faculty development programs should be linked to a post-tenure evaluation system.
6. Innovative approaches to post-tenure evaluations, such as the growth contract, are needed.

Evaluation is a serious responsibility of the music administrator, and the advice of a personnel committee is an essential part of the process. In tenure track cases, the yearly expectation is for a recommendation of unconditional reappointment, reappointment with some stated condition, or nonreappointment. Regardless of the recommendation by committee, chair, dean, or anyone else, documentation and justification for that recommendation are critical. One dare not recommend nonreappointment in today's world without reasons—good *documented* reasons—for arriving at that judgment.

In the case of terminating a tenured professor, the same advice applies. There had better be plenty of documentation—of problems, of suggestions made to solve those problems, of failure of the individual in question to respond positively. There are numerous reasons for dismissing a tenured professor—dishonesty, moral turpitude, or failure to meet teaching responsibilities, to name but three. An Associated Press release in 1989 tells of a midwestern university that dismissed a tenured professor who "was accused of harassing his colleagues" and of misusing university resources.

A great deal of courage is called for in dismissing a tenured faculty member, and yet it may ultimately be the only action that will remedy a problematic situation. If the welfare of students and the department is at stake, it may be the only decision an administrator can make.

In conclusion, quantity of performance can be measured in various ways, but quality is usually measured in terms of opinions, values, and perceptions held by students, peers, alumni, and others. Quality is usually expressed in words and phrases, but unfortunately, words and phrases cannot be added, multiplied, or averaged. The final number or the final recommendation, regardless of how sophisticated the process, still represents a collection of human judgments. The challenge is to arrive at a process that accurately reflects the worth of the individual to the department, college, or university.

How, then, does one handle musicians on college campuses in matters of evaluation? As one would handle other human beings—with care, deference, respect, objectivity, fairness, courtesy, and empathy.

The matter of evaluation is truly complex and is constrained because of the difficult human elements involved. Each of us comes from a different setting with unique conditions. No one evaluation system will work for everyone. A high level of trust is called for so that faculty members do not feel that a system or instrument is being developed to "get" them. It must be perceived as being "helpful" in improving instruction and in securing rewards, and in fact, it must *do* those things.

Public Schools

Differences of opinion arise when, in evaluating the work of a teacher, the teacher perceives his role or the objectives of the music program as different from those perceived by the evaluator. Under the circumstances, one can see why it is extremely important that the function, goals, and objectives of the music program be defined as clearly as possible. Even where clarity exists, individuals will still disagree about what is expected of them. These disagreements may be serious, depending on the extent and importance of the area of disagreement. Not every discrepancy between what a music supervisor or director expects of his teachers and what the teacher is doing is serious enough for drastic action or polarization. However, if the discrepancy is sufficiently serious, then the music supervisor needs to determine a course of action. Often it is merely a matter of supplying the teacher with some pertinent information or providing him with some in-service training.

If it is a matter of inability, a lack of a particular skill, musical or educational, then every opportunity should be given the individual to develop that skill. Where talent or ability is completely lacking to such an extent that even training cannot remedy the situation, it becomes the supervisor's responsibility to consider changing the assignment so that the skill which the individual lacks is not called upon to the same degree or does not bear the same importance.

Occasionally, an individual may possess the skill necessary to achieve a goal but be completely uninterested in using it. If lack of motivation interferes with instruction, then drastic courses of action may be considered to motivate the individual. Although this implies a threatening tone, it is not so intended. The course of action will depend on the individual, the skill involved, and the situation. Failure to utilize a skill is often due to improper feedback or communication from the students, the administration, or the community. Such failure may be merely an attention-getting device. Supervisors need to make frequent visits in this kind of situation to give appropriate attention and even to supply the necessary feedback or information regarding the quality of the individual's teaching performance.

For example, one of the reasons many teachers avoid teaching twentieth-century music and twentieth-century devices is because their own education did not prepare them for current musical exigencies. They may have the musical ability to do so, but lack the incentive. Encouragement and on-the-job demonstrations can help the teacher become more comfortable and perhaps even adventuresome in pursuit and presentation of "new" music. In spite of the fact that they have the essential talent, they may not have the requisite knowledge. In the matter of recognition, it may be that insufficient recognition or approval is given to individuals who pursue these areas of music.

Transfer of assignment or termination of employment is not always the solution, particularly when a teacher possesses the potential for success in his present assignment. Actually, as indicated earlier, transfer or termination should be considered only after all other courses of action have failed. The key to successful personnel procedures is matching individuals and their musical skills to the classroom situations that ideally fit their capabilities. This will obviate much of the difficulty that arises when discrepancies between skill and teaching assignment occur.

In music, it is not unusual to find some outstanding teacher not performing as expected because he may be punished for doing so. He may even be rewarded for performing at a substandard level. For example, when attending a concert, the music supervisor may find that the entire time is being devoted to "pop" music of an ephemeral nature. Apparently it makes the "kids" happy and provides the teacher with gratification in knowing that the students "love his class—he or she is really with it!" The parents sing his praises as a teacher because classes and concerts are always "so much fun."

By the same token, this could be a teacher who is perfectly capable of making music of greater depth and significance equally exciting but is afraid of "turning off" the students or even the parents. The music administrator's or supervisor's challenge is to see that similar gratification and approbation are given this teacher for providing a balanced program that includes all facets of music and music education. Administrators will have to convince teachers that, in the long run, their careers will not suffer and that such performances can be equally rewarding in terms of the acclaim and recognition they will receive from the more musically knowledgeable members of the community. They can still teach in a manner that is satisfying from a student's point of view, without sacrificing musical principles.

When desired student behavioral change occurs, it is of critical importance that such change be acknowledged and rewarded. Too often individuals in responsible positions fail to respond, regardless of what occurs. If the members of the music administration never attend the concerts given by schools under their jurisdiction, then the implication is that they do not care how well the school and its music director are performing. If the administration gives attention only to problem situations, then those who need attention may actually create problems to obtain the necessary gratification.

The evaluative process in personnel matters is essentially to identify the problem, if one exists, and then to analyze the possible cause. Once this has been accomplished, the evaluator should select a course of action for solving the problem. Finally, the entire process remains incomplete until the supervisor or director evaluates the results of his action. Evaluation is basically controlling quality and determining courses of action to solve problems and thereby improve the quality of musical offerings in a school. All problems, however, cannot be easily solved. At times, a music administrator will have to be content with a partial solution because it will result in an amount of progress and change sufficient to make the situation more tolerable. In some instances, to demand or seek a full solution may undermine the measure of success achieved and destroy a program that may in time bear fruit. It will be another instance in which "the operation was a success, but the patient died." In the case of the teacher who performed only pop music, if he introduces one or two pieces of significant literature in his next concert, he is taking a step in the right direction. Rather than condemn the teacher for still having a limited diet, compliment his progress and encourage him to attempt more.

Classroom Visitation

The functions of classroom visitations are varied. In some cases, the number and timing are dictated by edict. A board of education or a state tenure law may make a certain number of classroom visits within a designated period of time mandatory for a new teacher. Unfortunately, this type of visit is primarily for the purpose of participating in evaluative procedures to determine the desirability of the teacher. If possible, this type of observation should be left under the aegis of the supervisory department, and only when extreme circumstances dictate should the director of music become involved. This statement should not be misconstrued to imply that the music administrator does not visit or observe in the classroom. On the contrary, this is his most effective way of dealing with, and helping, the individual teacher. It is merely that it is easier to help people if they are not always working under the threat of being rated. This applies to supervisory visits as well.

Classroom visits open up communications on a face-to-face basis. One teacher greeted her new supervisor in a large city in tears. She had been in the system seventeen years and had never had a visit from "downtown." She thought that they had forgotten her and didn't even know she existed. She was overjoyed to know that someone cared and was even interested.

Visiting a school can also supply the administration with information about the school, its pupils, and its administrators that does not always appear in written reports. All of this information is of the utmost importance when making decisions that affect curriculum and programs in a building.

Essentially, classroom visitation should be thought of in a positive sense. Its purpose is to assist in the improvement of instruction. It may be to help an inexperienced teacher or to assist an experienced one. It may be to assist some noncertified individual, or it may be to implement a group project. At times the purpose of classroom visitation may be to help a principal who needs assistance in dealing with a specific problem in his building.

Conducting an Observation

When observing a class, be certain to remain long enough to assure the teacher that he has been given ample opportunity to display his ability. However, stay only long enough to ascertain the quality of instruction. It is better to observe for something specific. Plan the visit so that it will be systematic and determine beforehand the specifics that need to be observed. Of course, be flexible enough to shift focus as the situation demands. Do not be hasty in forming conclusions, and reserve judgment on techniques or materials until you have had a chance to see the whole lesson and discuss it with the teacher.

No one likes criticism. Some can handle it better than others, but no one enjoys it, no matter how sincerely it is offered. It is therefore imperative that supervisors and directors understand the nature of every individual with whom they have to deal and be aware of each person's needs as they offer help. This requires tact and diplomacy. However, the music administrator need not avoid the issue or abrogate responsibility. Concern for the student and instruction is always the prime consideration, and an administrator must weigh the best way to achieve the goal of improving the instructional process.

When discussing the lesson, provide the teacher with alternatives. Try to get the teacher out of ingrained patterns. Remember a good music administrator releases a teacher's potential; he does not restrain that potential. If one sees something that is effective, encourage it, even if it does not always comply with traditional methods or established procedures.

In the authors' opinion, the practice of note taking during an observation is questionable. Avoid profuse writing, but jot down a few comments unobtrusively to remind yourself of something, positive or negative, that you want to call to the teacher's attention. Whatever is written should be shown to the teacher so that he does not think that you are preparing a secret dossier.

BE SENSITIVE

PROVIDE ALTERNATIVES

JOT A FEW NOTES or WRITE A LOT...

The music administrative staff should prepare an observation form to be filled out and given to the teacher after each visit. This *[handwritten: USE A FORM]* not only informs the teacher of specifics referred to in the discussion but also serves as a reminder for follow-up visits. Some school systems are now using portable tape recorders and cassettes when observations take place. Later the tape is given to the teacher so that he can hear the lesson. Such a record becomes a form of self-criticism and evaluation. The observer may or may not add comments *[handwritten: TAPE RECORD LESSON]* to the tapes. However, it can also be unnerving to a teacher. Let each teacher decide whether tape and/or written comments are utilized.

When talking to a teacher, avoid using cliché-ridden terminology. When making constructive criticism, conflict may be created. At all costs avoid polarization. Generally, direct comments to what occurred or what needs to be done *to improve learning for students.* If there are personal matters involved, be concerned only with their effect on the learning situation. The best type of criticism is that which engineers self-analysis. Remember that you are not there to establish authority. Be considerate. From the moment an administrator or supervisor walks into the room, it is no longer a normal situation!

Some supervisors and administrators have attempted to make videotapes of classes and use them for evaluative purposes. This is totally unfair and should not be done. First, no matter how unobtrusively a camera is introduced into a classroom, it alters the atmosphere to such an extent that much of what occurs is artificial. Second, videotaping is such an effective in-service device, as in *[handwritten: ?]* microteaching; it would undermine its positive values. Finally, to obviate the first two objections would require such extensive preparation and expense that the information gained in return for evaluation would be completely out of proportion to the results. Reserve videotaping for the function that it can serve best, instruction and training.

Under no circumstances should any observer undermine the *[handwritten: ?]* teacher's authority in the classroom. Remember that when the observer leaves, the teacher remains to face the class.

As indicated earlier, most evaluative visits are left to supervisors. However, the music director is always on call to assist in the process. As a matter of fact, administrators should respond to *any* call in some fashion.

Above all, administrators must realize that all teachers are individuals requiring an individual approach and individual attention. All problems cannot be solved, and some may resolve themselves. A sensitive administrator will establish priorities in dealing with staff. He must decide where he can achieve the most progress in the quickest amount of time when assisting a teacher.

Dealing with Incompetencies

No teacher should be considered incompetent until there have been several observations by at least the principal or the assistant, a music department head or a music supervisor, and the music director. A teacher should be given every opportunity and ample assistance to prove his competency, and only when all efforts have failed should any action be taken.

Throughout these proceedings, visitation records should be kept. As indicated earlier, these records should be given to the teacher and chief personnel officer for the school system. Contrary to popular opinion, tenure laws do not protect incompetent teachers. If enough proper evidence is available, even tenured teachers may be dismissed. Too often administrators lack administrative courage and find due process of law too troublesome. It is easier to avoid the issue. Under these circumstances, the fault lies with the administration. Too many individuals are content to rely on the cliché that tenure protects the incompetent teacher. Tenure laws were established to guarantee academic freedom, and in a democratic society it is essential that a teacher, who is a public servant, be protected. For example, without tenure laws, one might hesitate to play music by composers from a nation in conflict with the U.S. government or even fear the use of religious music under certain conditions. Tenure guarantees a music teacher's freedom to be artistically honest and should be protected. Unfortunately, if administrators are not courageous in the defense of tenure, its purpose will be obscured by charges that it protects the incompetent.

Under the headline "Dismissal of Teacher Was Not Inhumane," the Durham, North Carolina, *Morning Herald* (August 22, 1983) told of the dismissal of a seventh-grade science teacher by the Durham County Board of Education. Supporters of Miss X argued that the dismissal was inhumane because it deprived her of full retirement benefits, as well as current income, from then (when she was fifty-one) until such time as she could collect those full benefits. Some suggested that she obtain another job with the state so that she could continue to add to her retirement. The writer argued that while loss of income and some retirement benefits are personal tragedies, it does not make the school system irresponsible in taking the action it did.

"To many parents, black and white," said the writer, it would have been inhumane to continue to have their sons and daughters assigned to [her] classes." The board of education acted only after two years of observations and seventeen hours of hearings. During this process, the board paid her salary, provided her with resources, and treated her with dignity. The decision to dismiss her was not a

[handwritten margin notes:]
- KEEP WRITTEN RECORDS w/ COPIES TO TCHR + ADMIN.
- PROVIDE RESOURCES FOR IMPROVEMENT
- FOLLOW DISTR. DUE PROCESS

capricious action. The writer concluded that "to fire her for incompetence is necessary, not inhumanity."

Proper evidence in incompetency cases should be based on information gathered about experiences in the classroom and children's growth, not on personal appearance or personality conflicts. These latter factors are considered important only when they interfere with learning in the classroom. When teachers are confronted with bona fide evidence of incompetence, they usually do not wish to jeopardize their careers. They should be given the opportunity to resign. *Never* allow one's evidence or concern to be considered on a personal basis. No matter how much the observing supervisor may feel threatened, he must remain detached, objective, and impersonal.

At no time should any one music administrator undertake the responsibility for dealing with this type of incompetency alone. He should enlist the aid of all personnel involved in such matters.

Managing Personnel

J. Sterling Livingston, in his article "Pygmalion in Management," used an analogy with G. Bernard Shaw's play *Pygmalion* to approach the matter of improving the performance of individual faculty members.[25] In the play, the conflict revolves around the issue of whether one person, by his effort and will, can complete the transformation of another person. Many music administrators play similar roles to motivate capable faculty members to improve and stimulate their performances, whether in the classroom or in concert.

In the play, Eliza Doolittle explains to Colonel Pickering:

> You see, really and truly, apart from the things anyone can pick up (the dressing and the proper way of speaking, and so on), the difference between a lady and a flower girl is not how she behaves, but how she's treated. I shall always be a flower girl to Professor Higgins, because he always treats me as a flower girl, and always will; but I know I can be a lady to you, because you always treat me as a lady, and always will.

Although outstanding administrators always treat their faculty members in such a way that they produce superior performances, too many leaders unintentionally treat their colleagues in a way that leads to performances that are lower than what they are capable of achieving. In other words, the way one treats one's colleagues is subtly influenced by one's expectations of that individual. If the expectations are low, then the performance in the classroom is frequently poor and suffers. It is almost as if a law were in operation that performance in the educational structure rose or fell with the administrator's expectations. Duh....

Like teacher & student

The influence of an individual's expectations on another's behavior is not a recent conclusion. At the turn of the century, Albert Moll determined in his clinical experiences that subjects behaved according to the manner in which they were expected to.[26] Robert Rosenthal of Harvard University demonstrated in a series of experiments that a "teacher's expectation for her pupils' intellectual competence can come to serve as an educational self-fulfilling prophecy."[27]

If an administrator is of the opinion that a faculty member will perform poorly, it is almost impossible to hide his expectations, because the message is usually communicated, even unintentionally, without conscious effort. In fact, individuals in these leadership roles usually communicate most when they are seemingly doing the least communication. For example, the silent treatment is in effect communicating a negative feeling—perhaps even more effectively than a serious verbal criticism. What is critical is not so much what one says but rather how one *behaves*. Obviously, the manner in which the administrator treats individuals on his faculty is the key element to high expectations and high performance.

It is essential, however, that when he is dealing with high expectations, the goals must be realistic and achievable. To encourage the unattainable is self-defeating. In setting higher expectations, he is dealing with motivation, and when the performance goals (expectations) exceed the attainable, the function of motivating becomes discouraging. In his violin method Dr. Shinichi Suzuki taught us that we underestimate the potential and capabilities of young children. But one must also realize that musically, though not necessarily technically, there are limitations that can only be overcome by maturation, growth, and development.

"A skillful music administrator with high expectations of his faculty members will provide an environment that stimulates self-confidence and growth, their capabilities will develop, and their productivity will be high."[27] Without realizing it, the administrator is Pygmalion.

NOTES

1. Ron Ross, "The Fine Art of Faculty Recruitment," *Music Educators Journal* 67, no. 9 (May 1981), p. 49.
2. Peter Drucker, *Management: Tasks, Responsibilities, and Practices* (New York: Harper and Row, 1974).
3. College Music Society, 1444 Fifteenth Street, Boulder, Colorado 80302.

4. Chronicle of Higher Education, 1255 Twenty-third Street, NW, Washington, D.C. 20037.

5. Luttons Music Personnel Service, P.O. Box 13985, Gainesville, Florida 32604.

6. National Association of Schools of Music, 11250 Roger Bacon Drive, No. 21, Reston, Virginia 22090.

7. National Association of College Wind and Percussion Instructors, Division of Fine Arts, Northeast Missouri State University, Kirksville, Missouri 64501.

8. A. J. Drucker and H. H. Remmers, "Do Alumni and Students Differ in Their Attitudes Toward Instructors?" *Journal of Educational Psychology* 42 (1951).

9. J. A. Centra and F. R. Creech, *The Relationship Between Students, Teachers and Course Characteristics and Student Ratings of Teacher Effectiveness*, Project Report 76-1 (Princeton, N.J.: Educational Testing Service, 1976).

10. Educational Testing Service, Princeton, New Jersey 08541.

11. Kenneth Eble, *Career Development of the Effective College Teacher* (Washington, D.C.: American Association of University Professors, 1971).

12. Peter Seldin, *How Colleges Evaluate Professors* (Croton-on-Hudson, N.Y.: Blythe Pennington, 1975).

13. Peter Seldin, *Changing Practices in Faculty Evaluation* (San Francisco: Jossey-Bass, 1984).

14. J. A. Centra, *How Universities Evaluate Faculty Performance: A Survey of Department Heads*, GREB Research Report No. 75-5bR (Princeton, N.J.: Educational Testing Service, 1977).

15. J. A. Centra, "Self Ratings of College Teachers: A Comparison with Student Ratings," *Journal of Educational Measurement* 10 (1973).

16. N. L. Gage, "The Appraisal of College Teaching," *Journal of Higher Education* 32 (1961).

17. A. H. Maslow and W. Zimmerman, "College Teaching Ability, Scholarly Activity and Personality," *Journal of Educational Psychology* 47 (1956).

18. H. G. Murray, "The Validity of Student Ratings of Teaching Ability," Paper presented at the Canadian Psychological Association Meeting, Montreal, 1972.

19. J. A. Centra, "Self Ratings of College Teachers."

20. Alexander Astin and Calvin B. T. Lee, "Current Practices in the Evaluation and Training of College Teachers," *Improving College Teaching*, ed. Calvin B. T. Lee, Washington, D.C.: American Council on Education, 1967.

21. William Hipp, "Practices in the Evaluation of Music Faculty in Higher Education" (Ph.D. diss., University of Texas, 1979).

22. Milton Hildebrand, "How to Recommend Promotion for a Mediocre Teacher Without Actually Lying," *Journal of Higher Education* 43 (January 1972), pp. 44–62.

23. Allan Tucker, *Chairing the Academic Department: Leadership Among Peers*, 2nd ed. (New York: Macmillan, 1984).

24. Christine M. Licata, *Post-tenure Faculty Evaluation: Threat or Opportunity?* (Washington, D.C.: Association for the Study of Higher Education, 1986).

25. J. Sterling Livingston, "Pygmalion in Management," *Harvard Business Review* 47 (July-August 1969), p. 81.
26. Robert Rosenthal and Lenore Jackson, *Pygmalion in the Classroom* (New York: Holt, Rinehart and Winston, 1968), p. 1.
27. *Ibid.*, p. vii.
28. Livingston, "Pygmalion in Management," p. 89.

SUPPLEMENTARY READINGS

Centra, John A. *Determining Faculty Effectiveness.* San Francisco: Jossey-Bass, 1979.

Colwell, Richard. *The Evaluation of Music Teaching and Learning.* Englewood Cliffs, N.J.: Prentice-Hall, 1970.

Doyle, K. O., Jr. *Student Evaluation of Instruction.* Lexington, Mass.: Lexington Books, 1975.

Dressel, Paul, et al. *Evaluation in Higher Education.* Boston: Houghton Mifflin, 1961.

Eble, K. E. *The Recognition in Evaluation of Teaching.* Washington, D.C.: American Association of University Professors, 1971.

Eckard, Pamela J. "Faculty Evaluation: The Basis for Rewards in Higher Education." *Peabody Journal of Education* 57 (January 1980), pp. 94–100.

Gronlund, Norman. *Measurement and Evaluation in Teaching.* New York: Macmillan, 1965.

Hildebrand, Milton, and Wilson, Robert C. *Effective University Teaching and Its Evaluation.* Berkeley, Calif.: Center for Research and Development in Higher Education, 1970.

Hills, John R. *Measurement and Evaluation in the Classroom,* 2nd ed. Columbus, Ohio: Charles E. Merrill, 1981.

Kronk, Annie K. and Shipka, T. A. *Evaluation of Faculty in Higher Education.* Washington, D.C.: National Education Association, 1980.

Kunz, Don. "Learning to Live with Evaluations." *Change* 10, no. 2 (February 1978), pp. 10–11.

Miller, R. I. *Developing Programs for Faculty Evaluation.* San Francisco: Jossey-Bass, 1974.

———. *Evaluating Faculty Performance.* San Francisco: Jossey-Bass, 1972.

Rose, Clare, and Myre, Glenn F. *The Practice of Evaluation.* Princeton, N.J.: ERIC Clearinghouse on Tests, Measurement, and Evaluation, Educational Testing Service, 1978.

Seldin, Peter. *Successful Faculty Evaluation Programs: A Practical Guide to Improve Faculty Performance and Promotion/Tenure Decisions.* New York: Coventry Press, 1980.

STUDY QUESTIONS

1. How do you develop a pool of candidates for a music position in higher education? How is this similar to, or different from, what one does at the precollege level?

2. What are the considerations in putting together a search committee of five people?
3. What is the role and purpose of affirmative action in the hiring of music personnel?
4. What do the terms *affirmative action* and *equal opportunity* mean?
5. What key questions should you ask a candidate for a position in music?
6. How do you structure the interview/audition experience?
7. What are the purposes of music faculty evaluation?
8. How are music faculty evaluated, and by whom?
9. What is the evidence one should assemble in evaluating music faculty?
10. How would you go about developing a plan of evaluation for music faculty?
11. Is the evaluation of music teachers in the public schools different from the process in higher education? If so, how and why?
12. How do you handle a music teacher who is incompetent, lazy, and, by all measures, doing a poor job of teaching?

6

Faculty Development and Improving Instruction

Faculty development is an elusive matter. There are many variations on the theme. On some campuses it is not mentioned, is ignored, or is even forbidden. On others it receives lip service. On a few it is an item of high priority. In any case, its purpose is to improve instruction in the classroom and encourage personal growth.

The American Association of University Professors (AAUP) newsletter, *Academe*, asked for a response from its constituents to the statement "My institution (does, does not) have an effective faculty development system." Only 6 of 150 responses indicated the existence of an effective faculty development system. (*Academe* left the meaning of "effective" up to the respondent.)

John Centra conducted a survey in 1977 to find how effective faculty development programs were. Just over half of the 2,600 degree-granting institutions in the United States then provided some kind of staff development. Of this group of 1,300 + institutions, 756 responded to Centra's survey. It was found that first- and second-year teachers were moderately involved in programs. Those with fifteen or twenty years' experience were only slightly involved. Providing grants for teacher improvements was found to be common and was rated both effective and popular. Another practice, not widely used but considered effective, was the growth contract. Respondents said one of the least effective practices was the annual teaching award.[1]

Institutions of higher education face the harsh reality of decreased funding, declining enrollment, lack of faculty mobility, demands for accountability from all sides, and advancement of the age of retirement. So what do you do *with* or *for* that faculty member who is now fifty and has already mentally retired, yet is still on the faculty? Have you thought about the fact that he still has twenty years to go for his *real* retirement? That is practically a generation! In student terms, it is five generations. (In fact, the mandatory retirement age for faculty may soon be entirely eliminated, extending the time frame even further.)

Past approaches to faculty development have included changing the curriculum, seeking brighter students, recruiting Ph.D.'s from the best graduate schools, establishing new governance systems, and undertaking self-studies.

Faculty development has been attempted by bringing in new faculty—men and women with new ideas and fresh perspectives. In one music department this past year there were two fortunate appointments. An assistant professor of violin began the fall with one student string quartet. In the spring he had five ensembles functioning. He attracted five new string majors for the coming fall. He visited two local high school orchestras regularly and worked with the directors in any way he could—and he was welcome! He is now a state officer in the American String Teachers Association (ASTA)—his first year in the state. In a few months he breathed new life into the string program, and his outgoing personality and enthusiasm made him a welcome addition to the faculty. There is a new sense of optimism in that department.

Another new appointment in the area of music history and composition had a difficult start when it developed that the person's expectations were a bit unrealistic. However, when that issue was resolved, the teacher proved to be successful and made valuable contributions to three departmental committees. By the end of the year, students were singing his praises but still saying, "He's tough." At the end of the year, he had a composition recital of student works—and a few of his own—that was a delight.

Other faculty members are not immune to the successes of newcomers. Those successes are inspirational to all, and the more sensitive and conscientious ones will ask, "How can I do a better job?"

In the recent past, efforts at faculty development or enrichment have been largely cosmetic in nature or based, at least in part, on faulty assumptions about the way in which faculty members, as well as students, learn, change, and grow. There are very few guidelines to follow and not a large number of real successes.

One of the more massive attempts to improve teaching and learning has been at the University of California, where a special million-dollar appropriation has been made for this purpose throughout the nine-campus system. Since the money was available for only one year, guidelines had to be drawn up hurriedly, campus liaison people were identified, proposals were solicited, and projects funded. Three kinds of projects were supported: evaluation of teaching effectiveness, summer grants to faculty members for the improvement of individual courses, and seminars or small discussion courses for entering students. Evaluation of this effort disclosed that the impact was highly selective: the students and faculty involved appeared to have benefited, but the effect on the larger population has not yet been observed.

Developments in Great Britain
(1977)

In *Teaching Professors to Teach* Seldin includes, among other things, case studies and methods of faculty development used in British universities.[2] One clear trend in British education, reports Seldin, is the active involvement of students. Independent-learning schemes flourish, and self-paced learning is very much in vogue.

Almost all institutions in Great Britain now offer some kind of staff training. In many, this is limited to an induction course of two or three days for new faculty members. At others, both new and veteran academics are taking an active part in courses, conferences, workshops, and seminars devoted to teaching-learning topics. Time at these meetings is spent exploring lecture methods, small-group teaching, project teaching, assessment of students, and examination preparation.

These efforts are not embraced by all, by any means. As a matter of fact, it is estimated that only 10–15 percent of British academics have taken part in the various faculty development opportunities. But it is a start. Critics say that if faculty members are to be motivated to participate in, and benefit from, a training program, they must see it as challenging, relevant, and important to their own needs at that particular time. The importance placed upon teaching and its improvement through the institution's reward system is a powerful influence on the teacher's participation in training programs.

Seldin reports that at the University of Surrey there is an Institute of Educational Technology. The institute offers an annual resident course in teaching-learning and specialized short courses in topics such as individualized learning, small-group teaching, objective testing, and educational aids. The course on teaching and learning is an intensive full-time seven-day resident course that examines a range of teaching techniques and provides a forum for the examination of problems in teaching and learning. The course is limited to fifty persons and is offered to faculty from any university, regardless of subject specialty.

At the heart of this course is the notion that every faculty member must develop an understandable teaching philosophy that is more demanding that "I teach as I was taught." The principal aim of the course is to get professors to bring to their teaching the same critical and creative attitudes they bring to their research activities.

Recently, the Association of University Teachers and university administrators in England agreed that mandatory training of university teachers should be given to probationary faculty. (The reason was an impending legal action.) As things stand in Britain, a teacher dismissed after three years for poor teaching has his case automatically reviewed by a tribunal. The tribunal must be satisfied that adequate training was available and that the dismissed teacher failed to avail himself of it or underwent the training but emerged still a poor teacher. But a teacher is immune to dismissal if adequate training is *not* available.

An interesting concept in British universities is that of staff development officer. This person has funds to expend on training activities for faculty. He can run workshops, invite in outside experts, and train others in departmental units to assist new faculty members to become more effective teachers. He is someone with whom faculty members can easily identify. Staff development officers generally have training in psychology and/or management techniques. They work closely with faculty governing and advisory committees. And, most of all, they have been, and are, successful teachers.

The Association of University Teachers and the University Authorities Panel adopted an agreement in 1974 that covers many areas. One of its most meaningful passages states, "Where appointments have a probationary period, it is incumbent on universities to provide training for the probationer of a helpful and comprehensive nature. Advice and guidance by a senior colleague nominated for this task and encouragement to attend formal courses of instruction should be included."

Developments in the United States

One can only wonder at how music teaching in institutions of higher education in the United States might improve through structured experiences specifically geared to the many kinds of music instruction.

Analysis of the ratings of overall teaching effectiveness for more than eight thousand teachers with varying years of experience shows that those in their first year of teaching generally receive the poorest ratings (average 3.54 on a five-point scale).[3] Teachers with one or two years of experience and those with more than twelve years of experience receive similar ratings, an average of about 3.75. Slightly higher are teachers in the three-to-twelve-year range, with an average of 3.83. First-year teachers are usually learning on the job; most of them have had little formal training in graduate school on the process of teaching.

The slight decline in rated effectiveness in the later years of a teaching career has implications for teaching improvement programs. Some teachers acquire substantial administrative or research responsibilities in their later years, along with a decline in teaching improvement; others become bored and indifferent. Faculty development programs therefore need to be concerned with revitalizing older teachers as well as providing assistance to those just entering the profession. Gilbert Highet points out that changes occur over time in the subject matter within a discipline, as do teachers' relationships with their students. He believes that many teachers in their later years assume too much knowledge on the part of the young, while their own grasp of the subject matter has become more firm.

Here are some ideas that a music unit head might use to cajole, inspire, or motivate faculty members in the college or school setting to change and grow:

1. *Sabbatical leave:* A key concern here is the extent to which a sabbatical will improve teaching effectiveness. How will research, travel, and visits with other professionals enrich classroom activities and the faculty member's ability to make a significant contribution to the department?

While sabbatical leaves are often thought to be only in the province of higher education, such is not the case. Forward-looking school systems offer similar opportunities to their faculties, and by compensating the faculty member on leave the *difference* between his salary and that of a replacement, the school district incurs no added expense. The faculty member on leave may need to seek additional funds for support of his semester or year away, but such support can come from any number of sources. And a program such as this says to staff members, "We value what you do, we'd like you to be even better, and we'll help you accomplish this particular effort at improvement by providing partial compensation and by keeping you on our payroll for insurance and retirement purposes." This kind of statement is a powerful morale booster for faculty.

2. *Rotation of assignments:* Faculty should be encouraged to teach different courses and interact with students at different levels. A movement of teaching assignments among lower-division, upper-division, and graduate courses, where appropriate, can be extremely stimulating. The wisdom of having senior faculty working with incoming freshmen has been borne out time and again. A simple change of times of day and days of the week of teaching assignments can even help a faculty member feel a sense of "newness."

In the public schools teachers often become entrenched in

WHERE SHOULD
THIS PERSON BE
TEACHING ?

MATCH THE
PERSON TO THE
JOB.

"their" schools. While instrumental-music teachers, who are accustomed to traveling, are less likely to fall into this trap, there remain many music teachers who have worked to build "their" programs. And, in the case where there is careful vertical articulation, one can understand this feeling of territoriality. Nonetheless, there are teachers who *ought* to change levels or schools once in a while, who would *like* to change but are fearful of doing so. The encouragement to make such a change could produce big dividends in renewed vigor and enthusiasm—and a sense that a new beginning can occur.

3. *Teacher exchanges:* This may be one of the most attractive ways to set the stage for change. There have have been many successes in teacher exchange programs where faculty with parallel assignments have swapped jobs for a semester, a quarter, or a year. One department in a midwestern university set up a job exchange with the public school system in the city where the university is located. The department chairman worked with the school administration to lay the groundwork and secure the necessary approvals. Then he quietly lined up four colleagues who agreed to join him as guinea pigs in the experiment. The next step was to announce in a faculty meeting, "Professors A, B, C, and D are going to join me in a one-week teacher exchange with the X County Schools. Who would like to join us?" A total of nine members of the university department participated in the project. Everyone returned to his original position with a new appreciation for the difficulty of teaching on "the other side." And, of course, there are the predictable examples of higher-education faculty exchanging positions with other professors and of public school teachers changing places with their counterparts. Such exchanges take a great deal of time and patience to arrange, and excellent matches are hard to find. It is also difficult to find people who are willing—let alone eager—to participate in such efforts.

4. *Off-campus or out-of-district appearances:* The music executive can be very helpful in arranging for off-campus appearances for members of his faculty. It is an honor as well as a responsibility to make a presentation on a different campus. This challenge brings out the best in a teacher. Most teachers are unable or unwilling to promote themselves for such opportunities; the executive can more easily seek these opportunities for them.

School districts are often seeking individuals with expertise to present in-service workshops. Many music teachers in the schools are exceedingly capable, but are overlooked for such opportunities.

5. *Revolving load credit:* Where a college department has four divisions with an average faculty load of twelve credit hours, the music executive can develop a schedule whereby *three free hours* are assigned to one division each semester. That means that each division will have three free hours once every two academic years. The faculty members in that division submit proposals to receive the three free hours—that is, a net reduction of their teaching loads of three hours. The proposals speak to the question of how this is going to make him a better teacher, more effective in the classroom, a more vital contributor to the department. A committee (and ultimately the executive) decides which proposal is most imaginative, has the greatest potential for success, and is most needed. The professor then pursues the project with reduced load and moves into the next semester with renewed enthusiasm, vigor, vitality, and excitement.

6. *Research projects:* The academic year, with its January terms, intersessions, and summers offers times for faculty to pursue research projects, field studies, and visits to other campuses. The music executive frequently has access to information not available to faculty members and can be an effective catalyst in this regard. School systems will often hire teachers in the summer to develop or revise curricula or even to create new programs of study. Such experiences can serve to raise horizons and broaden attitudes.

7. *Campus visitors:* It is hard to overestimate the importance to faculty motivation of bringing an outside expert to the campus or school district. If the teacher, author, clinician, researcher, conductor, performer, or artist is actually chosen by the faculty members themselves, they will then have a stake in the productivity of the person's visit. There are many successful practitioners in higher education who have a great deal to offer your campus, and they are eager to be asked. People from industry, business, labor, and the arts have much to offer both students and faculty in the school or college setting and can be an important catalyst for change.

School systems will often bring visitors to their programs as well—members of professional symphony orchestras who will come for a day to conduct clinics or master classes for students and faculty; guest conductors who will work with ensembles prior to an important concert or contest; and general music specialists who will reside in the district for several days to teach and to work directly with teachers in implementing a new series that has been adopted.

8. *Conferences:* Some faculty attend anything and everything that comes along. Others need to be pushed, shoved, and even taken to professional meetings. Here again, the alert music executive can assist faculty to secure spots as "presenters" at professional meetings and can encourage the submission of papers or the presenting of musical programs or artistic exhibits.

School districts should make it as easy as possible for music teachers to attend professional conferences, for it is in those surroundings that one sees the latest in materials, hears inspiring performances and presentations of various kinds, and comes away with ideas of how they can do a better job on Monday morning. Many school districts have citizens committees that raise funds (some have chartered foundations) for instructional improvement. Conference attendance is one of the best—and least expensive—ways of providing highly concentrated experiences for school music teachers that can result in substantial gains in performance as well as attitude.

9. *On-campus workshops:* Workshops that focus on improving instruction can be very useful. Some faculty have never considered teaching strategies other than the lecture approach. Some have never really considered the meaning of a lesson plan. Some have never developed objectives for a single class session, let alone goals for an entire year. Expert advice and guidance can be secured to help faculty become better, more effective, and more thoughtful teachers through a variety of workshops aimed in these directions.

Workshops on college and university campuses aimed at school music teachers are a way of life throughout the country. Many teachers find attendance at these workshops to be a fast way of accumulating new and up-to-date knowledge and techniques. Such workshops usually count toward master's degrees and provide the enrollee with continuing-education units (CEU's) toward professional advancement.

The price tag on these ideas varies. If you have zero dollars but willing colleagues, you can cover for each other to provide for sabbatical leaves. Assignments can be rotated. Teacher exchanges can be arranged. Revolving load credit can be planned and off-campus appearances can be encouraged. If you have between $500 and $1,000, you can dream up ideas for research projects. You can pay partial or full expenses to a professional meeting. You can bring outstanding persons to the campus for performances, lectures, short residencies, or workshops. If you have more than $1,000 to expend on the development of faculty members, you can do any of the above to some degree.

The processes of change are subtle and ill defined. A successful faculty development program will not necessarily answer all, or even most, of the problems of the department or the institution. If, however, some positive changes can take place in attitudes, processes, or structures, the effort will have been worthwhile. At its best, a program of faculty development can contribute to the growth of the faculty member, can set the stage for improved learning, can improve faculty morale, and can enhance the reputation of the institution or school district.

■

ELEMENTARY AND SECONDARY SCHOOLS

As indicated earlier, there are many avenues open to a school music administrator for staff development and the improvement of instruction. They include:

1. attending in-service training workshops
2. developing and organizing instruction guides
3. observing demonstration lessons
4. participating in textbook adoptions
5. conducting research and advanced study
6. visiting curriculum centers
7. attending professional meetings and clinics
8. participating in microteaching exercises

Workshops

No teacher-training program can possibly prepare a teacher for every emergency or for every situation. In-service workshops serve two functions: to inspire and challenge in the broad sense and to deal with a specific problem.

Workshops should emanate from the needs of teachers to improve instruction for pupils. They may be directed toward providing basic information that may be readily available or they may be organized to offer a fresh approach for a program that is stagnant. This applies even to those workshops that introduce new concepts, new materials, or new media. However, once the nature of the workshop and for whom it is intended is decided (a grade level, a special area, systemwide, or a single school), it then becomes the responsibility of the administrator and the staff to set the machinery in motion for implementation. They need to organize committees, disseminate information publicizing the workshop, and notify those affected, whether attendance is required or optional. Certain social amenities need to be observed if a guest is presenting the workshop, or even if it is entirely a local meeting. These amenities are designed to set people at ease and may enhance the general atmosphere of the workshop. To assure the success of these meetings, someone in a responsible position should prepare a comprehensive checklist that includes materials and equipment needed, communications and information that need to be distributed, and any other pertinent considerations. The checklist should include the following:

1. Give the working title and brief description of the workshop.
2. Identify the workshop leader—a flexible person capable of shifting with valid new ideas introduced.
3. Include in all announcements and publicity the date, time, and location.
4. Consider the time frame.
5. Prepare name tags.
6. Determine whether some form of credit will be given and the nature of it.
7. Provide follow-up materials and evaluation sheets.
8. Determine what instructional media will be used.
9. Plan the room setup (including how many tables and chairs will be needed).
10. Buy refreshments.
11. Hire photographer.
12. Plan audio or video tape of presentation.

Regardless of the nature of the workshop or institute, it is intended to change the behavior of the teacher in the classroom. The need for it may not originate with the music administrator or his supervisors; it may result from a teacher's request or a pupil's concern. It may stem from a change in the nature of the school or the influence of outside sources (e.g., a law affecting new graduation requirements). It is the administration's responsibility, however, to be sufficiently sensitive to recognize the concern when it manifests itself and then proceed to act upon it.

How the workshop is organized will vary. Democratic procedures are generally the most acceptable. No single administrator should feel automatically compelled to assume full responsibility. Faculty and staff should be invited, indeed encouraged, to suggest the names of workshop leaders. A list of such presenters might be circulated for comment and polling. Occasionally an administrator sees or hears a speaker or a performance that is so compelling that he must have it for the staff. This is the exception. Even under these circumstances, however, it helps to consider and consult with those for whom the workshop is intended.

Guides or Courses of Study

A "music guide" or "course of study" is a compilation of recommended music materials, methods and experiences with suggestions to aid the teacher in organizing and presenting them. Actually, the chief function of this printed material is to help teachers provide better learning experiences for children—the improvement of instruction. In addition, however, guides are most helpful in providing printed information for new teachers or laypeople who want to know about the school music program. (They provide a public relations service.) Although the ones who learn most from a guide are those who prepare it, the guide is useful as a means of providing some assistance not only to all teachers but also to administrators such as principals and curriculum coordinators. All guides should contain the aims and the objectives for the specific area for which they are prepared. They should reflect the current philosophy of the total school music program and should serve as guidelines, not directives. They are intended to free the teacher rather than impose uniformity. If a teacher is to plan educational-musical experiences for the needs of individual learners, he needs optimum freedom and flexibility to function within the governing principles dictated by the educational-musical philosophy of the school.

Guides and courses of study are intended to be informative and helpful. They should be developed cooperatively and primarily by the people who will be using them. Often outside professional assistance may be required. Although the actual productive work will take place among the local personnel, committees are stimulated by the ideas of others. When this is done, the consultants should definitely be informed of their functions and specific purposes in appearing before a group so that they may prepare the appropriate materials and ideas. When experts are given responsibility for directing the development in certain areas of the music guide, they should also be given the status of regular committee members; however, they should not be allowed to use the status of their authority to dictate the program. In fact, a guide should never be dictated by the people in authority and handed down from on high.

The organization for developing the course of study will depend on the local situation. If the staff is small, it may operate largely as a committee of the whole. If the teaching group is sizable, a division of labor may be effected through creation of subcommittees. Those in charge of recommending members for committees should be familiar with their personal characteristics, backgrounds, reactions to pupils, and educational positions. A cooperative and open-minded attitude is a most desirable quality. The influence of members on the other personnel in the system is another important consideration, since committees must have sufficient prestige among the faculty so that the results of their work will be accepted and respected.

The music administrator should take the initiative in organizing committees and assist them in their preparation. The people who make up the study committee should represent as many points of view within the system as possible. However, they must not be the kind of people who are obstructionists or who are unable to resolve differences. Committee membership should include males and females, from various ethnic and religious groups. Administrators and curriculum specialists in the system should be included.

The committees may be organized in several ways—by grade or school levels; by subject areas such as instrumental, general, and vocal; or by specific types of activities within a subject area. It is desirable, however, that there be coordination of the work of all areas. In initiating a committee for a guide or course of study, the director must give each committee an adequate perception of its role in the total plan and a clear sense of direction and purpose.

All teachers should in some way be involved in the study. Although it is usually physically impossible, as well as undesirable, to assign all teachers to committees, there are activities that can keep them aware of the need for continuous growth. Occasional group meetings can bring everyone together to hear important presentations, progress reports, and evaluation of accomplishments. A large number of teachers can be used in experimental programs. All teachers should be urged to send in written comments and evaluations of the methods with which they are working, descriptions of their most successful activities and programs, and suggestions for new methods. Their reactions to grade placement of instructional units and their needs for textbooks, audiovisual aids, and creative materials can be quite valuable.

It is desirable that participation on these committees be rotated among the staff members, but continuity should be retained by overlapping some committee members. Some with expertise may be invited for just a particular meeting, while others will be retained throughout the study.

The administrator or the supervisor concerned should help the committee by arranging for a suitable working environment and see that appropriate procedures for democratic interaction prevail. A member from the music administration usually serves as chairman, but need not always do so. It is helpful if a supervisor serves as chairperson, primarily because he has certain facilities available. However, he may offer the use of these facilities as a committee member, even if a teacher acts as chairperson. All guides should be considered as tentative and be reviewed at least every five years.

Although they will vary in format, curriculum guides should include, in addition to the statement of philosophy, aims, and objectives, a plan outlining the "scope and sequence" of the music course or the area that is being covered. Aims may be stated in broad, general terms, but objectives should be presented in terms of "behaviors" that can be identified and measured.

Specific instructions and procedures for teaching activities are particularly useful for new teachers. Lists of resource materials, including supplementary song material, records, films, and other pertinent information should be included. Philip T. McClintock prepared a "checklist for the examination of curriculum guides in music" that may provide some direction when preparing or examining other guides in music (see Appendix E).[4] All guides should be used at least one year experimentally before being put into their final publication form. The experimental edition should include a tear-out sheet containing information that would allow the teacher using the guide to register reaction and suggested changes. In smaller communities, it is usually desirable to have a special committee just to edit the materials and supervise its publications. The editing committee is mainly concerned with achieving uniformity in the publication so that all teachers in the community may use it easily. In larger school systems there is a publications department to oversee the process.

When planning a guide to instruction, one should not overlook the possibility of its being used by school administrators and school officials. The guide can be an excellent aid in the efforts of the music administration to provide school principals with the information that they need to determine the scope of their school music offerings.

Improvement in instruction will not result automatically from the mere issuance of a new guide or course of study. Improvement occurs only as teachers develop better learning experiences for children. Nonetheless, teachers who are genuinely interested in providing better experiences for their children can receive immeasurable assistance from well-designed courses of study.

Observing Demonstration Lessons

A most effective method for improving instruction is to have a teacher who might be having difficulty visit a classroom being taught by a successful music teacher in an analogous situation. The key word is *analogous*. One should not have the teacher observe a situation that is completely antithetical and expect a positive reaction. Visiting classes of successful teachers is especially useful to new teachers.

Since the visiting teacher may observe methods and techniques for teaching under actual "combat" conditions, it is much more convincing. It is helpful if the demonstrating teacher or supervisor is aware of the specific problem that concerns the visiting teacher. This will enable the demonstrator to focus on this problem when preparing his lesson. If there is no specific concern, then the observing teacher should be given some background on what to expect and the nature of the lesson. It is desirable to plan a postdemonstration conference between the teachers, at which time the observing teacher will have an opportunity to ask questions and gather additional information that might be of assistance.

Another type of demonstration lesson is one that is planned by the administration to introduce new procedures, new equipment, new materials, or new curriculum guides. These lessons are given to large groups of teachers and may be presented by an outstanding teacher, a visiting clinician, a member of the supervising staff. If it is a guide, it may be introduced at several buildings by members of the workshop who helped develop it. (Videotapes and specially prepared "microteaching" excerpts are also of immeasurable value in this type of situation. They will be discussed as a separate item later in this chapter.)

The demonstration will be most effective if the need for it emanates from the teachers. However, it will fall to the administrator to initiate such a program if changes and developments occur because of action taken by the administrative authorities in a school system. For example, when the Detroit Board of Education decided to change to nongraded primary units in the elementary schools, not only was it necessary to retrain the elementary classroom teachers, but music specialists needed to readjust to teaching music to this type of school grouping; therefore, numerous demonstration lessons were given by supervisory personnel and outstanding teachers in the specific buildings where the change was introduced.

Observation visits need not be confined to the local school system. Teachers should be encouraged to visit neighboring school systems where outstanding teaching is also occurring. No opportunity to observe a demonstration that will contribute to a better classroom lesson should be overlooked.

MENTOR IN NEARBY DISTRICT

"ADOPT AN UNCLE"

Textbook Adoptions

Textbooks are merely tools or resources utilized by teachers and students to facilitate learning. They are not the curriculum, nor should they determine the direction a course should take. Too often basal series are selected on the basis of being the best one available after comparisons are made. Before examining any books, the committee should determine the objectives, the scope, and the sequences of its school program. It should then search for books that best fit this scheme, even if books from several different series need to be adopted. (In this computer age textbooks may ultimately be a composite of pages selected by each individual school system from several publishers.) It is advisable that a school system set up a schedule for textbook adoptions on a regular basis. In most school systems such a schedule will vary from six to eight years. When one knows well in advance of an impending adoption, it becomes possible to experiment beforehand with all of the new series music texts under consideration.

When the appropriate time arrives, it may be necessary to submit a budget for the textbook committee, depending upon the school system. If teachers are paid to participate in this kind of workshop—the practice in most large cities—then one must determine the number of meetings and the expenses involved, including costs for consultants from outside the school system, secretarial services, use of buildings, and numerous other small items for which a board requires budgeting.

Just as writing a new curriculum guide can be a valuable experience for those participating, so is serving on a textbook selection committee. The committee should consist of men and women, classroom teachers and special music teachers. There should be representatives from a variety of ethnic groups to see that different views and prevailing attitudes are represented. The committee should include a member of the principal's group and, if possible, a general curriculum specialist. In some communities, committees are encouraged to utilize an outside consultant from a local or neighboring university's music education faculty to participate. As indicated earlier, the committee chairperson is usually a member of the supervisory staff. It may be the music administrator, depending on the available staff or how he envisions his role in relation to the task. Thus, if he has proven expertise as a junior high school general music teacher, he would certainly be chairperson of a committee selecting a basic junior high textbook for general music classes. However, if the committee is selecting a series for string instruction, then an outstanding string teacher in the system would be appropriately appointed chairperson of that group if there were none in the administration.

The director or chair of the selection committee, with the aid of the music administrator, then should prepare a "Preliminary Philosophy and Pertinent Information Bulletin." This bulletin should contain the prevailing statement of aims and objectives for the area of music for which the series is being selected. The bulletin should review the purpose of the committee to formulate criteria for the new music text or series, to examine and evaluate available texts, to recommend a text or series for grades or a course, and to establish the procedures and responsibilities of the committee.

Another section in the bulletin should include certain evaluative features to look for when examining texts, such as physical characteristics of the book; authors; organization, content, and style; publication data; teacher's manuals; student editions; supplementary materials; and prices. Above all, do not forget to include a tentative work schedule—a timetable for decision making.

All publishers being considered should be notified about the adoption process. This notification usually comes from the office of the assistant superintendent in charge of curriculum and instruction. The information bulletin should be sent to the publishers, and each member of the committee should receive copies of the books being considered.

The early meetings should be devoted to establishing evaluative criteria, reviewing reports from teachers who have used the books experimentally, setting up a schedule of time allotments for presentations by textbook publishers, and determining what the basis will be for the final selection. The music publishers involved are then notified and invited to make individual presentations at specific dates and times. Avoid having overlapping presentations, and be certain to provide time for a lengthy question-and-answer period. The evaluation criteria should include not only musical content but the text's treatment of the various ethnic and racial groups that make up our nation (see Appendix E).

Research and Advanced Study

Essential for the continued growth of the music program in any school system is a concerted effort on behalf of research and development in music. The research may consist of a project in advanced studies or personal investigations. If it reflects creative thought and sound processes, it should be explored. One must remember that if it is an experimental program, a time limit should be placed on it and a period of assessment should follow. Incidentally, it is not necessary that every research project be successful. We often learn as much from negative findings as we do from successful ones. Careful research projects may yield results that can be applied immediately in the classroom and rehearsal halls.

In the name of research, music departments are often able to secure needed equipment. Some of this equipment will have lasting value long after the research has been concluded (e.g., word-processing and computer equipment).

Assisting individuals outside the school system in the conduct of research programs may become burdensome and time-consuming. However, if such research is valid and has the potential for making contributions to music education, one must contribute when possible. Such participation indicates a positive attitude toward the benefits that the entire profession derives from these efforts, and so, as the music administrator in your community, you should encourage other music teachers to involve themselves in these activities.

Most school systems build into their salary schedules financial incentives for advanced study. The music administrator should encourage music teachers to pursue advanced degrees for self-improvement and to keep the program from stagnating. Appropriate recognition should be given these individuals, and if they are working on a project that has a definite effect or has ramifications for a school music program, they should be given and facilities to explore and develop these projects. This attitude helps keep a music program dynamic and alive.

Music Curriculum Centers

It is not always physically feasible or economically possible that every classroom have every piece of desirable equipment or materials in it. Model centers placed at strategic points can serve as warehouses to circulate the material based on need and demand. They may also provide demonstrations and instruction on how to use the equipment and generally contribute to the overall in-service program.

Usually the music center is equipped with professional books and a variety of basic music series. It should have available for circulation kits, such as those containing instruments of the orchestra, related art material, and visual aids. The center should contain such equipment as Autoharps, resonator bells, sets of percussion instruments, and ethnic instruments. Each center should house a recording library with listening stations for teachers and students. The center should contain duplicating machines and other equipment essential to provide music for teachers and the classroom. In Glendale, California, the curriculum center in the administrative office circulated trunks containing materials and special equipment to enrich the classroom offerings.

Equipment, such as that student composers use for composition, computers may be distributed through this facility. One advantage of the loan system is that teachers and schools may borrow equipment and material for an extended period of time, so that if it proves sufficiently useful, they may decide to purchase it through their own school funds.

Each center should be staffed with a music consultant, a director, and a secretary-librarian. The music center staff is responsible to the music administrator for planning and presenting workshops for individuals and for entire schools. This center can be a dynamic influence in keeping a school system well equipped and up-to-date and is especially useful in rural areas, where a county system can provide this service throughout its district.

Attendance at Professional Meetings

Unless professional meetings are scheduled on days that do not conflict with school schedules, in many large school systems attendance at them is unfortunately reserved for members of the administration because of the economics involved. This is most regrettable, since teachers benefit from these meetings in many ways. Such meetings not only are inspirational but offer opportunities to exchange views with colleagues in the field. Current materials and equipment are exhibited, and the many demonstrations and clinics not only help keep people in the profession current but often lead to the generation of other creative ideas for use in the classroom. Music administrators, directors, and supervisors should work with principals to arrange to cover classes as much as possible to enable teachers to attend professional meetings. It might even be to the administrator's advantage to teach the classes for a day. Unfortunately, in many large systems the administrator would rather avoid making a decision about who should go. Regardless of who attends a professional meeting, there should later be some form of report about it for all teachers and staff. Not only is this an obligation to the school system that has given those in attendance released time and possibly some financial assistance, but it can be utilized as another opportunity for in-service education. Doing this tends to mitigate somewhat the resentment that those who were unable to attend might feel. (Many music teachers attend professional meetings on weekends and in summers whenever possible.)

A good music administrator will not only encourage but try to make it possible for teachers to take advantage of these meetings to improve themselves. Every effort should be made to see that the budget provides for this need. Naturally there will be limitations, and when they occur, the music administrator should develop an equitable arrangement that rotates this opportunity so that the benefits are offered to as many as possible.

Attendance at professional meetings should not be confined to national and state meetings. There are many local and university workshops that offer similar opportunities for improving instruction.

It is especially important that members of the school music administration also be active in professional organizations that service the total field of education, not just music. It is not enough to belong! They must participate and accept responsibility in these organizations so that music may be represented appropriately. In addition, they will grow and better understand music's role in the totality of education.

Microteaching

Another vehicle for improving instruction is the utilization of microteaching. However, before becoming immersed in it, one must be fully informed of its use and abuse. Microteaching is basically a technique evolved out of an idea. It is not a panacea. Its use can be either helpful or destructive to the individual, depending on how it is utilized and applied.

Microteaching is based on the principle that by isolating a single concept or skill to be learned and examining it in miniature form, one can learn as much about instruction as one can learn from actual teaching in the classroom, since microteaching is actual teaching under specific conditions. An advantage to microteaching is that although it is a practice session, it is real teaching. It enables the teacher to try out, strengthen, and improve teaching behavior during the course of several brief sessions.

For microteaching to be properly utilized for in-service analysis, it is important that it be conducted in such a manner that it is absolutely clear to the teacher that he is not being evaluated. The entire emphasis must be placed on instructional assistance, not rating. Although it is important that the microteaching session be videotaped, it is not an essential part of the process. When a videotape machine is not available an audio tape recorder may serve the same purpose, even though the visual aspect of the teaching is omitted.

Essentially, microteaching is selecting a single special technique, skill, or lesson and teaching it to a small group of children in a short specified amount of time. The process is built around the sequence of teach-analyze-reteach. Its purpose is to focus the teacher's attention on teaching behaviors and provide an opportunity for controlled "practice" teaching. Teachers are actually given an opportunity to see what they do when they teach a single aspect of a music lesson.

To be an effective in-service vehicle every effort must be made to reassure the teacher of his security. First, the taping is done with a small, limited (four–eight) group of children who are not regular members of the teacher's class. Second, the taping is usually done in a room other than the teacher's regular classroom. And third, the objective of microteaching and the problem to be analyzed are clearly defined before the teacher begins taping or recording. The entire filmed presentation should not take more than eight minutes.

As soon as the lesson is completed, the students fill out prepared forms to indicate what they learned and how they perceived what the teacher was attempting to do. The supervisor then reviews notes with the teacher, and the teacher reviews the tape. (Incidentally, it is not necessary that the entire tape be replayed. Once the appropriate point is made or observed, the rest of the tape may be set aside.) It can be disconcerting or even defeating if the supervisor speaks excessively or gets involved with matters that were not agreed upon initially. When the analytic part of the process is completed, the teacher again teaches the lesson to a different group of students.

"If teachers had a microteaching clinic as a part of the professional resources—like workshops and professional libraries—available to them, they could use it to systematically improve their instructional skills and to try out new curricular materials."[5] In addition, a microteaching lab could be utilized by supervisors and teacher to serve as a model for demonstrating or introducing new materials or new techniques to other teachers. A model for a microteaching experience might be structured as in Figure 6–1.

If the selected problem is to introduce the concept of rondo form to a group of fourth-grade students, the teacher would plan a series of short lessons. He would then focus on the first step, which would be to introduce the concept in a microteaching laboratory. In setting up the controlled situation, it would be determined that a small number of fourth-grade students not known to him would be invited to serve as participants. It would have to be determined whether they would be selected at random out of a general music class or from a special class, such as band or orchestra. It might be arbitrarily decided that the lesson is to be seven minutes in length. The supervisor would then instruct the teacher in procedures to facilitate taping and specifics regarding the lesson. It might be predetermined that the rondo form would be introduced via the Orff method, whereby the teacher presents a rhythmic theme A, each child responds with a contrasting theme B, C, and so on. However, after each child presents his theme, the class responds with A. Result—a rondo.

The presentation is then made and analyzed as shown in Figure 6–1. The feedback is real and immediate. A record is then kept of the original teaching performance for comparison with subsequent reteaching. At the reteaching stage, it is often more interesting and beneficial to focus on the same technique with new students and a fresh start than to redo it under the same conditions. However, after a series of lessons it may even be determined that the Orff approach does not lend itself to the purpose of the lesson and a new approach might be considered for teaching the rondo.

It is imperative that music supervisors understand that microteaching does not apply to every situation. To be effective, it must focus on a single idea; it must fit a specified lesson. Such a lesson might be just on learning how to hold a violin bow, but it would not necessarily apply to an orchestra rehearsal. The example of the microteaching lesson introducing the rondo form in a listening lesson within a given amount of time would be valid; however, it could not be used for an entire listening lesson. To develop an entire lesson, it would have to be broken down into its various components and each would have to be studied independently:

1. introducing the concept of rondo,
2. developing ability to recognize a rondo in a simple song,
3. developing ability to recognize a rondo in more complex forms, and
4. writing an original rondo.

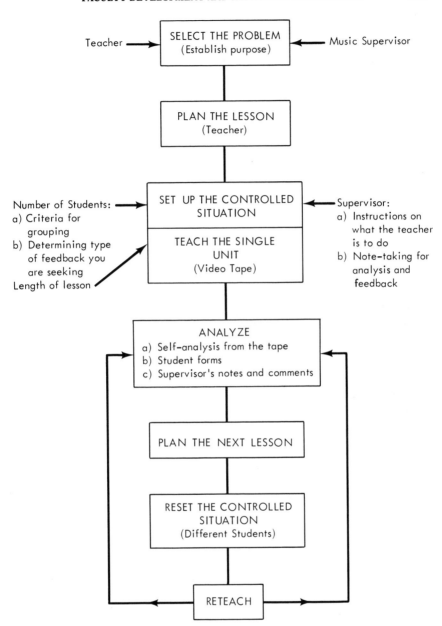

FIGURE 6–1

From each of the four components, a separate microteaching lesson could be developed.

Best of all, microteaching can be used as a device by supervisors to show teachers opportunities to involve students usually overlooked. Its use applies to experienced teachers as well as to new teachers. Many of the constraints of the normal classroom may be eliminated, and controlled conditions can be developed. By reducing the complexities of the typical classroom, the teaching-learning environment can be manipulated to direct attention to a limited number of specific techniques.

Supervisors and administrators constantly search for ways to improve instruction. Microteaching offers an opportunity for teachers to become involved in the process through self-analysis. In a microteaching clinic supervisors can assist teachers in a concentrated way that may eliminate wasting hours sitting in the back of a classroom to the discomfort of the teacher, students, and supervisor. A word of caution: microteaching is not to be construed as a device to eliminate the important need for visitation and interest in what the teacher is doing in his own classroom. It merely eliminates some of the anxiety and tension that occurs when retraining is done in the teacher's classroom with his own students. In a sense, it is artificial in that no regular classroom resembles the microteaching model. The success of microteaching will depend on its judicious use for the appropriate situation. Its potential for the improvement of instruction is unlimited.

NOTES

1. John A. Centra, *Faculty Development Practices in U.S. Colleges and Universities,* Project Report 76-30 (Princeton, N.J.: Educational Testing Service, 1976).
2. Peter Seldin, *Teaching Professors to Teach* (Croton-on-Hudson, N.Y.: Blythe Pennington, 1977).
3. J. A. Centra and F. R. Creech, *The Relationship Between Student, Teachers, and Course Characteristics and Student Ratings of Teacher Effectiveness,* Project Report 76-1 (Princeton, N.J.: Educational Testing Service, 1976).
4. Philip McClintock, "An Examination of Curriculum Guides in Music with Reference to Principles of Curriculum Planning" Mus.Ed.D. diss., Indiana University, 1970).
5. Dwight Allen and Ryan Allen, *Microteaching* (Reading, Pa.: Addison-Wesley), p.6.

SUPPLEMENTARY READINGS

Bergquist, William, and Phillips, Steven R. "Components of an Effective Faculty Development Program." *Journal of Higher Education* 46, no. 2 (March–April, 1975), pp. 177–211.

———. *Handbook for Faculty Development.* Washington, D.C.: Council for the Advancement of Small Colleges, 1975.

Bergquist, William H.; Phillips, Steven R.; and Quehl, Gary H. *A Handbook for Faculty Development.* Washington, D.C.: Council for the Advancement of Small Colleges, 1975.

Centra, John. "Plusses and Minuses for Faculty Development." *Change* 9, no. 12 (December 1977): 47–48.

Freedman, Marvin. *Academic Culture and Faculty Development.* Orinda, Calif.: Montaigne, 1980.

———, ed. *Facilitating Faculty Development.* San Francisco: Jossey-Bass, 1973.

Furniss, W. Todd. *Reshaping Faculty Careers.* Washington, D.C.: American Council of Education, 1981.

Menges, Robert J. "Teaching-Learning Experiences for Colleges and Other Adults: A Selected Annotated Bibliography." Evanston, Ill.: Northwestern University, The Center for the Teaching Professions. Occasional Paper Number 12, revised January 1977.

Morris, W. H., ed. *Effective College Teaching.* Washington, D.C.: American Council on Education, 1970.

McKeachie, Wilbert, Jr. *Teaching Tips: A Guidebook for the Beginning College Teacher,* 7th ed. Lexington, Mass.: D. C. Heath, 1977.

Nelson, William C., and Siegel, Michael C., eds. *Effective Approaches to Faculty Development.* Washington, D.C.: Association of American Colleges, 1980.

Seldin, Peter. *Teaching Professors to Teach.* Croton-on-Hudson, N.Y.: Blythe-Pennington, 1977.

Webber, Robert. "Improving College Teaching: An Annotated Bibliography." New Rochelle, New York: Change, August 1976.

STUDY QUESTIONS

1. What is meant by "faculty development"? Give examples.
2. What are ways that the music administrator can provide encouragement for faculty members to grow?
3. How would you go about setting up a program for faculty development in a public school system? In a college or university music department?
4. What role can workshops play in faculty development? How would you set up a workshop experience for a music faculty?
5. How would you set up a microteaching exercise around a specific teaching problem? Diagram the procedure.

7

Designing and Planning Curricula

*T*he primary function of any music administration is to develop and improve instruction for students, whether at the elementary, secondary, or university level. This can best be accomplished through the curriculum—not the guides, the courses of study, and syllabi published by a board of education or a university faculty but, rather, the ongoing experiences offered students that enable them to grow and develop in a school or academic environment. The guides and courses of study are intended merely as written guidelines for teachers in developing the experiences they will offer in their classrooms. Syllabi show the class plan and what is expected of students throughout the course. With this in mind, curriculum planning is defined as organizing the content to be used purposefully by the school or music department as a stimulus to learning. The guides then become means toward an end and not ends themselves.

In a broad sense, the term *curriculum* encompasses those instructional activities planned and offered to students which are based on "planned interaction of pupils with instructional *content*, instructional *resources*, and instructional *processes* for the attainment of educational objectives."[1] To further illustrate these relationships, the U.S. Department of Health, Education, and Welfare prepared a design shown in Figure 7–1.[2] Note that the staff's educational objectives are based on the identified needs of the students and community. Content, resources, and processes interact with pupils and each other to reach these objectives.

A curriculum that provides for all students must offer a variety of opportunities that enable them to be selective. It must include experiences that will prepare them for the remaining years in this century as well as those of the next, yet it cannot overlook the significant musical contributions of the past.

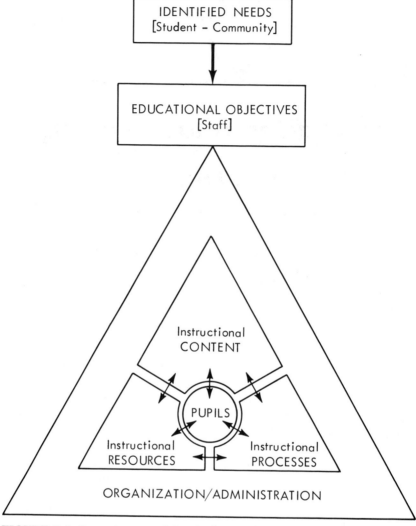

FIGURE 7–1 Some Aspects of Curriculum and Instruction and Their Interrelationships.

In higher education all music curricula are built around a core of studies required of all students. Depending on the academic degree sought, there are state requirements, particularly in areas requiring state certification, such as music education. In addition, the curriculum contains broad professional requirements and specific professional training for those pursuing performance degrees. Another component of music degrees is general education—studies in mathematics, social science, laboratory science, English, communication, and other nonmusical fields. In many institutions of higher learning, the curriculum is planned in terms of numbers of hours with semester or quarter credit assigned to each block of time.

Many performance-oriented schools require some form of recital for graduation. However, it has been advocated by many professional organizations (e.g. MENC and NASM) that when the student is not pursuing a performance degree, the recital requirement might be waived if he has demonstrated performance skills in compensatory situations.

REALLY? [handwritten margin note]

In higher education the course syllabus usually replaces the curriculum guide. Although there is little consistency in the requirements for syllabi, it is desirable that one should be made available for all areas of instruction.

To introduce changes in the curriculum, music administrators should follow these five steps:

1. Evaluate student needs, school philosophy, and effectiveness of current curriculum.
2. Develop a program of instruction.
3. Implement or develop instructional procedures and strategies for the new program.
4. Prepare instructional material.
5. Evaluate both program and instruction in keeping with its objectives.

Existing programs require these steps:

1. Establish the need for the new program and develop a rationale.
2. Research existing programs and determine if there is duplication or overlap with them in any new program.
3. Establish a rationale for a change if it involves revising a newly established program.
4. Determine the cost in dollars and personnel.
5. Devise the program and present it for consideration at departmental, college, or university level.
6. Revise as is necessary and desirable.

When music administrators function in this manner, they truly become architects of future music programs.

FORCES INFLUENCING CURRICULAR CHANGE

Curricular concerns will vary from community to community. There is no set pattern. Leo Chamberlain and Leslie Kindred, in their textbook *The Teacher and School Organizations*, identify the forces that shape these demands as being custom and tradition, textbooks, pressure groups, philanthropic foundations, colleges and universities, the mass media, public opinion, government legal requirements, and professional influences.[3] The authors of this text would add a tenth item—economy.

A few words about each are offered below, but first it is necessary to point out that no one of these forces is fully responsible for what is taught in a school. The competent administrator must work directly and vigorously with all of these forces to bring about the changes necessary for an effective curriculum. His constant goal should be the ultimate achievement of music and music education as a part of the core curriculum, to offer opportunities for musical experiences to all children, according to their interest and ability.

In these times, when segments of the public are concerned about whether education of uniform quality is being offered throughout a community, one cannot assure them that it is, as long as music is regarded as a "piecemeal elective." Until music, or at least a fine-arts subject, is required for graduation, some students will have exposure to music throughout their school life and others will have virtually none. (This requirement was initiated in the New York City public schools in the late 1970s.) Until music is taught as a comprehensive art form, even those enrolled in music courses or organizations cannot be assured of uniform quality, since unfortunately much instruction is mechanical, such as learning to perform in an orchestra, band, or chorus. Our persistent focus in all music classes should be the development of a comprehensive "knowledge" of music. Students should learn to think and react musically in a musical situation. Every administrator must keep this concept foremost in planning curricula.

Custom and tradition determine the conventional curricular offerings and are a reflection of past attitudes. According to some educators, it takes approximately fifty years for a new, worthwhile idea to permeate the entire educational system of this country. The greatest resistance to it may come from the forces of "custom and tradition." Yet these same forces have helped preserve some of the desirable aspects of a curriculum that might otherwise have been eliminated. (At Cass Technical High School in Detroit, a strong music program was preserved. During the post–World War II period in Detroit, special teachers were retained in music even as other large cities moved to self-contained classrooms.) One has to distinguish between those attitudes which interfere with progress and those which protect desirable programs.

Textbooks, through their content, can determine the direction that a curriculum may take. It is true that a textbook is essentially a resource tool or teaching aid, but it is also a source of information on which instruction can be structured. It can be an asset or a deterrent to good instruction. As a result, textbooks and textbook publishers too often play a major role in controlling the content of a course of study. A competent administrator will give appropriate direction to avoid this pitfall.

Today there are many books available on the market to meet the changing needs of most educational institutions. However, departments of education are coming more and more to depend on the development of their own supplementary materials to provide immediate solutions to imminent crises. (For example, an "Afro-American Song Book" was prepared by the Detroit Board of Education because at that time there was insufficient material in the current basic series. In San Antonio, units on Mexican-American music and art were prepared by enterprising teachers.)

Textbooks are improving, however, and one can find ample, varied material in every series. Even the learning sequences are similarly structured, so that it becomes a matter of individual taste regarding a particular feature of one book rather than that of another.

Too often a selected textbook determines the curriculum. In reality the reverse should be true: the educational philosophy of the community and the needs of the students should determine the choice of the textbook. It is the music administrator's responsibility to see that this occurs through democratic procedures. These procedures were discussed in Chapter 6.

In the future, texts will be custom-made of materials from a variety of sources. The *New York Times*, in an article by Edwin McDowell, reported:

> McGraw-Hill, Inc., one of the nation's largest book publishers, has developed the ability to customize college textbooks to suit the needs of individual professors—or even individual students—in 48 hours. . . . This system was developed in a joint venture with the Eastman Kodak Company. It will enable teachers and professors to order anywhere from 10 to 20 books and select the contents according to their needs and specifications.
>
> "It [the textbook] can even be personalized with the instructor's name, school and class number on the cover." In the future it will not be necessary to just select a series but it will be possible for music departments to order combinations of series and selections.[4] (1989)

Pressure groups can be a positive, as well as a negative, force. Although they invariably represent a vociferous minority, they are effective because the majority of people are apathetic about curriculum and curricular reform. In their positive aspect, they can help arouse the apathetic majority, and their enthusiasm can be utilized, if done so judiciously.

One of the critical challenges to school administration is the manner in which it is able to deal with pressure groups, both positive and negative. The perceptive administrator is able to distinguish between pressure and a genuine need emanating from a basic community concern. The emphasis in the school curriculum on Afro-American studies was both a direct response to pressure and the satisfaction of a long-neglected need. In this instance, needed curricular reform was actually initiated and supported by outside pressure groups in many of the nation's large cities.

Many school systems can point to cultural and community pressures as the source of their fine music programs, whereas others may have succumbed to pressures that have virtually eliminated basic music instruction because of shortsighted planning. Incidentally, it has usually been more difficult to eliminate a successful music program that is based on substantial learning experiences than one that has all the characteristics of a "frill."

There are literally hundreds of *philanthropic foundations* concerned with education. Almost all of them are privately endowed nonprofit organizations seriously committed to improving public welfare and education. They have stimulated a great deal of experimenting with new courses and developing new concepts.

The programs supported and developed by foundations have influenced many new directions and initiated curriculum reform. In Dearborn, Michigan, at the Edsel Ford High School, an entire humanities approach through the English curriculum was initiated as a result of a study funded by the Ford Foundation.

Published reports such as the Rockefeller Panel report on *The Performing Arts: Problems and Prospects* have caused communities and school systems to appraise their own role in the arts. Other reports of similar nature have forced schools to examine and revise their programs.

Through admission requirements, *colleges and universities* have exerted considerable influence on the school curriculum—often at the expense of the arts. This is changing, and music educators need to keep informed about which colleges and universities seek students with balanced education. Much of the confusion about entrance requirements is a result of misinformation and anxiety over admissions.

Most high schools belong to accrediting associations administered by the colleges and universities in their respective regions. In this manner, higher-education institutions have played a significant role in determining class sizes, teacher qualifications, and materials utilized in instruction. Many outstanding high school programs are a direct result of institutional experiments by university scholars.

The *mass media* have had a tremendous impact on curricular change. Marshall McLuhan, in *Understanding Media: The Extensions of Man*, indicates that the whole nature of education is changing as a result of the tremendous developments in mass communication.

The arts have especially benefited from these developments. Artists and fine musical organizations can now be a part of one's evening at home and provide entertainment of the highest caliber. There is much more information and knowledge available to students today as a result of the accessibility of fine music through the media. Educators are still trying to determine how the media can be put to their most constructive use.

Public opinion is probably the most potent force to offset undesirable pressure groups. In the final analysis, it is the public that has the last word in curricular reform. It controls the nature and content of the curriculum through its governing body, the board of education, and through its chief employee, the superintendent. Failure to comply with, or to understand, the role of public opinion has led to many of the difficulties that schools find themselves in today. It is therefore essential that the public and the school administration educate themselves to properly interpret the weight and implications expressed by public opinion.

Legal requirements generally stem from recommendations by state boards of education or state legislatures. It is recognized that states have the right to legislate regarding content in certain areas of the curriculum. Unfortunately, they do not perceive the full extent of their responsibility and often act under the influence of pressure groups or vested interests. This militates against fine-arts programs, which still tend to be regarded as peripheral, rather than core, subjects. Yet state boards of education can be effective in retaining balanced programs, by lobbying for legislation against such imbalances if they recognize the values inherent in the humanities.

By far the most significant of the forces affecting change can be *professional influences*. It is a truism that change in a school curriculum can be implemented only as far, or as fast, as the other forces will support the program. It is therefore the professional educator's responsibility to assume leadership in working with all of these forces to bring about the desired changes.

There are other professionals in the school structure, such as the superintendent and principals, who will also determine the nature and emphasis of music in a school program. If a superintendent or curriculum director of a school system is interested in developing a music program, the chances for success are far better than if he is opposed.

Other professional agencies, such as the Music Educators National Conference, the American Choral Directors Association, the American String Teachers Association, the National School Orchestra Association, and the American Bandmasters Association, can also serve as pressure groups to bring about desirable changes where music programs are in difficulty. In addition, they help to call attention to worthwhile projects that contribute to improvements in the music curriculum. The Music Educators National Conference periodically organizes a Commission on Teacher Education to prepare competency statements and explore possible revisions for bringing the preparation of teachers of music up to date.

Full scores are now fairly standard with school music publications, but they came only after a concerted effort on the part of the American String Teachers Association and the various Band Associations insisting that they be made available.

Finally, the one force over which there is little academic or musical control and yet has the most pervasive effect on the curriculum is the national or local *economy*. It especially affects the arts because in our society the arts are still treated by many as desirable but not essential for existence. And yet the National Council for Basic Education includes the arts as a part of its basic required instruction.

A successful music administrator will be sensitive and aware of all of these forces in working to bring about effective change. He will not rely solely on any one of them but utilize and fuse as many elements as the situation warrants.

An effective curriculum assists and somewhat assures the child of continuous, sequential musical growth through a comprehensive and balanced instructional program. The offerings in any school district should reflect the attitudes and philosophy of the music staff, the administration, and the community. The courses should include consideration of the interests and the needs of *all* of the students. To do so, the curriculum must be developed cooperatively, remain flexible, and be sufficiently open to invite scrutiny and study by all groups that influence change.

CHANGING THE CURRICULUM

Musical learnings are the responsibility of the whole school. They cannot be assigned to one teacher and forgotten by the others. Education in music begins in the pre-school years and continues until the student graduates from high school; it does not come about as the result of a course in the junior high school years. It is, rather, the product of everything musical that happens in twelve or thirteen years of schooling, indeed of everything musical that happens through a life-time.[5] ᴇʀɴꜱᴛ ꜰɢᴀʀʏ, 1965.

Only the administrator of the total school music program is in a position to see the complete continuum and plan for it. It is not something that just happens. It is a direct result of careful planning and direction. To develop a curriculum according this concept requires the involvement of many people. Leadership roles need to be assigned at virtually every level of the sequence if a careful, well-conceived plan is to be developed.

1961!

J. Lloyd Trump and Dorsey Baynham, in their text *Focus on Change*,[6] indicate that *change* is now an accepted part of the school scene. If effective plans with appropriate objectives can be developed, enlightened administrators should be sympathetic to proposed constructive revisions in the school curriculum and assist in the process. They need not fear change.

There are two types of curriculum change, whether it be in the schools or the universities, *change in human behavior* and *instructional change* or *change in content.* Change in curriculum should not be confused with merely improving instruction. To some, curriculum improvement may mean merely changing certain subject emphases without changing fundamental goals or course structure. To change the curriculum, one must change the way one perceives the entire structure. It means changing the goals and even the processes.

The most difficult yet effective change occurs when a teacher, especially an experienced one, changes the way he has been conducting his music class for years. As indicated earlier, the Contemporary Music Project of the MENC-Ford Foundation has done much to effect both forms of change through its composer-in-residence program and its focus on comprehensive musicianship in the 1960s.

The curriculum should reflect contemporary knowledge of the subject area if it is to be regarded as both relevant and valid. Although there has been much abuse of the term *relevance,* an idea is fundamentally relevant when it has widespread applicability and is in touch with the social and cultural realities of the community. This principle assists in establishing the relative importance of ideas in the study of music. One of the things that a music administrator is confronted with when determining the validity of the curricular offerings is the extent to which they reflect the music of all times, utilizing contemporary techniques and knowledge. He must also ascertain their implications for learning values in a social and cultural setting. The emphasis, of course, is altered with the passing of time and changes in the social and cultural milieu.

MUSIC IN GENERAL EDUCATION

Music in general education, more commonly referred to as "general music," is the core of the entire music program in the schools. It is the trunk of the tree with the various special organizations serving as branches. It should pervade the entire program. Because it does not receive the attention and acclaim afforded special groups, the general program in music is often slighted, but no concerned administrator will permit it to suffer. As the core offering in the entire program, it should provide experiences for every child interested in music.

The major component, referred to as "basic musicianship" in higher education, involves specified theory and music history/literature courses, as well as their related offerings. These will vary from one institution to another but are required to meet the minimum standards established by the National Association of Schools of Music (NASM). Each degree program then establishes its own curriculum with specialized areas, such as music education or performance, surrounding the basic musicianship component.

Balancing Special Programs

The vocal and instrumental organizations in a school system are the performance-oriented offerings in the school music program. Although within the context of each one there should be appropriate allocations of time devoted to general music education, the motivating force of special groups is performance. This does not negate the teacher's responsibility to teach music in the comprehensive sense of developing musical understanding. Incidentally, one does not just "teach" comprehensive musicianship. Rather, it is a *way* of teaching that is reflected in musical response from the students. Too often music educators try to categorize comprehensive musicianship into specific activities and compartments such as composing (organizing sounds), analyzing, and performing. This compartmentalization is merely the means toward developing students who think and respond in musical situations as musicians. Comprehensive musicianship actually involves every musical activity. It is evident in the way students react in musical situations. Music administrators must be constantly alert to see that this is done in the schools under their jurisdiction, whether they work through their supervisors or are themselves in direct contact with individual teachers.

To do this, music administrators must attend concerts in schools regularly. They must be firm in their convictions of the importance of this task. Incidentally, comprehensive musicianship can be attained through a variety of musics and in many different types of performances. As long as there is evidence of it, whether it be in performance or in a classroom of students being exposed to experiences that lead to comprehensive knowledge, the medium itself is not of prime importance.

In one school system it was the practice of the director of music education to review with the department heads and directors the contents of programs that were performed each year. A chart was prepared, and the degree of representation of the various periods and styles performed was discussed to determine if the music was truly representative of all periods in music history. This exercise proved to be successful in making teachers aware of historical imbalance in programming and focused on where they placed their musical emphasis or preferences. This is only one aspect of responsibility to the totality of music assumed by the music administrator. County school music administrators and supervisors, and in fact every teacher, should check his programming in a similar way.

If educators are to accommodate individual tastes and preferences, it is mandatory that schools maintain a variety of performing groups. Incidentally, to do this there must be some orderly procedure that provides information regarding students as they move from building to building, from grade level to grade level. Too often students are lost in transfer because no one has prepared the necessary organizational steps. This is really a clerical and administrative procedure, which, if not allowed, can undermine a well-planned program.

But even more significant is the responsibility that the chief music administrator has to see that no one special area suffers because of a lack of interest or inertia on the part of the faculty. He must constantly strive to strengthen every part of the special program, whether it be orchestra, band, chorus, or small ensemble. Opportunities to participate in each of these musical organizations should be available at every grade level beyond the established starting point, to accommodate a student's legitimate interests in performing music. Music administrators are in the best position to see that this is accomplished. Incidentally, every music class or private lesson, no matter what its level, should be taught comprehensively. The only difference between levels is the degree of involvement and sophistication.

A balanced curriculum in the secondary schools includes special courses in music theory, music literature, and music history. They need not be presented as separate entities but may be grouped under one or two combinations of these titles. As indicated earlier, these elements are fundamental to comprehensive musicianship and are taught in all music offerings. However, we are referring here to special classes that place particular emphasis on these subjects. It is as much the administration's responsibility to see that provisions are made for these classes as for the others.

Related arts or humanities programs may not fall under the aegis of the music program, but if they do not exist in a community, the music administrator should assume leadership in initiating such programs. Where they do exist, the administrator should maintain an active role in enriching them. He should work with the art department, the language arts department, the drama department, and the social studies department to see that music's role in the humanities is properly presented. But even more significant, administrators and their colleagues need to see that the humanities permeate the entire curriculum, grades one through twelve. In universities, degree requirements generally include a certain number of credits in the humanities. It is such requirements that help distinguish between studying at a conservatory, at a music school, or in a department of music at a college or university.

Any course that will add a new dimension to the school music program should be considered and investigated. Creative thinking and imagination will vitalize or revitalize the curriculum and stimulate enthusiasm. For example, in Wichita, Kansas, such creative thought resulted in the development of a piano-mobile; in Philadelphia it resulted in the acquisition of organs, percussion instruments in the elementary schools, and electronic synthesizers in the junior high schools; and in Cleveland a supplementary education center for the arts was created. Detroit began preschool violin programs, elementary troubadour harp programs, and electronic organs in junior high schools in inner-city areas. Arkansas was able to send professional ensembles all over the state, particularly through rural areas by means of a trailer equipped for such presentations. All of these programs were the creations of imaginative teachers and administrators who were willing to be embarrassed by an occasional failure rather than being so careful that they failed to innovate at all.

Computers

No single development in the latter half of the twentieth century has had greater impact on instruction than the development of the computer. This device has already revolutionized our industrial, recreational, and educational life. It has enabled our society, including its educational system, to increase its efficiency with greater speed and more accurate information, and has provided expanded opportunities for more highly individualized instruction. When the computer was introduced into education, there was great concern about its excessive cost. However, like all technical innovations, as its use increased, cost was reduced. We now have reached the time when we can foresee each classroom having its own computers to assist with instruction and research. Today virtually all children have access to computers at home or in school.

As we approach the twenty-first century we find that the computer is no longer a gimmick or a toy. It is an instructional tool that is utilized by every area of instruction, including music, at both the school and university levels. There have been many computer systems developed. In selecting a computer, one needs to find an instrument that is well suited to teaching music. It should possess high-quality graphics and a self-contained sound system. Programs should be able to be stored on small, inexpensive discs and be quite compact so that teachers can easily carry an entire unit throughout a building or even home.

Outside of the actual performing organization, computers may be used in almost every aspect of instruction. They can provide supplemental drills or, if one is involved in a spiral curriculum, reinforcement of various concepts. They have the capacity to take a student through a complete series of theory exercises or tests that would be determined by the students' ability and their rate of speed in learning. Computers can interpret scores and offer suggestions for improvement. Through humorous devices, they can offer encouragement and hold students' attention at times when they otherwise might be discouraged.

Probably one of the most important aspects of computer instruction is the ability to operate at a student's own learning pace. Students can progress at their own rate of speed and do not have to rely on class norms. Computers can present new materials to students in a very systematic manner, allowing each student to enter the system at his individual level of achievement or previous experience.

Contrary to some opinion, computers can provide creative activities for students. They can compose music in any style. They can choose from any programmed melodies, harmonies, rhythms, timbres, and even voicings. The advantage of a computer is that the student can have feedback as soon as he puts material into the instrument. Students who have difficulty with traditional instruments find a great deal of pleasure in working with computers. They may add or change notes easily on the computer and never have to reach for the pencil or manuscript paper. Any school system with an eye to the future of its program must include computers in its thinking. We cannot ignore this new development and its capabilities as an aid to instruction. Computers are not the teaching tool of tomorrow; they are already here. The challenge of the future is to make them more effective.

CURRICULUM IMPROVEMENT IN THE UNIVERSITY

Jim Hammons has pointed out that actually most college faculty look to their chairpersons, when appropriate, for encouragement to effect curricular change.[7] When an effort to bring about effective change emanates from faculty members, they expect their administrator not only to encourage them but also to facilitate their efforts. Purposeful change is evidence of an effort to improve one's instruction, and such efforts should be rewarded and reorganized if needed rather than discouraged.

If one is to provide the necessary leadership to bring about desirable changes, one must be knowledgeable in the areas of curriculum and instruction. Most resistance from the top to such change is a result of administrators being insufficiently well informed in these areas. To improve the performance of a chairperson in curriculum development, Hammons refers to an article by Melvin Blumberg and Charles D. Pringle, "The Missing Opportunities in Organizational Research: Some Implications for a Theory of Work Performance," which groups these factors for improvement under four categories: ability, motivation, opportunity, and climate.[8]

Ability is the potential to achieve what one is capable of achieving. Much of this characteristic is imbedded in the selection process. If participation in curriculum reform and teaching in the change process require special skills, individual faculty members or curriculum leaders should be selected on the basis of possessing these skills. Furthermore, once selected, they not only need encouragement but also require support, continuous training (change is a constant process), and ample opportunity to bring about desired change.

Motivation is a complex, intangible drive. Whereas ability deals with the potential to act, motivation is that which impels one to act. There is probably no greater incentive than one's internal drive; however, externally, the expected rewards for changing to improve instruction must be made worthwhile.

Opportunity refers to those factors which may be beyond the individual's direct control but do determine whether that person has the chance to perform. Too often chairpersons or other instructional leaders are burdened with class loads that are excessive in relation to their responsibilities as leaders in curricular matters. In addition, curriculum leaders require support in such matters as budget, secretarial assistance, and print and nonprint media if they are to be efficient managers and educational leaders.[9]

Climate is an individual's perception of his work environment. Its parameters consist of such concerns "as the reward systems, workload, status differentials, and autonomy."[10]

EVALUATING CHANGE IN CURRICULUM DEVELOPMENT

As society and music increase in complexity and change becomes even more accelerated, it is essential for music education that music educators both in the colleges and in the schools become more specific about what they hope to accomplish, how they intend to achieve their goals, and how they will know if they have accomplished these goals:

> . . . Where am I going
> How shall I get there, and
> How will I know I've arrived?[11]

These questions need to be answered in such a way that ambiguities are resolved and clichés are dispelled. They must contain well-defined behaviors that can be evaluated within a given time and long-range aims that can be measured only in terms of the future and maturation. However, even long-range goals need to be stated in such a way that anyone conducting long-term research may measure or evaluate them in an identifiable manner at the end of a reasonably specific time, no matter how distant it may be.

On the other hand, music administrators must not be caught up in rejecting certain aspects of music as an art form that defy measurement. Aesthetics and attitudes, or the affective domain, are equally important in music, and it is a misguided idea that some of these areas comprise universals that can be measured only as fixed behaviors. Opinions and judgments change as one matures, and provisions for growth must also be considered.

One must not confuse evaluation with measurement. They are completely different and serve different functions. Evaluation deals with determining the quality of an offering, while measurement determines the amount or extent of the offering. Often under Title I "evaluation procedures," schools were required to count the number of students attending the program with a perfunctory "Did you like it?" This was a form of measurement. The real impact would be to determine the effect that the program has on a child's attendance at musical programs fifteen years later or other evidence of involvement. This would be "evaluation."

The evaluative process is governed by the established objectives as they relate to the growth and development of the student. However, objectives must not be so restricted as to materials and procedures that they obviate flexibility. Objectives are not arbitrary products of a music department's staff. In developing them, one has to consider many factors. First and foremost, objectives should relate to the art of music and what it does for and to people. In addition, the needs and aspirations of a community and society as a whole must also be considered when establishing goals. This includes the student needs, interests, and maturation. This information is then absorbed, evaluated, and organized into a statement of goals.

Once a music department has some ideas where it is going, it must determine how it shall get there. Instructional patterns are developed and a series of musical experiences are then constructed to assist the student in reaching his destination—an education that will aid and guide him in a changing society. To provide for these experiences, one has to allocate space, resources, personnel, and students. Budget must be provided, and all facets that contribute to a desirable learning situation must be taken into consideration. An appropriate faculty needs to be secured to implement instruction, and a climate conducive to learning must be created.

When this has all been accomplished, one needs to measure the success of the program to see if it has arrived. In order that the evaluation be reasonably valid, the program has to be measured in terms of whether the student truly reflects the objectives initially stated. If one were to diagram the entire process, it might appear as shown in Figure 7–2.

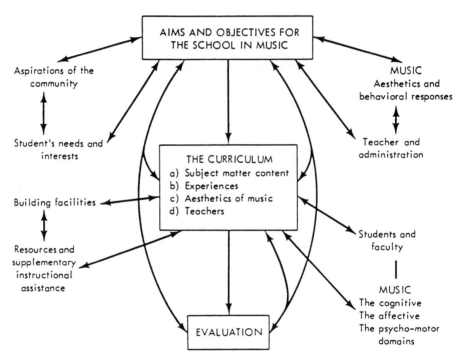

FIGURE 7–2 The entire system is dependent upon open lines of communication and feedback moving in either direction. It is bound together by a complete loop evolving from the evaluative process.

A small community, for example, might be concerned with becoming more self-sufficient culturally. It has no string program in the school, no civic orchestra to stimulate and encourage orchestral performances, and many students who do not want to play in the band but are interested in playing string instruments have no outlet. Informed people are sufficiently concerned that their children are not being exposed to the great cultural heritage reposing in the orchestral literature and their aesthetic development is being truncated.

The individual in the position of leadership in music education is equally concerned and, with his staff, sets up a five-year plan to develop a school string program that will fulfill the need expressed by the community. A string staff needs to be employed, facilities need to be provided, and equipment must be secured. In the meantime, as the staff is being assembled, incipient stages of the curriculum are being planned. Appropriate experience in a well-designed sequence will be organized by the music teachers and music administrators, and to be certain that the program is more than just performance-oriented, specific goals in aesthetics and the affective domain will be identified.

At the end of the year, the entire program should be evaluated. This evaluation should be based on the criteria established when developing the overall aims. When the program does not meet its criteria for a successful experience, adjustments should be made. It might be that the students are not developing a particular skill that was a goal for the first year, or it might even be that there has been insufficient sustained interest. At any rate, the bases for the evaluation should be examination of student growth, student development, and student response. Objectives may be revised, and changes made in the curriculum sequence, after each evaluation. At the end of five years, the entire program should be given an overall evaluation, and as a result, the string plan might take a new direction or be continued as it exists. On the other hand, if evaluation reveals that the program does not meet the criteria as reflected in the aims and objectives, there may be other ways of achieving the original goals, so that the project might be abandoned in favor of another approach. This is merely a broad description of a new program and how a music department would evaluate its success and progress. In an actual situation, each item would be specified and evaluated on its own merits as reflected in its criteria for success.

EVALUATING PERFORMANCES

Aesthetic judgment is a difficult area to evaluate. One cannot apply a simple rule to every aesthetic decision. There are many variables that one must consider. A music supervisor or administrator needs to take into consideration the nature of the situation as well as the values of the community and those who comprise it.

When evaluating a performance, there are technical aspects of it that are fairly fixed. Such universals as tone quality, phrasing, and rhythm are fairly standard, but the more subtle aesthetic values are not as easily identified, particularly when one is concerned with raising musical standards. (Certain musical arrangements of the baroque and classical periods have been so oversimplified that they have lost the characteristics of those periods.) This standard, incidentally, is not to be confused with recognizing that when one assesses the performance, it should be considered in the context of that idiom and not evaluated in terms of another genre.

To help resolve this dilemma, a good rule to apply is that it is far better to aspire to a musical performance higher on the aesthetic scale and fall slightly short of it than to set your goals at an extremely low end of the aesthetic scale and achieve it. For example, a musical performance that attempts to realize a performance of music that might have a standard of 80 on our imaginative aesthetic scale of 100 and only achieves 70 percent of its goals is far more commendable than that of a performance of music that rates 25 on the same musical scale and realizes 100 percent of it goals. If one is only interested in music of low aesthetic value, the students cannot grow in aesthetic perception and value judgment. On the other hand, one should be equally critical of a performance that is so far beyond the technical and aesthetic level of the students that it does not even achieve a 50 percent rating.

As long as music administrators are responsible for standards and aesthetic values, they must determine some criteria for evaluation. Without criteria, they are unable to enforce or justify their position regarding aesthetic standards.

One should not interpret this to mean that any music supervisor or director arbitrarily imposes his own aesthetic values, which may have origins other than the music being performed, on those being evaluated. These judgments must be made in the context of the society and social milieu from which they originate and are being performed. One does not pass judgment as to whether or not a gospel song is more or less significant than a Lutheran hymn. If it is a gospel song, it must be performed in the best tradition of gospel singing. If it is a Lutheran hymn, then the standard for that musical form prevails. Each idiom must be examined in terms of its significance to those performing and as to whether or not its function contributes to the growth, development, and understanding of the people involved.

Respect for the performance styles of ethnic groups outside the orbit of traditional Western music is extremely important, and music administrators need to be better informed about them. When dealing with traditional Western music, aesthetic values that apply to this tradition need to be equally enforced. One enforces standards for each milieu, but does not assess one in terms of the other.

■

EVALUATING FOR CHANGE

It is possible to develop a way of producing desirable change that employs evaluative processes. It is essentially a systems approach and has proven most effective in industry. This is basically the same approach utilized, whether consciously or not, by the Music Educators National Conference in its Goals and Objectives Project (1968–1970), under the leadership of Frances Andrews, and its subsequent Action Plans.

The initial step in any systems approach is the formulation of specific statements of what needs to be done and what the department or profession as a whole is able to do. A word of caution: these goals or objectives should be stated as precisely as possible, but they should not be governed by restrictions of materials or procedures that would limit the program. Such factors are introduced later—that is, once the objectives have been determined. If a department decides that its chief objective is to increase the use of contemporary music in concert programming, it will not specify initially what literature or which ensemble will be utilized until the objective priority has been established. It may then focus on one particular type of organization or on all ensembles or even on a particular level of instruction before it even considers implementation.

The next step might be to establish precisely what is meant as "contemporary music," and the staff may then discover a need for improving specific musical skills if the objective is to be achieved in a qualitative manner. Before a total program is embarked on, it would be desirable to set up some model programs in a specific school that might be interested in utilizing more-contemporary ideas. If it proves successful, this school's program could then serve as an example for other schools. Many innovative musical programs were introduced in the Detroit public schools by using Cass Technical High School as just such an example.

Dr. Bobby Jordan, the principal of a high school in DeKalb County, Georgia, at a workshop in the summer of 1989 at the University of Tennessee—Chattanooga when discussing how to initiate and implement the concept of "discipline-based music education" (DBME) in his school (see p. 152), suggested an approach that he utilizes to determine whether DBME has been employed in teaching music in the performing groups in his school. After a concert or performance, he asks two basic questions:

1. What have the students learned about music besides performing the compositions beautifully? (DBME involves history, criticism [judgment], aesthetics, and performance.)

2. Does the teacher cover *all* musics, not only traditional periods but also various ethnic and popular musics?

Related questions pursued by Dr. Jordan are as follows:

1. Has the teacher developed *course objectives,* and how well have they been met? (These are established at the beginning of the academic year and reviewed at the end of the year.)
2. Has the teacher provided details regarding the anticipated curriculum? (He then reviews them with the teacher at the conclusion of the year.)
3. Is the teacher *to define what* he is teaching?
4. Dr. Jordan also subscribes to professional journals affecting the discipline of music and shares and discusses the views expressed therein with his teachers. In addition, he appoints his music teachers to curriculum committees in music and areas pertinent to the music program. What is most significant is that Dr. Jordan lets his music teachers know that he fully supports a balanced curriculum.

Change, even in music and music education, is inevitable. It is better to plan and attempt to guide it rather than have it sweep over us like a tidal wave and leave us inundated. Too many music programs have been eliminated because no one anticipated change and planned for it.

NOTES

1. Dale Chismore and John F. Putnam, eds., *Standard Terminology for Curriculum and Instruction in Local and State School Systems* (Washington, D.C.: U.S. Department of Health, Education, and Welfare, 1970), p. 2.
2. *Ibid.*
3. Leo Chamberlain and Leslie Kindred, *The Teacher and School Organizations,* 4th ed. (Englewood Cliffs, N.J.: Prentice-Hall, 1966.)
4. Edwin McDowell, "Facts to Fit Every Fancy: Custom Textbooks Are Here," *New York Times,* October 23, 1989. p. 21.
5. Karl Ernst and Charles Gary, eds., *Music in General Education* (Washington, D.C.: Music Educators National Conference, 1965), p. 9.
6. J. Lloyd Trump and Dorsey Baynham, *Focus on Change.* Chicago: Rand McNally, 1961.
7. Jim Hammons, "The Department/Division Chairperson: Educational Leader?," *Community and Junior College Journal* 54, no. 6 (March 1984), p. 69.
8. Melvin Blumberg and Charles D. Pringle, "The Missing Opportunity in Organizational Research: Some Implications for a Theory of Work Performance," *Academy of Management Review* 17, no. 4 (1982), pp. 560–569.

9. Hammons, "The Department/Division Chairperson," p. 74.
10. *Ibid.*
11. Robert F. Mayer, *Developing Attitude Toward Learning* (Palo Alto, Calif.: Fearon, 1968), p. vii.

SUPPLEMENTARY READINGS

Blackburn, Robert, et al. *Changing Practices in Undergraduate Education.* Berkeley, Calif.: Carnegie Council on Policy Studies in Higher Education, 1976.

Bluhm, Harry P. *Administrative Uses of Computers in the Schools.* Englewood Cliffs, N.J.: Prentice-Hall, 1987.

Dressell, Paul L. *College and University Curriculum.* Berkeley, Calif.: McCutchan, 1971.

Fraude, Velma. "Not Only Little Angels Play the Harp." *Music Educators Journal* (October 1969), 56, no. 2, p. 37.

Gary, Charles. Curriculum Handbook for School Administrators. *Music Educators National Conference*, Washington, D.C., 1967.

Getty Center for Education in the Arts. *Beyond Creating: The Place for Art in America's Schools.* Los Angeles: Getty Center for Education in the Arts, 1985.

Greer, R. Douglas. *Design for Music Learning.* New York: Teachers College Press, 1980.

Hagemann, Virginia S. "Are Junior High Students Ready for Electronic Music," *Music Educators Journal* 56, no. 4 (December 1969), p. 35.

Hodsoll, Frank, ed. *Toward Civilization: A Report on Arts Education.* Washington, D.C.: National Endowment for the Arts, 1988.

Music Educators National Conference. *The School Music Program: Descriptions and Standards*, 2nd ed. Reston, Va.: MENC, 1986.

Motycka, Arthur. *Music Education for Tomorrow's Society.* Jamestown, R.I.: GAMT Music Press, 1976, pp. 1–20.

Saniford, Clarence. "Music in General Education: Are High Schools Doing Their Part?" *Music Educators Journal* (April 1969), p. 83.

STUDY QUESTIONS

1. What steps and procedures are needed to introduce change in the curriculum?
2. What are the forces that influence change in the curriculum? Discuss each one.
3. What are the four categories that contribute to curricular change in higher education? Discuss each.
4. Select a desired change for a music program, and diagram the steps and procedures to bring about the necessary change and measure its effectiveness.

8

Budget and Finance; Facilities and Equipment

*T*here are probably no more frustrating responsibilities confronting a music administrator than matters dealing with budget and finance. However, one can neither ignore nor dismiss them. Virtually every decision under consideration affects budget, directly or indirectly, and if one is to be an effective administrator, one must learn to deal with budgetary matters in a responsible way.

Practices regarding budgets are as varied as the universities and communities that use them, so no attempt will be made to present model budgets here. What is important is that there be some basic understanding of the structure of a budget and that the design reflect some underlying philosophy that can be interpreted in educational terms. A budget should reflect short-range and long-range planning.

Budgets should be designed out of a recognition of educational needs, not expediency. After all, educational needs should determine priorities in a music school or school system, with a music department, and even within an individual building in order to determine the kind of education students receive!

SOURCES OF FUNDS

The chief source of funds for a school system prior to 1973 was the locality. (Local dollars made up 60 percent of the local school support, while the state carried 40 percent of the cost.) This was the locus of financial responsibility. It was even the practice in many states to limit state aid to the local per pupil expenditure or the local tax base rate. The second major source of income was the state. However, in

[handwritten margin note: WHERE DOES $ IN YOUR DISTRICT COME FROM?]

1973 the figures were reversed. The public schools are a responsibility of the state, and under current practices, ultimately the state has the responsibility for their operation. In practice, however, the state delegates this responsibility to the local board.

There were two court cases in California and Texas in the early 1970s that led the movement away from local property taxes as the principal source of support for the schools. Both cases were based on the premise that many school districts, because of their tax base, were unable to offer their children equal educational opportunity, let alone education of the quality being offered in wealthier districts in the state. The decisions in both cases, as well as in others, led to the current financial equation.

Unlike the local board, the state is much more susceptible to political maneuvering because policies are determined by elected state officials with party affiliations. Since they are somewhat removed from the local situation, however, they are not as sensitive or as accessible as the members of the local board of education. Making financial decisions removed from the concerned area does have the advantage of minimizing sustained local pressures by vested interests. On the other hand, state legislatures, under these circumstances, may not always understand the needs and pressures of a critical local situation.

The last major source of revenue available to a board of education is the federal government, which in recent years has assumed a larger role in funding local schools in an effort to equalize educational opportunities and raise the level of education in economically "depressed" or "deprived" areas. This has created some interesting controversy. For years conservative educators have been concerned that federal aid would mean federal control, despite the fact that for years the government has subsidized construction in education and aid to states for school food programs, vocational training, and special education with a minimum of interference. This concern has proven to be somewhat unfounded to date. Grants to local boards of education are made within guidelines established by the legalities of the specific educational act and the context of *one's own proposal*. Recipients of grants are required to evaluate the program and account for the money spent; however, this is a good business practice and cannot be construed as interference.

[handwritten margin note: WHAT ABOUT FUND-RAISING?]

In essence these three—local, state, and federal governments—are the sources of income available to public schools, and budgets are constrained by the total dollars from the three sources. Occasionally, grants from foundations or private contributions may be received, but they cannot be considered in overall budget planning. These contributions become the property of the board of education and do not belong to a single individual or, in the final analysis, even to a school building. It is the board's prerogative to distribute these funds in the way it deems to be in the best interest of children and education. Its only guidelines for the use of private contributions are usually established by the contributor.

At the college or university level, sources of funds include tuition and fees from students, support from the state legislature (for public colleges and universities), private contributions from various constituent groups (e.g., alumni, friends), grants from foundations or special-interest groups with specific projects in mind, and contracts with governmental agencies or corporations to pursue specific or even general research. In addition, most colleges and universities have endowment funds—accounts created by contributors to support scholarships, lectureships, or even provide for support for a professor. The "prestige" universities will have several endowed chairs occupied by distinguished scholars who will have a salary, travel money, equipment, graduate assistant help, and other perks that come from the earnings from the endowment.

The music executive at any institution will have one or more sources of funds around which to build a budget. In many cases he will be involved in one or more fund-raising activities to supplement these funds. (Fund-raising and grant-seeking are discussed in Chapter 9.)

RESPONSIBILITIES FOR BUDGET

The total budget for a school system is the responsibility of the superintendent, and for a university, the university president. It is the usual practice for this individual to submit the budget to the governing authority (the board of education, the trustees, or the regents) after consulting with the business department or chief financial officer and other administrators. Any anticipated expenditures from the music department that may require adjusting or reorganizing within the budget structure should be submitted to the responsible person in advance or during the budget preparation period. This procedure applies to both higher education and public schools.

One practice in some school communities is to assign a lump sum to departments, which in turn divide it within the department according to educational considerations. Another practice—one that is more prevalent—is to assign amounts to various expenditures according to the budget categories, such as repair, supplies, or music, and according to previously planned considerations. This is especially true at the college level. Some of the items are then subject only to authorization by the music administrator. Depending upon the limit set by the board of education or the board of trustees, other items would then require consultation with, and approval by, others higher in the line-and-staff organization.

In most systems, one cannot transfer funds from one category to another without approval from the appropriate office. This creates confusion in the minds of some administrators because they assume that when a sum of money has been assigned to the music department, it does not matter for which category it is utilized. One needs to know existing practices within one's own system before making these assumptions. It is advisable that every embryonic music administrator acquaint himself with the financial structure and the rules that govern administering funds within the school system or university.

WHAT IS THE BUDGET PROCESS IN YOUR SCHOOL?

WHAT IS THE PURCHASE PROCESS IN YOUR SCHOOL?

Budget Categories in Schools

Budgets are usually divided into several categories: supplies (office, studios, and classrooms), equipment (musical instruments, office equipment, music stands, classroom instruments, computers), textbooks and supplementary book material, pianos (they may be a part of the equipment), and maintenance (piano tuning, repairs, etc.). Instructional salaries are usually considered as part of the personnel department's budget. However, they are considered a cost item when determining per pupil expenditures in the schools or credit hours generated at the university level.

When preparing budgets for projects or other educational activities that require the submission of a budget, all of the above should be considered. Remember to include ancillary services, such as secretarial help and staff assistants.

Budget Categories in Universities

There are many items that overlap with those listed for schools. However, since a considerable number are in different categories, the two budgets are treated as separate entities.

A sample university budget in a school of music or department would, like the Indiana University School of Music, include the following:

Academic salaries (in schools this is handled by a personnel department)

Academic assistant salaries (associate instructors)

Administrative staff (professional level)

Clerical and service-maintenance staff

Wages (hourly students and nonstudents)

General supplies and expenses:
    Computing services
    Motor vehicle charge
    Publications
    Class and lab supplies
    Telephone
    Telephone, long-distance
    Transportation
    Office supplies
    Copy-machine costs
    Printing and duplicating
    Postage
    Honoraria
    Computer, lease and rental
    Computer software
    Equipment rental
    Mailing-list rental
    Space rental
    Repairs and maintenance
    Service maintenance contracts
    Advertising
    General supplies and expenses
    Freight and hauling
    Membership dues
    Expendable equipment

Fringe benefits:
    Recruitment
    Library
    Retirement program
    Travel
    Graduate fee remissions and scholarships
    Student employment

BUDGETS FOR NEW BUILDINGS

In a school system or university, two types of budgets are the concern of a music administrator. The first, which we have been discussing, is the annual budget. The second is ad hoc in nature and deals with specific buildings or programs. It is generally referred to as "capital outlay."

Each time a new school, a new building, or a remodeling of an existing school or department of music is planned, the music administrator should be certain that sufficient funds are allocated to provide the students in that building with the minimum amount of equipment and supplies necessary for an educationally desirable environment. This budget should be a part of standard policies. It should be revised periodically to conform to current educational practices and changing costs.

PLANNING NEW BUILDINGS

When determining needs for a new building, one must first consider the nature and philosophy of the program being planned for that community or university. Some responsible official must then ascertain the anticipated enrollment that will be served in the various music classes and activities in that building. Based on these anticipated needs, decisions are made for housing in the building. It is too limiting to rely entirely on past building plans designed for outmoded or past practices and philosophies. (For ideas about new buildings and renovations to existing space, see *Planning and Equipping Educational Music Facilities*, by Harold Geerdes.)[1]

A good example of a single-purpose building is the practice building at Indiana University. It was determined that the School of Music accommodations did not provide sufficient practice rooms for current and anticipated enrollments. Once the research and study were completed and accepted, funds were allocated to construct a separate building entirely devoted to providing the necessary practice facilities. Funding came from a combination of state money, private donations, and the university's budget allocation for new buildings. All of the previously mentioned concerns were taken into consideration, the entire building was constructed of single-module practice rooms of various sizes, to accommodate a variety of situations (piano, smaller instruments, small ensembles, etc.)

Teaching is affected by the physical environment. It can greatly influence the degree of success or failure achieved in a new unit. When music is only one area of instruction in a school building, music administrators need to be alert and even aggressive in seeing to it that the music department is given an opportunity to voice its concern for housing, storing, and maintaining the facilities provided in its unit and securing appropriate equipment.

PLANNING A NEW UNIT

When planning a new unit, the director or dean should be certain to involve and consult with those who will occupy the new building—not only the music staff but the administration and the various building committees. At these meetings the basic philosophy governing music education in a school community should be clearly stated and reviewed. This also applies to a university, the only difference being that in the latter the faculty is the community. Decisions affecting the following items need to be made with due regard for the philosophical position:

1. musical activities
2. classroom floor space
3. practice rooms
4. musical equipment
5. instrument storage space
6. chalk and tack boards
7. audiovisual aids
8. storage compartments
9. cabinet storage
10. room acoustics
11. strategic placing of electrical outlets
12. music library
13. sinks
14. office space
15. security

The director or the designated supervisor in the schools should make preliminary sketches of the unit and check the sketches in relation to the remainder of the building. This individual should keep a detailed checklist of miscellaneous items such as chalk and tack boards, audiovisual aids and installations, bookcases, computer installations, and closets. He should examine the latest classroom equipment to determine the type of chairs, instrument storage racks, and movable furniture that will be needed. All of these items should be selected on the basis of the prevailing educational philosophy, aims, and objectives as they relate to that specific program or school. For example, if there is to be a great deal of emphasis on related arts programs, then rooms must be designed to meet the needs of such classes.

It is advisable and desirable to meet with the school architect and the building architect, if they are different individuals, to discuss the materials being utilized and acoustical planning; do not minimize the importance of soundproofing. It can limit the effectiveness of any musical unit in relation to other classes as well as within its own confines. Check the location of the music unit in relation to other instructional areas. It should be segregated as much as possible from other sources of sound. The music suite should have easy access to the auditorium stage. There should also be easy access to a ramp area for loading and unloading equipment. Although the music administrator must accept the architect's concept in terms of the total building plan, he should be responsible for applying and checking its relationship to the music unit's use. In the case of remodeled space for music or new construction, the advice and counsel of an acoustical consultant is essential. One should not assume that architects and construction firms know about musical sound.

At the university level, a faculty member or member of the administrative staff may be given the responsibility for supervising or working with the architect and construction firm to see that the school of music is receiving what has been agreed upon. This individual will follow the same procedures outlined for a school building, except that they have a single focus (a building only for music instruction and performance rather than a broad educational facility encompassing many disciplines).

Finally, all music administrators should take pride in the new construction. They should watch the building grow and follow reports on its construction. The director or dean should get to know the superintendent in charge of construction for this building. If one discovers accidental omissions or other problems, one should report them immediately to the proper authority. Do *not* wait until the building is completed! Not all school systems may permit their director or supervisor to take such an active role in new building construction (this is not a concern of the university), but all directors of music should seek these responsibilities if they want an active role in decision making for the future of their program.

■

PURCHASING EQUIPMENT

Procedures for purchasing equipment vary with boards of education, but certain practices are consistent. Boards, states, and universities usually set a maximum figure for the purchase of equipment without the submission of formal bids. Purchases made below this figure present little problem. However, if it is necessary for bids to be submitted, the variance in quality of construction and manufacture may be so great that it will be virtually impossible to assure a school system or music school of appropriate equipment, unless a specific, uniform program is established.

Like every other decision, the selection and purchase of equipment should be based on an established educational philosophy. Is the emphasis to be on building a program for the future or on reinforcing an established one? Will the budget seek to provide quality or quantity? This, incidentally, presents another problem. A policy of accepting only the lowest bid for the purchase of equipment leads to a point of diminishing returns. In some cases, the repair costs of a "cheaper" piece of equipment over a period of years would have enabled the music department to have purchased several pieces of far superior equipment during the same period. In addition, an instrument that does not produce a desirable sound even under the best of conditions is a liability throughout the life of that instrument. Over a period of years, purchasing large numbers of inadequate instruments to fill only numerical requirements for classes may provide inadequate tonal satisfaction. These instruments usually end up being a constant source of irritation for years to come. To assure quality control, one could argue for the *lowest* bid, providing it represents the *best* bid.

To assure music departments of proper music equipment, stringent specifications should be developed by those who ultimately use or supervise the use of this equipment. This procedure involves them in decision making and helps obviate future resentment regarding the material received. The instrument specifications, for example, fall into three categories: first-line instruments, second-line instruments, and third-line instruments. When selecting a standard for purchase, be certain that all dealers are bidding on the appropriate category. This helps obviate some of the current practice of bidding a third-line instrument against one in the first line and thus securing the bid because of lower cost. The same principle applies when purchasing equipment in the schools for the general music class or the choral department. Administrators must be alert and vigilant to see that all specifications are adhered to when making their decision regarding choice. It is the students who ultimately suffer when inferior equipment is substituted, and the board or university is actually being defrauded. The teachers who will use the equipment or a selected administrator should also inspect the equipment before final approval for purchase is given.

Many boards have permitted their music departments to include "acceptable tone" as a specification. This is especially true in higher education. This is usually handled by a committee or team of experts from the total staff under the aegis of the supervisory staff or department chair. They will hear questionable instruments and accept or reject them by a group decision, so that it is not a matter of personal opinion (see Appendix H, page 317).

Not all business departments are sensitive to these complexities. It is the responsibility of the music administration to work with business agents and try to educate them when necessary. This requires patience and understanding on the part of the music administration, who should also try to understand the complexities of the jobs of these representatives from the business office. They are also there to facilitate instruction, and anything that can be done to make their job easier will be appreciated. As indicated earlier, the teacher is the key to quality instruction, but even good teachers can be better if provided with appropriate and quality equipment.

MAINTENANCE

There is no more severe drain on a music budget than the item listed as "maintenance." On university campuses and in public areas such as schools where theft and vandalism are responsible for major outlays, it is advisable to have all equipment visibly marked, identifying it as the "property of" the school in such a way that to remove the mark would deface the instrument sufficiently to destroy its market value. This identification may add slightly to the cost of the instrument, particularly if it is done at the factory, but the savings in discouraging theft more than offsets this expense.

Pianos should be inspected and tuned on a regularly scheduled basis. It is impossible to develop good musical ears if they are constantly adjusting to poorly tuned instruments. In addition, it is better for the instruments and helps prolong their life. Piano tuners, like potential teachers, should be auditioned and interviewed to determine their competency. This can be done by giving them one or two pianos to tune. Depending on the size of the community, they may then be placed under contract or assignment to see that the regularly scheduled tuning is assured. At a university this individual may be given a staff or faculty position.

Some urban communities maintain their own repair shops, the repair person being a staff member. He usually makes regular visits to the buildings for routine maintenance, with some special provision being made for emergency repairs. Other communities may specify certain shops that have the necessary qualifications to handle appropriate repairs. Teachers or students may take or send the instruments directly to them. This procedure will vary according to the size of the department or school of music at a university. Some have their own repair person, who might even be a faculty member teaching repair techniques.

Regardless of who does the repairing and maintenance, some procedure should be established to see that it does not interfere with instruction. A student sitting in a classroom, biding his time until his instrument returns from the shop, represents wasted money in lost learning time. It is poor economy, regardless of the pennies saved by so-called good business procedures. Every effort must be made to find ways to minimize red tape that prolongs repairs and maintenance. In addition, it is advisable to maintain some record of the repair costs. When an official record is kept, it is much easier to approach a business department, superintendent, or dean for an instrument replacement. The statistics concerning repairs are concrete evidence and not opinion of cost factors, and the point of diminishing returns in so-called austerity or economy programs can be substantiated.

Some school systems will assign a budgeted amount for repairs to each building, which the teachers may spend at their own discretion. A department or school of music at a university usually has repair as a single item for the department. Another method is to have a maximum figure for repair that does not require official approval. Unfortunately, there have been too many abuses of this practice, and although it expedites matters, it has proven excessively costly. One way of dealing with this approach is to have each approved repair person submit to the department a cost list that automatically would cover almost every expediency. It is also information that teachers should have when advising students regarding repair shops.

It has proven to be worthwhile to establish specifications even for repairs, especially when large quantities of work are being bid on, as is done in the summer. These are difficult to meet, but they provide a basis for demanding quality service.

Certain pieces of equipment, such as bows, mouthpieces, strings, and pads should be kept on hand as supply items to avoid lost instruction time. (Incidentally, fiberglass bows have proven to be excellent substitutes for wood bows, which break easily, and as a result, good fiberglass bows are more economical over an extended period of time.) Strings, tail gut, valve buttons, and other small items that affect maintenance should be readily available so that instruments will not be incapacitated for extended periods by the breakage of such easily repaired items.

■

INSURANCE

It is increasingly difficult to acquire insurance at a reasonable rate. In most cases, the cost is so prohibitive that schools prefer to take their chances. If students are assigned an instrument for school and home use, it is advisable that they be urged to include the instrument on their home insurance. Universities often carry insurance on university-owned instruments, but when they are lent to students, coverage becomes the student's responsibility.

Music administrators should confer with their board business agent and determine the advisability of carrying some kind of insurance. This is often overlooked, even when it is easily accessible through a university or board of education total contract with an insurance company.

■
PROFESSIONAL ETHICS

Under no circumstances can a music administrator permit personal interests to interfere with his judgment when establishing guidelines, specifications, or standards. He must have administrative courage to take a stand in the best interest of education for his community on matters affecting purchases. One cannot be all things to all dealers. Music administrators should use their knowledge to advise appropriately and not base recommendations on expediency or fear of rejection by business interests.

The National Education Association, in the *NEA Handbook*, specifically establishes the guidelines governing ethical practices in regard to outside employment and compensation affecting school purchases. Every school music administrator needs to be fully aware of these guidelines and be certain that they are followed. They were developed to protect the students and the community, and everyone connected with the school system is obligated to adhere to, and enforce adherence to, them.

In addition, the music administrator must not indulge in practices that are in direct violation of copyright laws. Neither can he knowingly approve of members of his staff committing such acts. There are provisions that permit some duplication when it is done strictly for educational purposes. Because of legal implications, it is recommended that individuals needing to duplicate materials check current provisions of the law. Whenever possible, it is even safer to check with the publisher for permission.[2] Incidentally, on October 31, 1988, President Ronald Reagan signed legislation that required the United States to adhere to the Berne Convention, an international treaty. This treaty is the oldest, most comprehensive, and most protective international copyright treaty in the world. This means that the United States now has copyright agreements with twenty-four countries with which it previously had had no separate copyright treaties. This should be reviewed periodically with the staff to remind them of their responsibility in this matter.

The music administrator must follow the finance and business practices established by the board of education and diligently enforce them, no matter how frustrating the regulations may be. These practices have been established to protect all parties, and failure to follow them leaves one open to suspicion. No one conducting school matters can permit this to happen if he is to continue to be effective as an administrator or teacher.

NOTES

1. Harold Geerdes, *Planning and Equipping Educational Music Facilities* (Reston, Va.: Music Educators National Conference, 1987).
2. Charles Gary, "Working Within the Copyright Law," in *Voices of Industry* (Reston, Va.: Music Educators National Conference, 1990), pp. 65–72 (available either in book form or as an audiocassette.)

SUPPLEMENTARY READINGS

Aebischer, Delmar W. "How to Win Friends and Influence People." *Music Educators Journal* 57, no. 6 (February 1971), p. 45.

Althouse, Jay. *Copyright: The Complete Guide for Music Educators.* East Stroudsburg, Pa.: Music in Action, 1984. (Distributed by MENC.)

Berk, Lee Elliot. "Life Styles, Credits, and Moral Rights." *Music Educators Journal* 57, no. 7 (March 1971), p. 69.

———. "Music Education and Copyright Law: Infringements in Copying." *Music Educators Journal* 57, no. 8 (April 1971), p. 55.

Carter, E. Eugene. *College Financial Management.* Lexington, Mass.: Lexington Books, 1980.

Goldstein, William. *Selling School Budgets in Hard Times*, Fastback #215. Bloomington, Ind.: Phi Delta Kappa Education Foundation, 1984.

"Government Aid to the Arts: How and How Much," *Music Educators Journal* vol. 56, no. 7 (March 1970), p. 107.

Hartley, Harry. "1980s Education Scenario: From Tax Revolt to Governance Reform." *Music Educators Journal* (January 1981), p. 35.

National Education Association. *NEA Handbook* (1958–1959). Washington, D.C.: NEA 1959, pp. 62–63.

Roe, Jessica. "U.S. Adopts Berne Convention, Extends Copyright Protection." *International Musician*, December 1988, p. 1.

Seawright, James. "What Goes into an Electronic Music Studio." *Music Educators Journal* (November 1968), p. 70.

Prince, H. J. "Representing Faculty at the State Capitol." *Footnotes* (AAUP), Spring 1984, p. 1.

United States Copyright Law: A Guide for Music Educators. Reston, Va.: Music Educators National Conference, 1978.

Weeks, Richard. "Just a Little off the Top Please." *Music Educators Journal* (December 1982), p. 37.

STUDY QUESTIONS

1. How should budgets be designed?
2. What are the sources for funds at the public school level? What are the sources for funds for universities? Discuss the implications of each one.
3. Discuss the implications of purchasing from the lowest bidder. How does one proceed to protect the community so that it will acquire the most desirable products under the existing conditions?
4. Review the copyright law. What is one permitted to do in duplicating educational material, and when is one in violation of the law?

9

Fund-Raising and Grantsmanship

Fund-raising is the act of raising money or its equivalent for specific purposes. The "equivalent" may be scholarships, lectureships, equipment, uniforms, robes, an endowment, or the like. One former college president defined *fund-raising* as a "series of disappointments punctuated by occasional successes, most of which are unexpected." Fund-raising is much more art than science. It is full of inconsistencies. It should be understood that fund-raising is not just seeking and asking; it is also selling. The program, the cause, the event, or the institution must be "sold" to a potential contributor or investor so that he can see the value to him of associating with whatever it is you are selling.

Thus, on the one hand, we have the philanthropy of an individual, foundation, or corporation with resources to share and, on the other hand, a department, school, band, orchestra, choral group, or even larger institution with a need that can be addressed by the funds or other resources possessed by the philanthropist. In the best of all worlds, a partnership will be created between the two whereby everyone wins. The philanthropist or philanthropic agency has a need met, as does the receiver. They each gain. The challenge in fund-raising is to identify and describe a need in compelling terms and then find the individual or agency interested in, or willing to, meet that need.

Fund-raising has always been a part of the life of higher-education institutions, especially those in the private sector. During the last fifteen years public higher education has become increasingly involved in fund-raising, because state legislatures have been either unwilling or unable to appropriate sufficient funds for the operation of junior colleges, colleges, and universities for which they had responsibility. Job descriptions for positions of chair, director, or dean

169

in departments or schools of music now routinely contain the phrase "must be skilled in fund-raising" or "should have a record of success in fund-raising" or "should be willing to seek help outside the university for resources."

Even at the public school level, there are increasing signs that fund-raising is to be a part of the overall educational picture—not just the raising of funds to support trips, uniforms, and robes but also the broader educational enterprise. Development officials, whose responsibility will be to raise money to support educational projects, are being sought in several Florida school districts. Whether this kind of direction is taken by other states remains to be seen.

Those who conduct ensembles at the secondary level know that fund-raising is a fact of life. Rare is the band that can function in a quality manner and with a full program without an infusion of funds other than those provided by the board of education. Music is expensive. We know that. Instrumental music is equipment-intensive and needs more support than the board of education can give, even if it had the desire to do so.

Elaine Guregian, in publishing the annual report of school music budgets in the *Instrumentalist* for 1989, said that "educators at all levels consistently have contributed to half of their budgets through fund-raising with the rest coming from tax dollars . . . for the 1988–89 school year, that percentage of teacher effort has remained much the same, at 49%."[1] High school band directors now raise 59 percent of their budgets. Of the respondents to Guregian's questionnaire, 79 percent of those who teach high school reported "having booster organizations, and a resounding 92% conduct fund-raising campaigns." At this point, only 43 percent of the elementary, junior high, and middle school directors responding to the survey said they had a booster organization and 55 percent of them conducted fund-raising campaigns."[2]

It therefore seems clear that a person who has, or is seeking, a position of leadership in a college, university, or public school system in the field of music must have both knowledge and skills in the field of fund-raising, not only because he will probably have to do it but also because of needing to be a resource and adviser to colleagues.

HISTORY

Philanthropy is an old concept. The word comes from the Greek for the love of mankind, charitable giving for a worthy cause, or a desire to help mankind through acts of charity or deeds of practical beneficence. In the twentieth century B.C., the Babylonians were admonished in the Code of Hammurabi to take care that "justice be done to widows, orphans and the poor."[3] The tithing principle is hinted at in 1500 B.C. by the demand by Phoenician gods that the first fruit of all products be given to the service of religion. In 1300 B.C., Moses decreed that a tenth part of the harvest be set aside for religion and support of the poor. In 1170 A.D., Moses Maimonides sent letters asking community leaders in North Africa to raise funds to redeem captives—probably the first direct mail campaign.

Philanthropy has shifted from being overwhelmingly the support of religious institutions to greater support of the secular; in the United States at present, health and human services, the arts and humanities, and education are the recipients of 35 percent of all giving. When the category of "other" is factored in, the total percentage given to nonreligious causes is 54 percent.[4]

American philanthropy was likely born two decades after the Pilgrims landed when the Massachusetts Bay Colony sent three clergymen back to England to raise money for nascent Harvard College. They returned with £500. Until the end of the eighteenth century, colonial fund-raising was concentrated on higher education and religion. Gradually health, civic, social, and artistic causes entered the picture.[5]

Andrew Carnegie, who had already amassed a fortune of $30 million in steel making, published an essay in *Wealth* (1889) in which he said, "Millionaires should, instead of leaving their fortunes to their families, administer their wealth as a public trust during life." In that same year, John D. Rockefeller gave $600,000 to help found the University of Chicago, the first of millions the oil baron was to give that university.[6]

Soon after, social agencies such as the YMCA, the YWCA, and the Red Cross began raising money. Harvard began raising money from alumni. In addition, there were highly successful efforts by the National Catholic War Council, the Salvation Army, and the Jewish Welfare Board.

In 1920–1921 fifty representative higher-education institutions reported receiving gifts of $28,145,000. Thirty years later the same group received $112,790,000; allowing for the currency differential, this amount was $28.8 million greater in purchasing power than the amount received in 1920–1921. In 1960–1961 the amount ($345,953,000) represented an increase of 22 percent over the 1959–1960 total and twelve times greater than the amount received forty years earlier.[7] Clearly, fund-raising in higher education was big business. "American givers," said Scott M. Cutlip in 1965, "have come from the tin cup to the telethon in little more than half a century."[8]

■

POINTS TO CONSIDER

The sixteen points to consider represent advice from experienced and successful fund-raisers. They are not presented as absolutes. There will be those who will say, "I have done just the opposite and been successful." And that may indeed be true, for we remarked earlier that fund-raising is full of contradictions. Nearly every fund-raising effort is different from the ones before. There is a lot of common sense and a lot of instinct that comes into play as a person with a need or a cause approaches a person, foundation, or corporation for assistance. So, keeping in mind that disclaimer, consider the points below.

1. *Planning:* Any and every fund-raising venture must be carefully and thoughtfully planned before it can succeed. That applies to establishment of an annual fund, a phoneathon, a proposal to an arts commission, a request from your alumni, or a campaign to buy new choir robes. The more thorough the planning, the better. Goals and objectives need to be clear. People who are involved in the project should be a part of the planning and goal setting. Many fund-raising ventures have been unsuccessful because they got to a certain point where it became apparent that no one had thought about what to do next or had the answers to critical questions. Effective planning is essential.

2. *Suspect to prospect:* Suppose you have an idea for your music department that requires a gift of $5,000 to bring it to reality. You think of two people who might be interested in making such a gift. At this point, they are merely "suspects." In order to move them from "suspect" to "prospect," you use what the Fund-Raising School calls LAI (for "linkage, ability, and interest"). You try to find ways to link them to you and your cause. This may mean corresponding with them, sending them flyers, news releases, or human interest material. A determination must be made also about their ability to give $5,000. Do they have that kind of discretionary income—or perhaps some other source from which that money could come? And finally, an interest must be established. This gets the individual to the "I'd like to be a part of this project" stage. "The thing that got me there," the donor says, "was your providing me with material, your inviting me to that event, your introducing me to the people who would profit from this gift. I can see how vital it is. I want to help."

3. *People business:* Fund-raising is a people business from beginning to end. It is a contact sport, if you will. It is about people and relationships. A favorite aphorism in the field of fund-raising is "People give to people." A more accurate statement would probably be "People give to people with causes"—of "with ideas." It is one thing to establish a relationship with an individual with means and quite another to establish a relationship with someone in a foundation, a corporation, or a government agency. And yet the successful fund-raisers do just that. Through letters, phone calls, proposal writing style, documentation, and face-to-face meetings, the fund-raiser develops a relationship with a decision maker. And from those efforts come exciting results.

4. Team effort: While there are cases in which a donor has given to an institution or a cause because of the efforts of one person and one person only, fund-raising is more often a team effort. Members of the team can be the president, the development officer, the dean, the chair, the supervisor, the band or orchestra director, the parent, and even a student. More may be included—board member, alumnus, friend, classmate, colleague, peer. It is the music administrator's responsibility to put together the appropriate team for this purpose. If it is a campaign, the team will be large, varied, and complex. If it is the pursuit of a particular gift from a particular individual, the team may be two or three persons. But nearly all successful fund-raising ventures are successful because of good teamwork—never mind the critical nature of good leadership.

5. Real interests: It is often the case that we do not know of a donor's real interests. Mr. Smith was a horticulturist with a degree in the subject and an extremely successful business. When approached by his college for a gift, he told them, much to their surprise, that his real interest lay in the field of literature. He was "turned on" to the wonders of literature by a magnificent English professor, and what he really wanted to do was to establish a scholarship for students who were planning to become teachers of English. Mr. Brown was a star basketball player in college and went on to law school and became a highly successful and prosperous attorney. The university had him pegged for a major gift to either the athletic program or the law school. He said, "No, my family has always been interested in music; my three children all played string instruments in their various school orchestras, and nothing gave my wife and me more satisfaction. I want to do something for the music department."

So, how do you find out what interests people have? You ask them. They will tell you and tell you quickly. Knowing the real interests people have and the various needs or projects of the institution give the effective fund-raiser the opportunity to put together positive packages that will yield exciting results.

6. *Stewardship:* One of the easiest things to forget after the gift has been given is the stewardship of the giver. It is common to say thank you, but not so common to continue a program of cultivation of the giver. Donors appreciate being thanked, but appreciate even more being remembered. Such persons need to be invited to events, need to be informed as to the good their gift is doing, need to be introduced to "their" scholarship recipient. Who are the best prospects to become donors to an institution? Those who have given before, who are in the habit, who are already "sold." Thus, the action of stewardship is even more critical as one considers future need and future opportunities for collaboration.

7. *Money to raise money:* It takes money to raise money. Some institutions, groups, or individuals do not realize this. They set up an office to raise funds, but do not provide proper and sufficient clerical help, travel budget, research support, or postage and telephone costs. Or a campaign is set up without proper means of covering campaign costs—brochures, travel, long-distance service, consultants, and receptions. Part way through the campaign comes the realization that there has to be a way to cover expenses, so the goal is increased or some donors are approached to contribute to the cost of the campaign (not a popular cause, by the way). Members of a high school orchestra get involved in selling cheese products, but do not realize that they need money for printing brochures and buying advertising in the local paper. The university plans a phoneathon, but forgets to budget for the student callers—a modest hourly wage and a pizza party after each evening's effort. At every level of fund-raising, there are costs involved, both in time and in money. Expense money is not only the result of proper planning but also a commitment of support—a vote of confidence in the effort.

8. *Success:* People buy into *success*, they buy into *opportunity*, they buy into *quality*. Your conversation and your writing should be rooted in these assumptions. Everyone wants to back a winner. Those with funds to dispense are successful people. They have made money, have worked hard, have earned a position of responsibility. No one wants to give to a loser, to a person of low standards, or to an organization known for its shoddy productions. So tout the best that you have and work to make every part of your organization top-quality. Although not every school of music in the country can attract the best students and it takes generations to build a quality reputation, everyone has some part of their enterprise that is good, that is worthy, that perhaps is even exceptional. Quality sells! And people with means will *invest* in a program that is quality, that has endured, that has a future. You have but to tell the story—to the right audience.

9. *Remember, it's his money:* As one moves down the arduous path of converting a suspect into a prospect, of cultivating that prospect, and of getting to the point of asking that prospect for a gift, it is easy to forget that it is *his* money. It is also *his* time. Your project may not match his interests. If so, you had better shift gears quickly and get a new project or you will lose a prospect. Donors will give *their* money to causes that are of interest to them. If yours is not, then their gift will go elsewhere. Their timetables, too, may not be yours. Patience is a virtue, to be sure, but for fund-raisers it is essential. Some fund-raising and grant-seeking is very time-oriented, with a very specific time being set to bring the process to a conclusion. But much fund-raising, especially that aimed at individuals, is on a looser (i.e., slower and more protracted) timetable. Maintaining a positive relationship with a donor prospect is of critical importance. The lesson here is to work to create a match between a donor's interest and your project so that the gift can come your way.

10. *Borrow before you ask:* This strange-sounding concept has its roots in an Aristotelian saying: "The finest compliment one man can pay another is to ask him to do a favor." It is an extreme compliment to someone that you wish to borrow something from him—an art object, a boat, or a house—to utilize for a special purpose connected with the raising of resources. There is something about this that creates a bond between donor (or prospective donor) and recipient. It creates a "we're in this venture together" syndrome.

Now that the word *ask* has come up, it is time to point out that asking is the phase of the fund-raising process that most often goes awry. Many seekers of resources simply cannot bring themselves to ask for a gift eyeball-to-eyeball. And that is the number-one reason people do not give—they have not been asked! You do not have to apologize for asking. If your cause is deserving, no apology is necessary. If not, do not apologize—do not even ask. Some advise that you should not ask for money per se; rather, you should ask for a scholarship, a lectureship, an endowed chair, a room, a lab, a band uniform, or a grand piano. And in proceeding toward the "ask" (the word has now made a leap from verb to noun), you should remember that face-to-face solicitation will produce $50 to every $10 produced by telephone or to every $1 produced by direct mail. And it is good business to ask for gifts at the high range of a prospect's potential to give. People feel honored to be overasked.

11. *Keep people in the forefront:* Your project may indeed be to acquire a thing—a grand piano, for example. But you will have a great deal more success if you emphasize not the "thingness" of the object but what it will do for people. Faculty will perform recitals on it; so will students. It will be placed on a stage where guest artists will perform. The piano will be available to faculty and students, on a special basis, for practice. It will be in a hall where eighty performances occur each year, and it will be heard by as many as eight thousand people. On occasion, there will be critics in the audience. This piano will be the finest instrument in the department and will give students, in particular, an opportunity they have never had before. It is helpful to tug on the heartstrings a bit to strengthen the "people factor" in any project. It may be much better and more productive to phrase the ask as a request for a scholarship, a lectureship, a uniform, a choir robe, a tux, or a trip for a student rather than as a request for money. The basic concern in fund-raising is not money but people. What is important is what the gift can do for people.

12. *Publicity does not raise money:* It is not enough to develop four-color promotion pieces and expect their distribution to attract contributions. As one fund-raiser put it, "people don't give to billboards." This is not to say that publicity is not important or helpful. It is both. But at some point there has to be that ask—that time when one person asks another for a gift. As Brakeley puts it, "you can't fish when the fly is in the boat and you can't raise money without asking for it. Like milking a cow, you've got to sit right down and do it."[9]

13. *Start with natural prospects:* You will have much greater success in fund-raising if you begin canvassing those who have an interest in your enterprise. They may be alumni, parents, symphony subscribers, arts patrons, or others who have been touched by what it is that your institution does. They should be sought out, and their interests researched. Once their interests are known, it is up to you to develop ideas or projects that will engage them.

14. *The time will never be right:* If you wait for the right time for a campaign to ask for a gift, that time may never come. Many experts advise that the best time to ask for a gift is when the need is documented and the case determined. Using the excuse of timing, one can endlessly rationalize *not* asking. To do so is to risk psyching oneself out of ever asking. Irving R. Warner observes, "There is no such thing as a right or wrong time of year or month to have a campaign. When you have made your plans properly, it's the right time."[10]

15. *Buy a Buick:* Harold J. Seymour, one of the fathers of fund-raising in this country, observed several years ago that "nobody ever buys a Buick just because General Motors needs the money."[11] This oft-repeated statement suggests that people will not invest their resources—either money or objects—in an organization or institution that is in trouble, is on the ropes, or is perceived as being of poor quality. They will invest because they see a gain for themselves. That gain may be associated with a winner or a feeling that dividends of one kind or another will come to them. In short, they will invest because they believe in you and your cause, because they trust you, because they believe that you will be a good steward of their gift.

THE CASE STATEMENT

The case statement is the documentation that supports your case. It should convey excitement, proximity, immediacy, and the answers to key questions. It explains the plan, states the arguments for support, and shows how gifts can be made. In short, it tells all that needs to be told in good taste, logical order, and clear prose. It should be convincing, even compelling.

The case for your organization, institution, or project answers some or all of the following questions:

- What is the mission?
- What is your organization all about?
- How is the project relevant, important, or urgent?
- What is the problem?
- Are you equipped with the appropriate support to resolve the problem?
- What are the goals and objectives?
- What planning have you done?
- Has the need been clearly established?
- Have evaluation methods been established? If so, what are they?
- Will you accomplish what you set out to do in a reasonable time?
- Is your projected budget congruent with the tasks?
- What is your history of service or activity?
- Who will benefit from this project?
- Why should someone support your cause?
- What are the benefits to contributors?

━━━━━━━━━━━━━━━━━━━━━━━■━━━━━━━━━━━━━━━━━━━━━

WHY PEOPLE GIVE

People give to causes, institutions, and organizations for a variety of reasons: religion, taxes, guilt, fear, love, peer pressure, perceived need, respect, loyalty, recognition, tradition, altruism, nostalgia, friendship, gratitude, sympathy. They also give because they believe in the cause, they desire immortality, they seek power, they wish to impress others, they have low sales resistance, they serve on the board, or it makes them feel good.

But what is the number-one reason that people give? Study after study shows that it is *because they are asked.* Many people are ready to give and even want to give, but they will not take the direct action unless, and until, someone asks them. The lesson for fund-raisers is clear: *someone must ask someone for money.* Seymour states it succinctly when he says that "the essence of fund-raising is that somebody, with some good reason, has to see somebody about giving money for the advancement of some good cause."[12]

━━━━━━━━━━━━━━━━━━━━━━━■━━━━━━━━━━━━━━━━━━━━━

WHY PEOPLE DO NOT GIVE

To some extent the reasons people do not give are the converse of why they do, but let us enumerate them anyway:

- There is no linkage, no connection with the cause.
- They do not feel they have the money.
- They are not interested.
- They are opposed to the cause.
- The wrong person asks them, or they are solicited in the wrong way.
- There is no tradition of giving.
- No compelling case has been made; they are not convinced of the need.
- There has been no appreciation, no follow-up to a previous gift.
- They feel they cannot make a difference.
- They do not wish to be involved.

Again, the number-one reason people do not give is *because they were not asked.*

SELECTING THE PROPER VEHICLE

For the high school director who is looking for a way to raise $5,000 for equipment or $15,000 for robes or $25,000 for a trip or $80,000 for new band uniforms, there are numerous fund-raising modes from which to choose. Several companies do nothing but set up programs for raising a needed amount of dollars. Some deal in only one product or idea; others deal in several. If that is the direction you wish to go, how do you choose?

It is suggested that you think of two principles: quality and service. Some questions to ask: Is this a product I would be pleased to have in my own home? Could I sell this product to a friend or relative in good conscience? Is it the best product of its kind? What is the rate of return (profit margin)? How much time, effort, and manpower will it require to run the program? For what period of time does the campaign need to run? Can the effort be duplicated again next year? Is the product so good that you will develop a loyal clientele? What is the reputation of the company? Of the salesperson? How much assistance and service will the company and its representative provide?

There are countless other ways to raise money: special events (entire books have been written on the subject); raffles; proposals to arts agencies, foundations, government agencies, and corporations; communitywide appeals; one-on-one solicitation for specific projects; annual funds; telethons; phoneathons; and capital campaigns and alumni contacts, to name several.

The challenge for the music administrator is to establish and document the need and then ask, How can we meet that need? In some situations, many forms of fund-raising will be impractical, impossible, or intolerable. In reality, you may have only a few avenues open to you. You will have to find what will achieve the best results, not just for today but for the future as well.

PLANNED GIFTS

No chapter on fund-raising would be complete without reference to long-range giving—commitments that people make to institutions for a gift sometime in the future. It may be helpful to consider three instances in which people wished to make such commitments.

Professor Storey, a longtime faculty member at a midwestern

college, had purchased some stock many years ago. It had split five times and had become worth $50,000. Professor Storey decided to make a gift of this stock to the music department of his college. What were the results?

First, Storey's annual income from the stock rose from $1,000 per year (2 percent in dividends) to $3,400 (7 percent of the value of the stock, which the college was willing and able to pay because of selling the stock and reinvesting the proceeds). He and his wife will continue to receive this amount for their lifetimes.

Second, Storey had no capital gains tax of $11,200 to pay ($40,000 gain multiplied by 28 percent, his tax bracket).

Third, he received credit for a charitable income tax deduction for this year of $25,000 (the amount is limited to 50 percent of his adjusted gross income). The remainder can be taken over a five-year period.

Last, the college music department will receive the $50,000 upon the deaths of Storey and his wife.

On the occasion of her retirement Miss Ayles, age sixty-three, took out a $25,000 life insurance policy, on which she pays a premium of $225 per year. The premium is tax-deductible because the university is named the owner as well as the beneficiary of the policy. Miss Ayles received a $25,000 credit for a charitable gift the year she named the university as owner of the policy. Furthermore, she receives an ongoing tax deduction for premiums paid and the university will receive the face amount of the policy ($25,000) upon her death. The policy is not a part of her estate.

Sarah Gilbert, with homes in both Palm Beach and Greenwich, has decided to move permanently to Florida. Her Connecticut home, purchased in 1960 for $50,000, is now worth $600,000. She is willing to give half the proceeds from the sale of the house ($300,000) to Crumb College, provided she can receive interest on the amount during her lifetime. The college pays her $18,000 per year (6 percent of $300,000) and she is able to claim a charitable income tax deduction of $168,225 in the year the gift is made—an actual tax savings of $77,000 ($300,000 minus $25,000 [half the original purchase price] multiplied by 28 percent [Sarah's tax bracket]). She can use her onetime exemption of $125,000 from the sale of a residence. In addition, she receives $300,000, the other half of the proceeds from the sale.

There are many variations on these themes. One can make deferred gifts of cash, stock, bonds, real estate, tangible personal property, and life insurance. Income can come to the giver at once or at some future time. And tax savings can be considerable.

Irrevocable gifts include three types of charitable remainder unitrusts, charitable remainder annuity trusts, pooled income funds, charitable gift annuities, deferred charitable gift annuities, and retained life estate. No doubt other instruments will be developed in the future.

Finally, ultimate gifts can be made to charitable institutions through wills and bequests. Individuals can avoid estate taxes at the same time that they direct that a portion of their assets be given to the college or church of their choice.

The music administrator who desires the best for his unit will be actively seeking resources beyond the school building, the district, or the campus. With these extra resources, ideas can flourish, excellence can be fostered, and visibility to the community and beyond can be achieved. Nothing proclaims quality so loudly as an individual or a group saying, "I'll place my resources in your hands. I endorse what you are doing and what you stand for."

Most music executives have had little or no education or training in the area of fund-raising. The most successful are those who have ideas, dreams, and a vision of the future. They convince others that their enterprise is worth investing in. Success begets success. People want to be associated with a successful enterprise.

With imagination, ideas, common sense, a desire to rise above the crowd, and some chutzpah a music administrator can become an effective raiser of resources for the institution.

An increasingly important responsibility for today's music executive is the securing of grants as a way of raising funds to support programs in the music unit. While this responsibility may not loom large for the music supervisor in the public schools, it definitely does for chairs, directors, and deans in colleges and universities. Increasingly, the job announcements for such positions are stating the need for this kind of activity. Why does one seek grants? Who gives grants? How does one apply? What are the chances for success? Let us look at these questions.

WHY ONE SEEKS GRANTS

Whether one is in charge of a music unit in the public schools or in a college or university, one has a need for additional funds to support programs and ideas. Few music unit heads have *all* the resources they need to carry on a quality program. Therefore, one itemizes need; looks around for an agency, foundation, or company to meet that need; and proceeds to develop a proposal to meet that need.

The receipt of a grant may enable a program to move from average to excellent, may enable an idea to get off the drawing board and into the realm of reality, may provide for equipment or materials that would otherwise be only a dream.

When a school system or a college is a grant recipient, there is an immediate identification with a funding source such that each will benefit from the association. Indeed, a grant signals that there is a partnership between the unit with an articulated need and an agency with resources to assist in meeting that need.

The "quality of life" in a music unit is enhanced when a grant has been received. Students and faculty have the materials, the equipment, the physical plant, or the sheer money to do things that earlier were only dreams. A grant will help the music unit do a specified job better, more thoroughly, and with greater panache and sophistication.

The recognition that comes from receiving a grant cannot be underestimated. There is publicity attached to the receipt of a grant (some mandated by the grantor) and media attention to the grantee. It serves to raise the visibility of the recipient in the community such that other grants may be easier to come by.

If a good idea offering widespread benefits in its implementation simply cannot come to fruition without external assistance, then ways and means must be found to see that the idea is put into operation. A grant may well be the answer.

WHO GIVES GRANTS

The U.S. government, through its thousands of agencies, is the largest source of grant money in the country. The units that are most apt to grant funds for programs in the arts are the National Endowment for the Arts and the National Endowment for the Humanities.[13] One should also keep in mind the potential for direct grants from the Department of Education.

There are several thousand foundations in the United States. The *Foundation Directory* lists nearly three thousand foundations with assets of at least $1 million.[14] The information in this directory is arranged by state, interest area, and foundation. A description of each foundation will indicate the kinds of projects it is apt to fund. If key words such as *music, art,* and *education* are missing in the description, the grant seeker should quickly look in another direction.

Large corporations and even small companies give grants also and should not be overlooked as possible funding sources.

HOW ONE APPLIES FOR A GRANT

How one applies is *the* most critical question. First, one needs to know how the funding agency *wants* you to apply. Does it want only a letter at first? Does it want a summary of the idea? Does it want a full-blown proposal? Sometimes this information is readily available. Other times a phone call to staff members—those who actually manage the day-to-day operations—will provide the prospective grantee with the necessary information. Do not hesitate to call.

Assuming that a proposal is called for, one needs to craft a document that summarizes the idea and then places the details of putting the idea into operation into clear language. The Grantsmanship Center suggests a basic approach to proposal writing that includes summary, introduction, statement of need, objectives, methods, evaluation, future funding, and budget.[15] Variations of this outline are possible—even necessary—depending on the funding source and the idea to be funded:

1. *Proposal summary:* This element—commonly thought to be last, as most summaries are—should be written after all other portions of the proposal are committed to paper and should state in succinct form the most essential parts of the proposal. Certainly the "concept" of the proposal should be found here. But then the summary should be placed *first* in the document. Some readers will get only this far. If they are intrigued by the idea and captured by the concept that you have summarized so clearly and attractively, they will read on to find out about the specifics. Such a summary may be found in the cover letter to the funding source, but regardless of where it is found, you should assume that it is probably the first thing the potential grantor will read. Thus, the language should be concise, clear, and specific in describing the essence of your project, its cost, and who you, the prospective grantee, are.

2. *Introduction:* The introduction should be more than the offering of a teaser about the project for which you wish support. It should also tell the funding source about the organization you represent, how and why it got started, what is unique about it or at least what it is that is done particularly well, what the accomplishments are and who has recognized them, what the goals are, and what support the organization has received in the past. Norton Kiritz, the executive director of the Grantsmanship Center, recommends the use of a "credibility file"—a basis for writing paragraphs such as this in the future. Such a file would contain newspaper articles, letters of support, and any endorsement you have received for other efforts.

3. *Problem statement or assessment of need:* In this section there should be clear documentation that a need exists. While there should not be an excessive use of statistics, tables, diagrams, and charts (these are better saved for an appendix), there can be judicious use of numerical and tabular data to make your point. The need should be shown to be a reasonable one—and solvable if only the funding source and the applicant can form an alliance to get the job done. The funding source needs to see a logical connection between need and your organization's ability to meet that need. Furthermore, it should be clear in this part of the proposal that the problem outline is clear and that a solution is in hand, given the correct amount of time and money.

4. *Program objectives:* The pitfall here is that methods and objectives may become confused. An objective must be measurable so that the recipient and the funding source will know when, and if, the objective has been reached. Objectives should relate directly to the problem that has been described in the previous paragraph and should flow naturally from that discussion. If the problem has been clearly defined, then the objective should represent a relief—a solution—for that problem.

5. *Methods:* The questions that need to be answered in this section are several: How are you going to bring about the results that you have stated you want to see? Why have you chosen these particular approaches? What do you know about how others have gone about solving similar problems? Is there some way to predict that the methodology you have chosen will lead you to solve the problem you have identified, or are your approaches experimental? (There is nothing wrong with being experimental, but if that is to be your approach, it is better to admit it and then indicate why you believe it will be successful.) This section obviously calls for research into past practice. A grantor will want to know that you have done your homework, that you have considered other options but have chosen these particular ones because of their success rate in the past.

6. *Evaluation:* If the objectives stated are clear and precise, then the means for evaluating them to determine success or failure should be obvious. That is much more easily said than done. On the other hand, if you have to think long and hard about how to evaluate a particular objective, then it is perhaps the objective that is at fault: it may *not* be measurable. At that point, the objective should be rethought and restated. Evaluation may be subjective or objective. In subjective evaluation (secured through a Likert scale or similar instrument), you want to know how people "feel" about the program in question—those who are participants, if it is that kind of a program, as well as those who are observers. In objective evaluation you probably come out with numbers—a 10 percent gain, ten new pianos, a significant increase in test scores, or whatever. In certain cases, you may wish an outside organization to be the evaluating agency. But be sure that a granting agency will want to know just how it is that you intend to evaluate this program once it is funded and launched. Just how will you know of its success rate? A poorly conceived section on evaluation could easily torpedo a proposal.

7. *Future funding:* For onetime grant requests, this category is inappropriate. If you are requesting funds, for example, to outfit an electronic music studio, the project is complete when the funds become available and the equipment is purchased and installed. But for programs that are ongoing, the funding agency wants to know just how you expect to continue to support the project in the future. What funds are needed to keep the project going, and where will you get them? Other possible funding sources should be identified, and if it is possible to generate funds from program activity (e.g., admissions, fees), this will be a welcome bit of information for the funding source. In general, sources with funds do not want you to return again and again for similar requests or for the same request. Notable exceptions are state arts councils that regularly support symphony orchestras and other such groups with what is called in some states "general operating support" and that even allow those groups to submit requests on a biennial basis. Even organizations that request assistance for specific arts projects can return to the council on an annual basis where such a project has developed a history of excellence. If the continuation of the program or project requires funding for additional years, then the issue must be addressed in the proposal.

8. *Budget:* Every program or project has a financial element. The description and justification of the budget is a critical part of the proposal because it applies dollars, and thus value, to the goods and services that *are* the proposal. Norton J. Kiritz suggests dividing the budget into two parts: personnel costs and nonpersonnel costs. Personnel costs would include wages, salaries, fringe benefits, social security, and such services as bookkeeping and secretarial work, as well as fees paid to special consultants. Nonpersonnel costs would include space rental, equipment (lease or purchase), consumable supplies, travel, telephone, postage, and similar, miscellaneous costs.[16] In some cases, the amount under "cost" will be donated or paid in kind. In other cases, cash will be involved. One needs to know about matching requirements, if there are any. Some arts agencies, for example, require a two-to-one cash match for all grant requests.

A guide developed by the Cleveland Foundation is worth looking at.[17] There are similarities with, as well as differences from, the format suggested above. Following a letter of summary outlining purpose, background, amount requested, and time limits, there follows a six-step process:

1. Purpose and Definition of Project
    a. What is the basic purpose?
    b. How long will it take?
    c. Is it a new idea or a continuation of an idea that is already operating?
    d. How many clients are involved?
    e. How will the findings be implemented?
    f. Are any new methods/techniques involved in the project?
2. Priority of Project
    a. How serious is the need?
    b. How does this project compare with others?
    c. What is the target population?
    d. What immediate and long-range results are expected?
3. Financial Information
    a. What is the current operating budget?
    b. Will the project continue beyond the funding period?
    c. Have requests gone to other funding sources?
4. Background of Request
    a. How long has the applicant organization been in existence?
    b. What awards have been received?
    c. What is the tax-exempt status?
    d. Are there any cooperating organizations in the project?
    e. Is there support from the appropriate personnel in the organization for this project?
5. Personnel
    a. Who are the trustees/officers?
    b. What are their roles/responsibilities?
    c. What staff are required to implement the project and what are their qualifications?
6. Evaluation
    a. By what criteria will the project be evaluated?
    b. By whom will the project be evaluated?
    c. What kind of reports will be submitted—and when?

    d. What provisions will be made to implement short- and long-range results from the project?

    e. What evaluation techniques will be used?

The germ of a proposal to a funding source is an *idea*. The idea must be verbalized, fleshed out, and committed to paper in concise, clear terms devoid of jargon and flowery prose. The idea must be described as if the reader had no notion of what it was all about. A sense of commitment on the part of the individual writing the proposal needs to leap off the page so that the reader becomes excited about the idea too. In a proposal, questions must be answered before they are asked—about matters of finance, personnel, space, methodology, and evaluation—so that the reader will finish the proposal with a clear knowledge of the project rather than a multitude of questions and concerns.

One seeks a grant not just for financial support but to build a partnership. It is important for a grantor to infer from the proposal that here is someone with a need who wishes to form alliance with someone with financial resources to jointly solve a problem. The manner in which that will take place is in the text of the proposal, and the supplementary materials, in the appendix.

An idea can be absolutely first-rate, but if it is not well communicated, it will be lost in the shuffle of hundreds of proposals that land on the desks of funding agencies. The proposal should stay within the required parameters. Do not write beyond the limitations stipulated. The quality of the proposal is far more significant than the quantity of verbiage. Readers will *not* read beyond the established guidelines.

The receipt of grants will add a measure of quality to any music program. Grants serve to provide that which is impossible under normal budgetary constraints. And they are testimony to the many publics which a music program serves that an outside agency has recognized the character and integrity of this program and wishes to be involved and identified with it.

One should not minimize the time, energy, and effort needed to produce a well-written proposal. Time is spent in research, in data gathering, in personal contacts, in writing and rewriting. Is it worth it? You bet!

NOTES

1. Elaine Guregian, "1989 Survey of School Music Budgets," *Instrumentalist* 44, no. 1 (August 1989), p. 15.
2. *Ibid.*, p. 16.

3. Arnaud C. Marts, *Man's Concern for Fellow Man* (New York: Marts and Lundy, 1961).

4. The 1988 annual report of *Giving USA* lists gifts to religion, 46 percent; human services, 10 percent; health, 9 percent; education, 9 percent; arts and humanities, 7 percent; and other, 19 percent.

5. Scott M. Cutlip, *Fund-Raising in the United States* (New Brunswick, N.J.: Rutgers University Press, 1965), p. 1.

6. *Ibid.*, p. 33.

7. *Ibid.*, p. 242.

8. *Ibid.*, p. 526.

9. George A. Brakeley, *Tested Ways to Successful Fund-Raising* (New York: AMACOM, 1980), p. 164.

10. Irving R. Warner, *The Art of Fund-Raising* (New York: Harper and Row, 1975), p. 160.

11. Harold J. Seymour, *Designs for Fund-Raising* (New York: McGraw-Hill, 1966), p. 76.

12. *Ibid.*, p. 96.

13. National Endowment for the Arts and National Endowment for the Humanities, both 1100 Pennsylvania Ave., NW, Washington, D.C. 20506.

14. *The Foundation Directory*, 6th ed. (New York: Columbia University Press, 1983).

15. Grantsmanship Center, 1015 West Olympic Boulevard, Los Angeles, California 90015.

16. Norton J. Kiritz, "Program Planning and Proposal Writing," Los Angeles: *The Grantsmanship Center News*, 1974.

17. Cleveland Foundation, 1400 Hanna Building, Cleveland, Ohio 44115.

SUPPLEMENTARY READINGS

Allen, Herb, ed. *The Bread Game: The Realities of Foundation Fund-Raising.* San Francisco: Regional Young Adult Project, 1981.

Andrews, F. Emerson. *Attitudes Toward Giving.* New York: Russell Sage Foundation, 1953.

———. *Philanthropic Foundations.* New York: Russell Sage Foundation, 1956.

Blume, Hilary. *Fund-Raising: A Comprehensive Workbook.* London: Routledge and Kegan Paul, 1977.

Bremner, Robert. *American Philanthropy*, 2nd ed. Chicago: University of Chicago Press, 1988.

Broce, Thomas. *Fund-Raising.* Norman: University of Oklahoma Press, 1980.

Brody, Ralph, and Goodman, Marcie. *Fund-Raising Events: Strategies and Programs for Success.* New York: Human Sciences Press, 1988.

Carbone, Robert F. *Fund-Raisers of Academe.* College Park, Md.: Clearinghouse for Research on Fund-Raising, 1986.

Carter, Paul. *Handbook of Successful Fund-Raising.* New York: E. P. Dutton, 1970.

Compton, Everald. *Ten-Steps to Successful Fund-Raising.* Elms Court, England: Arthur H. Stockwell, 1978.

Flanagan, Joan. *The Grass Roots Fund-Raising Book.* Washington, D.C.: Youth Project, 1977.

Georgi, Charlotte. *Fund-Raising, Grants and Foundations.* Littleton, Colo.: Libraries Unlimited, 1985.

Grasty, William K., and Sheinkopf, Kenneth. *Successful Fund-Raising: A Handbook of Proven Strategies.* New York: Scribners, 1982.

Hutler, Albert. *A Guide to Successful Fund-Raising.* New York: Business Reports, 1977.

King, George W. *Deferred Gifts: How to Get Them.* Ambler, Pa.: Fund-Raising Institute, 1982.

Marts, Arnaud C. *Philanthropy's Role in Civilization.* New York: Harper and Row, 1953.

Mirkin, Howard R. *The Complete Fund-Raising Guide.* New York: Public Service Materials Center, 1975.

O'Connell, Brian, ed. *America's Voluntary Spirit.* New York: Foundation Center, 1983.

Payton, Robert L. *Philanthropy.* New York: Macmillan, 1988.

Phillips, Edgar H. *Fund-Raising Techniques.* London: Business Books, Mercury House, 1969.

Pollard, John A. *Fund-Raising for Higher Education.* New York: Harper and Row, 1958.

Porter, Robert A. *Guide to Corporate Giving in the Arts 2.* New York: American Council for the Arts, 1981.

Rockefeller, David. *Giving: Big Bucks, Bare Basics, and Blue Skies.* Washington, D.C: Independent Sector, 1986.

Schneiter, Paul H. *The Art of Asking.* New York: Walker, 1978.

Schneiter, Paul H., and Nelson, Donald R. *The Thirteen Most Common Fund-Raising Mistakes, and How to Avoid Them.* Washington, D.C.: Taft Corporation, 1982.

Silver, Morris. *Affluence, Altruism, and Atrophy.* New York: New York University Press, 1980.

Tenbrunsel, Thomas W. *The Fund-Raising Resource Manual.* Englewood Cliffs, N.J.: Prentice-Hall, 1982.

Vinegard, Sue, and McCurley, Steve. *101 Ways to Raise Resources.* Downers Grove, Ill.: Heritage Arts, 1977.

STUDY QUESTIONS

1. What is the difference between fund-raising and grantsmanship?
2. How does one learn about fund-raising?
3. How does one learn about the securing of grants?
4. What is philanthropy? What role does it play in American society?
5. What are some principles that are crucial for the successful fund-raiser to know and practice?
6. What is involved in building a case statement for your cause?
7. Why do people give? Why do they *not* give?
8. What are planned gifts? How can they be folded into a total program of fund-raising?
9. From what sources can music units secure grants?

10

Public Relations

*N*ever has the competition for the minds of people been more intense than in today's world. School and college administrators and the public are constantly required to make decisions that affect money spent and time consumed in education. To survive in academia, music as a subject must compete with other subjects for its share of the financial expenditures and allocations. Music educators must establish music, like all fields of education, with the public and the administration as an efficacious force in the lives of people. Music educators must convince their constituencies of music's contributions to the total community as a cultural and social force, a basic element of the complete education of people, young and old. To accomplish this, leaders in the fields of music and music education must articulate and interpret the significance of music in education. That is what public relations is all about.

Schools are supported by, and are the property of, the public. It is therefore advisable to keep the public informed about their schools and its music department. This is a matter not merely of information but of education.

It is not enough, however, to conduct a public relations program for the community only: it is equally important that the music department work to keep school administrators informed. Public relations for music education means, in part, educating the school administrators in new ways of thinking about the discipline. Such communication deserves high priority. This is taken for granted so often that it is not unusual for an administrator to have to be informed by an outside source of an event that affects his school, a fact that may prove embarrassing to him and the music staff. Such information should not be confined to developments and activities within the department but should include innovations, issues, and trends as they develop within the entire music profession.

It is equally essential to keep the music faculty both at the university and in the schools informed about events and developments that occur on public and private occasions or within the administrative complex. All too often music administrators shape events in their offices and neglect to keep informed the very people who are most affected by these decisions. To keep people informed, arteries of communications, including public relations, must be kept open and functioning in all directions. It is much easier to implement decisions that affect teachers if the faculty has been made aware of, and permitted to respond to them, in advance.

In every community there are key individuals who can be mobilized to support music in schools and universities. However, unless these leaders are kept informed, their potential for assistance will remain untapped. They need to be made aware of the goals of music education and the role it plays in the total scheme of education. This requires an organized public relations program, one that is oriented toward *communicating*—the key to successful public relations.

Good public relations is thus dependent on the school music administrator understanding the community and its needs. This includes knowledge of the racial and socioeconomic makeup of the community. He must be aware of, and sensitive to, the aspirations of all of the people who live in it. He should have a knowledge of the businesses and industries that are a part of his community and of its cultural and social climate. Anything or anyone who is involved in any way with education in the school system should be a source of information or aid. (This applies to the local university as well.) It is important that good relations be established and maintained with all of those constituencies.

At the university level, the music department or school of music must not consider itself a unit apart from the university. It should make itself an essential ingredient in the cultural life of the institution; it should be considered a significant element of community's milieu. This can best be accomplished by applying sound public relations procedures.

PURPOSE OF COMMUNITY-STAFF RELATIONS IN SCHOOLS

To maintain a good relationship between staff and community, a planned program that reflects the best qualities of the music program and school should be organized. It should be designed to appeal to the opinion makers in the community. It should never be intended as a cover-up for ineptitude or incompetency. The program should be based on good common sense, whether dealing with individuals face-to-face or with groups through publications and announcements. Its chief functions are as follows:

1. To interpret and inform the community about the school music program
2. To improve the learning experiences offered in the school
3. To promote interest in, and support for, the school music program
4. To eliminate confusion regarding the role of music in the schools
5. To ascertain whether the school music program is meeting the needs of the community
6. To make the public aware of the contributions that music makes to a child's growth and development
7. To include the community in planning and developing desirable programs
8. To involve the community in helping solve problems that affect music
9. To make the community aware of certain needed changes and what should be done to facilitate growth and progress
10. To promote a genuine feeling of cooperation among the school, the music department, and the community

Effective public relations involves two-way communication between the music administrator and a selected target audience—students, parents, colleagues, the administration, the general public, and government forces (legislators) who have impact on education. The success realized by the music executive is greatly influenced by his ability to communicate effectively with those targeted. An author in *Fortune* magazine once summed up public relations as good performance that receives appropriate public appreciation because it has been properly communicated.

In addition, communication serves to increase the effectiveness of the music administrator. Whether in the schools or in higher education, communication should make him more accessible to staff and community, and will help him gain support from people both in and out of education. To do this, the music administrator must establish effective contacts between himself, parents, other school personnel, civic groups, and the media. He should employ all of the available media and other resources:

1. Newspapers
2. School publications
3. Administrative publications

4. PTA in schools and similar school service or support groups at the university
5. Lay advisory committees
6. School- or department-made motion pictures of music activities
7. Students
8. School events such as concerts, assemblies, open house, and special observances
9. Performers
10. Radio and television (school-maintained, public, cable, and network)
11. Personal appearances
12. Performances, professional and school
13. Civic service groups
14. Adult education and recreation programs

At a state workshop in Indianapolis, Shirley Strohm Mullins, the orchestra director at Yellow Springs High School in Yellow Springs, Ohio, outlined fourteen steps that one should pursue when submitting press releases to the local newspaper:

1. See newspaper people personally (mailing is ineffective). "A smile is more effective than a paragraph initially."
2. After the personal visit, send out the press release.
3. Call later to see if it was received (follow-up).
4. Do not send a release too early or too late. Success of a release depends on the kind of newspaper—daily or weekly.
5. Newspaper editors get annoyed with musicians because musicians do not understand the problems of layout.
6. Small newspapers do more than larger ones.
7. Always thank the person who wrote the article (byline).
8. Know when you are wasting your time!
9. Do not scold or insult an editor if you did not get what you wanted or mistakes were made in the article.
10. Photography (check what size and what kind they use—glossy, black-and-white).
11. If students do it, give credit to "photo by"; this applies to papers as well as the photographer.
12. Prepare the negative.
13. Try to get papers to come out and take their own pictures.
14. Be sure you meet their concern—time and the like.

Remember, a press release is worth time expended. It builds esprit, promotes pride, and contributes to the students' self-image. Avoid being excessive. Know your situation and what your papers will or will not print.

COMMUNITY INVOLVEMENT

A concerned music administrator is civic-minded as well as school/university-oriented. He must take an active role in civic groups that indirectly contribute to the well-being of the area administered. It is time-consuming, but it is essential!

Music and music education involve working with people. It is impossible to avoid this function if you wish to have a flourishing music program. An integral part of school music administration is working with people, which cannot be done solely in the isolation of one's office.

Desirable public relations begins in the classroom, whether it be in a school or university. Since the signal objective of the entire administration program is to improve the quality of learning experiences offered the students, even public relations must focus initially on them. Universities are judged by the strength of their faculties, which is reflected in the nature of the instruction offered their students. Thus, the school or university becomes the focal point, and good working relationships must exist within the school or university as well as within the department. Through the students, working relationships with parents may be easily established. This affords direct contact with the community for building goodwill and support for the school music program. At the university, it can help ameliorate the traditional town-and-gown conflict.

As people not musically oriented see their children grow and benefit from constructive musical experiences in school, they will be more supportive of school music programs. Parents do not have to understand the aesthetics of music to know that acquiring aesthetic knowledge and developing good taste will make their children better educated. Focusing on what a program is doing musically for children is the best type of public relations.

Another vital segment of the community, often overlooked by the school music administration, is the professional musician. If the musical community supports the school music program, the public image of the music department is improved. In the past there has been considerable friction between the professional musician and the school music teacher. Each can enhance the other's functions. Both school and professional musician should utilize all of their resources by working together for better music everywhere. Generally this is not a problem in higher education, since many of the performance faculty are professional musicians who recognize their dependence on schools for future students.

Good working relationships should include members of the music industry as well. The Music Industry Conference has prepared *The Music Educators Business Handbook*, which is updated periodically.[1] This book is intended to promote better understanding between the school music department and the industry. In it, one can find almost every bit of pertinent information dealing with the industry. It is intended as a service to music educators and may be secured through the offices of the Music Educators National Conference.

Often the marching band in a parade or the high school choir at a civic meeting may be many people's only contact with the music education program. It thus becomes the music administrator's concern that these groups function with a high degree of efficiency, musicianship, and skill. High standards and good taste in musical performance should always prevail when dealing with the public.

OUTSIDE ENGAGEMENTS

Operating a "performance bureau" for both the schools and the university can be time-consuming for a music administrator, but it is well worth the effort in school-community relations. In a community like Detroit, the music department scheduled between 150 and 200 outside engagements annually. In smaller communities the number may not be as large, but it is equally important that this service be provided. To avoid exploitation of students' time and a performance that would infringe on professional agreements, strict regulations should be established governing these engagements. The head of the music department should administer the program in order to relieve the individual teacher or school of pressure that might be unduly applied by local school patrons. Teachers and school administrators must face these people on a daily basis, whereas music administrators can, in a sense, isolate themselves from the immediate situation. At Indiana University a performance bureau is maintained as a service unit. It determines fees and schedules, and operates much like an agency.

All requests for outside engagements by school groups should be submitted in writing, with full details as to time, place, nature of the sponsoring organization, type of group requested, admission charged (and, if so, for what purpose), and any other pertinent information. All responses should be returned in writing so that no misunderstanding will arise. (Forms may be prepared to expedite these matters; see Appendix J.)

No engagement should be approved that is in violation of the code of ethics agreed on by the American Federation of Musicians, the

Music Educators National Conference, the American Association of School Administrators (see Appendix N), and the National Association of Schools of Music. In a school, final acceptance of a performance request should be made by the school principal in consultation with the school music teacher involved, while at a university final approval rests with the dean or department chair. In some institutions of higher education, this process is governed by a performance committee.

Most decisions affecting these engagements are just good common sense. Travel and loss of class time should be kept at a minimum. The code is quite specific as to the types of activities that may or may not be approved. If handled properly, this service will not only promote good public relations but be an excellent means for motivating students to participate in music activities and enhancing the reputation of a school or department of music at a university.

KEEPING COMMUNICATIONS OPEN

Most school systems and universities publish some form of official staff paper, bulletin, or house organ that emanates from the superintendent's or the president's office and is distributed to all faculty and staff. Music administrators may use this publication to announce special events of citywide, countywide, national, or international interest. The space in such a bulletin is limited, so it should be used sparingly and judiciously (see Appendix I).

Every music department should publish its own newsletter or calendar of events. This publication could serve as a countywide or local publication, depending on the number of schools involved. At universities such a publication should serve the entire campus. It should be distributed to every staff member assigned to the department and the university and to key administrators. It should contain every piece of information that will help the staff be better informed about the music activities throughout the school and university system. No bit of information should be regarded as too trivial. It is better to make each issue short and distribute it frequently than to limit the number of issues and have them so lengthy that people find it an imposition to read.

In large school systems, it is advisable to hold an occasional "information session" with administrators out in the field. (A similar program should be utilized for county schools.) In addition to informing them about the aims and objectives of the school music program, it is helpful to renew standard information regarding basic equipment, materials, and texts. Time should be allowed for a question-and-answer period. Detroit, which is divided into nine regions, permits the various departments to do this on occasion. One should not abuse this opportunity and stay well within the allotted time. Universities periodically have reports from various schools presented at board of trustees meetings. (At Indiana University similar sessions are held on campus with state legislators.) These opportunities can aid immeasurably in securing support for the school or department music program.

Most institutions of higher learning have a separate office for maintaining public relations and disseminating news and publicity. However, these offices deal with items covering the entire campus and may not have the special interest or single focus necessary at times for a department or a school of music. It is therefore advisable for a music unit to have some means of publishing and highlighting its concerns and successes through channels directly responsible to its chief executive officer. Naturally, this must be done within the constraints of university protocol, and it should not in any way violate any of the institution's guidelines. Since universities depend a great deal on their ability to attract students, this public relations office for music is extremely important and must extend beyond just the local and campus environments.

MENC, in its Tips series, has an excellent pamphlet on public relations, which in its chapter on the media, points out that "the most important factor required for a successful public relations program is a disciplined plan of action."[2] To be successful, a public relations program must know what it wants to accomplish, must establish procedures to implement the pursuit of its goals, and must have a valid means of evaluating how well it is reaching its objectives.

■

IMPROVING SCHOOL-COMMUNITY RELATIONS

The most significant way to improve relations between school and community is to improve the "product." The better and more inclusive the school music program, the more likely it is to receive community support. Quality education merits better support.

In Warren, Michigan, the instrumental music teachers developed a unique progress report form that was distributed with the child's report card (Figure 10–1). This form not only enabled the teachers to provide specific information regarding the student's progress but also informed the parent of the specific instrumental skills being taught in the elementary schools.

WARREN CONSOLIDATED SCHOOLS

Music Department

TO: _____ _____ _____
(Instrumental Teacher)   (School)   (Date)

I, Mr./Mrs. _____, acknowledge receive of the Instrumental Music Progress Report. (Please sign and return with child to next lesson.)

Parent Comments: _____
_____
_____

WARREN CONSOLIDATED SCHOOLS
INSTRUMENTAL MUSIC PROGRESS REPORT
(WIND INSTRUMENTS)

STUDENT _____ GRADE _____ DATE _____
INSTRUMENT _____ SCHOOL _____

Individual Progress	1 2 3 4 5 6	Articulation	1 2 3 4 5 6
Comparative Progress	1 2 3 4 5 6	Correct Fingerings	1 2 3 4 5 6
Attendance		Tone Quality	1 2 3 4 5 6
(with equipment)	1 2 3 4 5 6	Playing Position	1 2 3 4 5 6
Attitude	1 2 3 4 5 6	Note Values	1 2 3 4 5 6
Effort	1 2 3 4 5 6	Rhythm	1 2 3 4 5 6
Preparation of		Time/Key Signature	1 2 3 4 5 6
Lessons	1 2 3 4 5 6	Intonation	1 2 3 4 5 6
Embouchure	1 2 3 4 5 6		

KEY: 1–2 Needs Improvement; 3—4 Satisfactory; 5–6 Excellent

COMMENTS: _____

1st COPY—Parent (to be distributed by classroom teacher)
2nd COPY—Instructor–school file

_____
(Instructor)

FIGURE 10–1

The school music administrator must be personally sensitive to school-community relations in the sense that he must keep in mind certain responsibilities that go with his office. He must try to see that all events are publicized and that board of education and school administration officials are invited. He must strive to maintain a high standard of performance both in and out of the classroom and must work to build a community feeling of pride and commitment to the school music program. Every effort should be made to cause each citizen to feel that it is his program and his accomplishment. Every achievement should be perceived as not just the success of the school music administration but a result of contributions from the community as a whole.

The Music Educators National Conference, under the direction of Joan Gaines, former director of public relations for MENC, prepared a tape and manual to assist administrators and teachers in holding workshops on "building community support." It contains all the essential information for organizing such a workshop, with special instructions to workshop leaders on utilizing necessary space and limiting numbers. The entire presentation is divided into three basic topics: Sharing Images and Cross Perceptions; Problem Analysis Through Role-Playing; and Ways to Build Community Support. It is a useful unit that every music administration may use as an in-service device for improving school-community relations.

NOTES

1. Music Educators National Conference, *The Music Educators Business Handbook* (Reston, Va.: MENC, 1988).
2. Elissa O. Getto, ed., *Tips: Public Relations* (Reston, Va.: Music Educators National Conference, 1987), p. 3.

SUPPLEMENTARY READINGS

Gaines, Joan. "Building Community Support for the Music Program." *Music Educators Journal* 58, no. 5 (January 1972), p. 25.
Music educators National Conference. *Promoting School Music.* Reston, Va.: MENC, 1984.

STUDY QUESTIONS

1. What are the functions of public relations?
2. What are some of the avenues available for an administrator to utilize in public relations?
3. What steps should one follow when submitting press releases?
4. How can one improve one's public relations?

11

Scheduling and Its Implications

*T*he function of a schedule is twofold: first, it represents an effort to organize someone's time, and second, it is a way of establishing priorities, whether this be intentional or not. One usually plans a schedule, whether it be his personal one or for a student body, on the basis of what is most important.

There are three types of scheduling that we need to deal with in this text: for administrators, for teachers, and for students. The administrator's schedule is a particularly important aid to functioning. It assists him in establishing commitments and work loads and helps anticipate certain demands. It is quite easy to become so involved with housekeeping chores that school or class visitations, individual teacher's conferences, and other essential duties are neglected. Concerned music administrators, however, need to plan their weekly, monthly, and yearly schedules well in advance so that what is most important to them is accommodated and ultimately accomplished. When this is done, matters of secondary concern may then be built around primary obligations. Planning should even include attendance at concerts and programs.

Unfortunately, one cannot anticipate emergencies or special meetings and performances called by those higher in the line organization or even by those who need assistance on a lower line or staff level. Of course, adjustments will be made, but if there is definite planning and commitment, those special calls or meetings may sometimes be adjusted for a previous obligation. However, one must be realistic, flexible, and judicious regarding such emergencies. Administrators should never fill their schedules to complete capacity, for doing so would eliminate the desired flexibility and opportunities for adjustment. They should keep some reserve time to handle items not accomplished or postponed because of other priorities.

Some individuals will hasten to point out that so-called house-keeping chores can be important and, when set aside, still remains on the desk. This is true. As indicated earlier, if these are routine matters, they may be handled by nonspecialized personnel. In addition, such chores are usually the kinds of activities or paperwork that can be handled outside of school hours. One may not like the thought of additional hours of work, but unfortunately, the higher one climbs on the line or staff structure, the greater is the demand for one's time. The busiest person in the school system and the one who usually puts in the most hours is the superintendent, or in a school of music, the dean.

■

FACULTY SCHEDULING IN SCHOOLS

Special music teachers or music coordinators who actually teach music in the elementary classroom will be governed by a school's schedule and prevailing attitudes toward music. This text will not attempt to discuss the merits of the length of different periods or the issue of whether skills of music should be introduced in schools by the special music teacher or the regular classroom teacher (see page 203 for MENC's position statement). As a generalization, one may assume that the younger the children, the shorter the periods should be. Forty-minute or one-hour music periods are too long for elementary children, especially primary children. When scheduling a music teacher's program, be certain that sufficient travel time between classes is built into the schedule. It is unrealistic to plan a schedule that does not allow time to move between classes, whether it be the teacher or the students who do the moving. This includes allowing appropriate time to travel between buildings. Without these considerations, music teachers cannot do an efficient job of teaching music.

Where classroom teachers possess the essential skills and are interested in teaching their own music, they should be encouraged to do so. This will free the music specialist to devote more time to the classes where his services are most needed. The specialist can always be on call to assist or conduct demonstration lessons for the more competent classroom teacher as the need arises. Incidentally, having the music specialist available for call from any classroom teacher applies to all school situations. However, the music specialist should be able to reserve more time to assist those teachers who are less able to present effective music programs, and this can be done only when schedules are kept flexible.

It is especially important that elementary schedules for music specialists be organized in such a manner as to permit considerable flexibility. It is unrealistic to have the elementary music specialist visit every classroom in a building for the same amount of time. This might be appropriate if the music specialist taught all of the music to all of the children in a particular building. However, even where special music teachers are employed for each elementary school in a system, such a practice is rare.

In Akron, Ohio, a formula was worked out to determine how much special music teacher's time would be allocated to each elementary building. For every two hundred children, the building was provided with one full day's services per week. Thus, a building with an enrollment of eight hundred to one thousand students would normally have a full-time music teacher, whereas a building with an enrollment of seven hundred to eight hundred students might have four days of service per week. The figures served merely as guidelines. A building might have eight hundred students with an interested principal who maintained an active, dynamic music program. Rather than try to find a one-day spot to fill a teacher's load, that school could conceivably have a full-time music teacher.

Where the classroom teacher does his own music instruction, supervisors or music specialists need blocks of time when they can be available to assist these classroom teachers in the conduct of their music programs. The chief advantage to a program in which the classroom teacher conducts his own music is that he can adjust his music schedule to accommodate the needs of his children as they arise. Where this kind of situation exists, it requires close supervision and assistance in organizing musical activities and seeing that they are carried out. Like all the general statements herein, this does not apply as stringently to an elementary classroom teacher who has the necessary skill, interest, and capability to organize and conduct his own music program. It is, however, the recommendation of the Music Educators National Conference that the skills of music be introduced by the special music teacher.

Instrumental schedules in an elementary school will depend on the attitude of the principal and the teacher in each building. Some teachers prefer that all of the instrumental students leave the class at the same time. Under these conditions, instrumental music classes will probably be taught in heterogeneous groupings. If the prevailing attitude is that the students leave the class a few at a time, then the instrumental music class will be conducted in a homogeneous manner. Some systems stagger the instrumental teachers' schedule so that the students do not always miss the same period. In Warren Township, Indiana, special classes operate under a rotating schedule among art, physical education, and music. Days are identified by the colors red, white, and blue. Thus, if music started on red, it would meet on Monday and Thursday the first week, Tuesday and Friday the second week, on Thursday the third week, and so on.

It is the music administrator's responsibility, through his supervisors, to see that music teachers' services in each of the buildings in the school district are properly utilized. Occasionally, some building principal might underestimate his need because of his own lack of interest in maintaining an adequate music program. It then becomes incumbent on the music administration to call this to the attention of the principal and take the necessary steps to ameliorate the situation.

FACULTY SCHEDULING IN COLLEGES

Unlike school schedules, which are fairly fixed once the length of the school day and the number of periods per day is established, universities and colleges follow no uniform pattern for scheduling. Schedules for faculty in colleges are based on the parameters established by each institution. Factors that affect university scheduling are (1) whether the university is on a semester or quarter system, (2) the institutions' regulations that determine minimum or maximum class loads, (3) what considerations are given to other assignments, such as administrative duties and research, (4) the nature of the class (laboratory, seminar, rehearsal, studio, research, etc.), (5) the number of contact hours expected for students' outside work, and (6) the number of hours credit given to that class. Even the latter is flexible, in that a performance lesson receiving six hours of credit might meet twice a week for one hour (two hours per week total), whereas a theory class receiving five hours of credit might meet from three to five hours per week. Essentially, most of the decisions affecting faculty schedules are determined by policies and practices of that particular institution and the educational philosophy of that university's leadership.

STUDENT SCHEDULING

Because of the nature of the music program, particularly in the secondary schools, it is almost impossible to avoid schedule conflicts unless special provisions are made for special music classes (floating period, a zero period that does not have academic classes, special modules, and other creative solutions).

Although scheduling appears to be a mechanical, administrative function, it remains a most important factor affecting instruction. Interestingly enough, one can almost ascertain a community's interest or an administrator's educational philosophy by examining a school's schedule. Where genuine concern for the fine arts exists, schedules are made to include them, even under the most adverse conditions. It is essential that the music administrator develop skills in constructing schedules so that he can aid concerned building administrators who wish to provide time for the arts.

Obstacles to school scheduling usually fall into the following categories:

Block scheduling

Tract scheduling (reading ability, IQ, etc.)

Core programs

Limited periods in the day

Conflicting philosophies among principal, staff, community, and others

Lack of communication between levels (elementary and secondary)

Personality conflicts and conflicts of interest involving counselors and teachers

Physical facilities

Academic emphasis and the "college obsession"

Activity periods substituting for regular in-school scheduling

Schedules are the products of much planning and should reflect the changing aims of the total school program. They should be regarded not as permanent or fixed but rather as being open and subject to continual review. A schedule design should be based on considerations involving students, staff time, curricula, and facilities. The design structure, in turn, is governed by factors that may be rigid or flexible. For example, the allocation of time is flexible, where as the plant facilities are fairly fixed. The number of students will vary from year to year, but when schedule planning occurs, the administrator is governed by fairly fixed numbers. However, depending on one's philosophy, even an imaginative administrator can make a plan reasonably flexible to adjust to the number of students.

Charles Gary, in *Scheduling Music Classes*, states, "Schedules are impartial, they do not deny a student the chances to participate in orchestra, band or chorus because they dislike music or twelfth grade oboists, but only because they were designed to do something else that educators considered more important."[1]

Solutions to the problems of scheduling music classes may be found in a variety of ways. Some schools have resolved their difficulties and expanded their offerings by utilizing elements of modular scheduling. Others have devised rotating schedules, with a movable period that falls at a different time each day. Still others have adjusted traditional schedules by reducing the length of each period so that there will be more periods in the school day. Examples of all these types of schedules may be found in *Scheduling Music Classes*, published by the Music Educators National Conference.[2]

MODULAR SCHEDULING

There is no magic in modular scheduling. It is merely rearranging the distribution and use of time. Modular scheduling is designed to meet individual needs and interests and to accommodate special concerns inherent in a subject. Since this text deals with music, to avoid being accused of approaching the subject with a biased view, let us use chemistry as an example. If there is going to be a laboratory unit that cannot complete its work in the allotted time, one could schedule a module that would extend the time, and then, on another day, the chemistry class would have a shorter period, perhaps when the assignment requires outside reading. Then, in turn, the music department could be given a longer period to prepare for an approaching concert or competition.

For too long a time, curricular objectives have been locked into rigid time frames. The semester ends in June, whether or not the class objectives have been attained. What is more significant is that educational leaders should be concerned with what concepts, skills, and attitudes students need to learn. Schedules should be sufficiently flexible to enable students to meet performance criteria in a class under the best time conditions and, once this is accomplished, allow students to pursue the prescribed performance objectives in other classes.

An excellent example of the utilization of modular scheduling is one described to Robert Klotman by David Amos at Patrick Henry High School in San Diego, California:

> Modular Scheduling of Music Program at Patrick Henry
> High School, San Diego, California, from 1969–1971.
> Department Chairman and Instrumental Director:
> David Amos; Choral Director: Robert Keller

Patrick Henry High School, in San Diego, California, is one of twelve high schools in the San Diego Unified School District.

The experimental scheduling and teaching methods were jointly sponsored by the district and the Model Schools Project of the National Association of Secondary School Principals.

During 1969–1970, the school day was divided into twenty-minute modules. During 1970–1971, a forty-minute-mod daily schedule was adopted. Unless the same class meets for two consecutive mods, there is a five-minute break between each mod.

Students are scheduled to attend classes during specified mods. During the mods where there are no regularly scheduled classes, a student has the option to schedule himself into various resource centers, discussion groups, teacher conferences, tutor assistance, library, music practice, test makeup, intramural sports, or various other learning centers where a faculty member or a teacher assistant is present to help the student with a particular subject area. The student schedules his daily open mods during the guidance or administration period (mod 3). The guidance teacher is the one who "guides" and assists the student in making his choice for the day's schedule; furthermore, the guidance teacher acts as a counselor for the entire three years of his student's high school career. Through this form of modular scheduling, student and teacher time, as well as the physical plant, are used to fullest advantage.

Teacher assistants, certified college students with training in a specified subject, are allocated to each department according to the number of students enrolled in the subject area.

Extensive use of educational TV is made. All rooms are wired for closed-circuit TV. In this manner, a single teacher could lecture to hundreds of students, if desirable.

The music department has a Listening Center, which is a practice room that has been converted to a resource room. It is equipped with record players, tape recorders, a full reference library, a piano, music paper, and study scores. A teacher assistant is in full charge of this room. Students may schedule themselves into the room to complete music assignments, study a musical composition that is to be performed by a school ensemble, receive assistance in music theory or literature, compose, or simply enjoy some good music. An electronic music center is also being planned for the near future.

Class offerings for the 1970–1971 school year were as follows:

Beginning class piano
Bands (Concert, Symphonic, and Marching)
Harmony-theory (a class in comprehensive musicianship)
Mixed choir
String orchestra (full orchestra met in the evenings)
Jazz ensemble
Madrigal ensemble

Girls' chorus
Music appreciation

Performing Organizations for 1970–1971 were as follows:

CURRICULAR	EXTRACURRICULAR (meeting regularly)
Marching band	Pep band
String orchestra	Improvisation chamber ensemble
Stage band I	
Concert band	Stage band II
Symphonic band	Full orchestra
Madrigal ensemble	German band
Girls' chorus	Various small ensembles
Mixed chorus	

Daily schedule of classes for Patrick Henry High School

Mod	Time	Instrumental Teacher	Choral Teacher
1	7:20	Band	Band
2	7:45	Band	Band
3	8:10	Guidance	Guidance
4	8:35	Harmony-theory	Girls' chorus
5	9:00	Harmony-theory	Girls' chorus
6	9:25	String orchestra	Madrigal ensemble
7	9:50	String orchestra	Madrigal ensemble
8	10:15		
9	10:40	(Lunch, sectionals, extracurricular	
10	11:05	ensembles, individual conferences,	
11	11:30	and listening center).	Mixed chorus
12	11:55		Mixed chorus
13	12:20		
14	12:45	Stage Band I	Music appreciation
15	1:10	Stage band I	Music appreciation

16	1:35	Beginning piano
17	2:00	
18	2:25	
19	2:50	
20	3:15	

This schedule seemed to have the least number of conflicts for the music students, within both the department and the entire school master schedule. The horizontal pairings and open mods allowed the greatest flexibility for combining classes on occasion and for faculty meetings and for student and parent conferences.

The Eckstein Junior High School in Seattle, Washington has an unusual schedule that permits it to involve almost one-half of its student body in music classes. It includes an activity period that occurs at a different time each day and in addition to before-school classes and other classes that alternate music with other subjects.[3]

Music educators also need to reconsider their inflexible attitude toward performing groups that require daily rehearsals of equal lengths of time. Perhaps they could use the time to better advantage if they met less often for a longer period of time or for different amounts of time on different days.

Meetings of the entire staff held for the purpose of discussing schedules before they are constructed often help resolve personality conflicts and power struggles over the use of student time. If a schedule is to be accepted, all affected by it need to be given an opportunity to express themselves, including teachers, students, and parents. The school music administrator can often alleviate much teacher anxiety involving schedules by working with the building principal to see that this is done.

COMPUTER SCHEDULING

Many schools rely on computers for class schedules. Contrary to a popular misconception, computers are not responsible for scheduling students out of music. Computers merely facilitate assigning students in compliance with a schedule developed by people—teachers and/or administrators. If schedules are designed to accommodate music students and music students are scheduled first, then they will be in the appropriate class. And even when conflicts occur the computer is capable of printing a list of these conflicts and those students listed may be individually hand-scheduled by a counselor or another designated individual. Incidentally, this concept of hand-scheduling when students' schedule conflicts occur is applicable to college and university students as well. Unfortunately, the college student does not have as many options as a school student has in his schedule of music major classes. The department or school of music rarely has more than one class of a particular subject, whereas in a school there may be several classes of English and history, for example.

Computers can be most useful in sorting and identifying groups and names. Because of their speed of operation, they can introduce much flexibility by setting up new schedules quickly and frequently. (This is especially useful in modular scheduling.) Furthermore, computers can be programmed to accommodate individual school needs and certain unique qualities that need to be identified in each program.

Rather than fear computers, music educators should study their uses and their abuses so that they may utilize them to improve and facilitate instruction. They can be tremendous time-savers and a means for improving efficiency in instruction. However, educators must never lose sight of the need for human control and human judgment in the final decision that affects a student's education and needs. This the computer is unable to provide.

In the final analysis, schedules are only as effective as the degree to which they accommodate the individual student. When the pupil is the major consideration, principals and teachers will cooperate to see that each child or college student will participate in a music program according to his needs and interests.

YEAR-ROUND SCHOOL

In the late 1960s and early 1970s, schools became interested in the year-round school plan, primarily because of overcrowding. It is true that some school buildings were used for summer school to assist students needing remedial work and that many had special summer enrichment programs, but for the most part, school buildings were closed, ostensibly for servicing. To some administrators, these closed buildings represented a financial waste. Universities generally are not confronted with this dilemma, since most of them maintain modified academic programs (summer schools). Most of the year-round programs designed during this period did not survive, because of a lack of funding and in some cases a lack of understanding as to how they were to be used effectively. Overcoming habit is difficult.

One of the early programs introduced was in the Dade County, Florida, schools. This new concept in school schedules, referred to as the Quinmester Project, was an effort to schedule a year-round program.[4] The schedule called for five nine-week sessions. Programs were designed so that "all courses were based on identified levels of musicianship as well as unique performance skills." Attempts were made to design courses that were nonsequential. However, entrance in a course was based on minimum competencies. Students were grouped according to achievement necessary to assure success. There was a sufficiently diversified number of offerings in music to accommodate any pupil's ability. This included making available a large number of alternatives in addition to the basic performance organizations—orchestra, band, and choir.

Under this program pupils chose to go in or out a "quin" (a nine-week unit) within a shorter period of time. Students then had opportunities for broader and more varied types of musical experiences. This program was introduced in 1971 and had moderate success, although it is not functioning at this time.

In 1973 the Sunnyside School District No. 12 of Tucson, Arizona, adopted a similar plan. This program is still in operation.

The Monroe County, Indiana, Community School Corporation Board of School Trustees in January 1977 undertook a "Pilot Project in Year-Round Schools for Grandview Elementary" school in Bloomington, Indiana.[5] On December 9, 1976, the board received a report from the Citizens' Advisory Committee on Year-Round School. That report included a recommendation to initiate plans to implement the forty-five–fifteen pattern of year-round school at Grandview Elementary School in the summer of 1977. This recommendation was based on a systemwide survey conducted by the committee, which showed that sufficient interest existed at Grandview to warrant exploration of the forty-five–fifteen plan for that school.

Some of their concerns were as follows:

A. Enrollment procedures
1. Although parents will be asked to make a commitment for keeping their children in the year-round program for one year, they should be allowed to opt out of the program at any time. A waiting list will be maintained to identify replacements for any child leaving the program.
2. Students will be allowed to opt into the program only at the beginning of a nine-week unit of time.
3. Students from other schools within the corporation may be placed in the year-round program only after all Grandview students have been accommodated. Parents of these children would be totally responsible for their transportation.

B. Remediation
   1. Plans should be made so that three two-week special reading and/or math classes could be offered in late September, early January, and late March. The need for these classes cannot be determined until the year-round program is under way and the educational needs of children are known. These classes could be taught by teachers working in the year-round program or by other teachers who would work only those six weeks during the school year.

C. Kindergarten
   1. Plans should be made to offer one section of kindergarten for twenty-five pupils. The teacher will only teach a half-day during those times that both groups are not in school at the same time. Parents will be responsible for transportation.

D. Special Education
   1. It is suggested that, at least at the outset, only speech and hearing services be offered in special education. There are no special education classes currently at Grandview School; therefore, it did not seem reasonable to initiate a class on the year-round basis at this time.[5]

As indicated, initially the year-round school was designed to solve problems of overcrowding. However, some proponents of the plan agree that it would not only improve learning but ultimately save money and help reduce teacher burnout. Furthermore, advocates felt that the year-round school would help interested teachers earn larger salaries and might even reduce boredom among students.

The school calendar currently in operation is a relic of the early rural society that dictated the need to have young farm people free to assist parents during the harvest. This requirement, however, has impeded learning by breaking the continuity one should have in studying. Studies have shown that children, especially those from disadvantaged families, tend to forget some of what they learned during the school year.

Because of its overcrowded conditions, California has in recent years been in the forefront in establishing year-round schools. In Los Angeles because of its serious overcrowded conditions, there are ninety-four schools on a year-round schedule. In the San Diego area, however, there are fifty such schools, "most of which have chosen the all-year schedule for the convenience it offers."[6] According to the National Council on Year-Round Education, in its 1985 meeting in Los Angeles, there were 325,000 students in fifteen states enrolled in year-round schools that year.

Those who advocate the year-round school point out that Japanese and European students attend school anywhere from 220 to 240 days a year. Another argument in support of the year-round school, according to Norman Brekke, superintendent of the Oxnard district in California, is that test scores have improved and "that it raised the morale among teachers and children and has contributed to a sharp decline in vandalism."[7]

In the summer of 1989 the New Orleans Parish School Board decided to add forty days to the school year at two city schools in disadvantaged areas as a part of a one-year experiment. Much of the estimated cost of $703,000 came from federal support. Even though this is a government-supported program, board member Woody Koppel indicated that the program would be evaluated on the basis of "improved test scores and deportment in the schools."[8]

It takes anywhere from thirty to fifty years for a significant change in the operation of schools to take its full effect. The year-round school concept is a significant development, and music administrators should begin preparing—or at least thinking about—it in case it should be initiated in their communities. They can then assume leadership roles in implementing it for the benefit of their community, students, and staff.

NOTES

1. Robert H. Klotman, ed., *Scheduling Music Classes* (Washington, D.C.: Music Educators Conference, 1968), p. 1.
2. *Ibid.*
3. Howard A. Doolin, personal correspondence (February 26, 1971); see also Klotman, *Scheduling Music Classes*, p. 12.
4. *Ibid.*
5. Monroe County Community School Corporation Board of School Trustees, "Regular Meeting, January 26, 1977," Vol. X, Report 95.
6. David G. Savage, "Board of Educators Ringing Bell for Year-Round Schools," *Los Angeles Times*, January 26, 1985, Metro Section, p. 1.
7. *Ibid.*
8. Associated Press release, "New Orleans Board to Vote on Year-Round School Program for Disadvantaged Students," Bloomington *Indiana Daily Student*, June 12, 1989, p. 3.

SUPPLEMENTARY READINGS

Landon, Joseph W. *Leadership for Learning in Music Education.* Costa Mesa, Calif.: Educational Media Press, 1975, pp. 256–274.
Thomas, George I. *Administrator's Guide to the Year-Round Schedule.* West Nyack, N.Y.: Parker, 1973.

Thompson, Scott D. "Beyond Modular Scheduling." *Phi Delta Kappan* 52, no. 8 (April 1971), p. 484.
Trimis, Edward. "Can Year-Round Scheduling Work for Your Program?," *Music Educators Journal* 77, no. 1 (September 1990), p. 50.

STUDY QUESTIONS

1. What are the functions of scheduling? Discuss each one.
2. What are the obstacles to scheduling music in the schools?
3. What are some of the solutions to overcoming these obstacles?
4. How would you go about constructing a year-round schedule that would accommodate a school music program?

12

Special Topics

ACCREDITATION

Accreditation is a process by which precollegiate and collegiate educational institutions join in association on a voluntary basis to assure themselves, their constituents, and the general public of the quality of their educational operation. Periodic evaluations of these institutions include examinations of mission, objectives, faculty credentials, library holdings, records, physical plant, planning for the future, finances, service to constituents, quality of student achievement, governance, and administration, among others.

There are institutional and specialized kinds of accreditation. "Institutional accreditation," for example, would include in its purview Mt. Prairie High School and Northeast University, with *all* its programs; "specialized accreditation," which in this context is the function of the National Association of Schools of Music, examines music programs *only* in colleges, universities, community and junior colleges, and non-degree-granting institutions that provide extensive education and training in music. The National Council for the Accreditation of Teacher Education (NCATE) specifically accredits programs in music-teacher education at the college level.

There are six regional associations that accredit both schools and colleges and are named for the region of the country in which they arose—Middle States, New England, North Central, Northwest, Southern, and Western. There are other national associations that limit their scope to particular kinds of institutions. "Institutional accreditation has two fundamental purposes: to provide public confirmation that what the institution is doing is of acceptable quality and to assist each institution in improving its own activities."[1]

The business of day-to-day operations of institutional accreditation in the United States is handled by the Commission on Schools (based in Boulder, Colorado) and the Commission on Institutions of Higher Education (Chicago). The former accredits institutions below the postsecondary level; the latter accredits postsecondary institutions.

In the early years of institutional accreditation, standards (some very specific) were set against which institutions were to be measured. For example, "there will be a productive endowment of not less than $200,000" and "class sizes will be limited to thirty." In more recent years the concept of standardization has been abandoned in favor of measurement of an institution against the purposes it seeks to serve—an acknowledgment of the increasing diversity of institutions. "Standards" have been replaced by "criteria," and "inspectors," or those who visited the institutions, became "examiners." The focus of evaluation became more qualitative and less quantitative.[2]

In recent years there has been an increasing emphasis on the "self-study," a process by which an institution—or a music department—looks at itself in terms of its mission, objectives, and goals. This process provides the data for accreditation decisions and enables institutions and departments to look at themselves, assess themselves, and plan for their own growth and improvement.

The Council on Postsecondary Accreditation (COPA) is a national nongovernmental organization that works to promote and ensure the quality and diversity of American postsecondary education. COPA periodically reviews the activities of the accrediting bodies it serves and provides other services directed at the improvement of accreditation.[3] Both the Commission on Institutions of Higher Education and the National Association of Schools of Music are recognized by COPA.

Regional Accreditation Associations

The evaluation process begins with the self-study, during which time an institution assesses its ability to meet the four criteria for accreditation:

1. The institution has clear and publicly stated purposes, consistent with its mission . . . ;
2. the institution has effectively organized adequate human, financial and physical resources into educational and other programs to accomplish its purposes;
3. the institution is accomplishing its purpose;
4. the institution can continue to accomplish its purposes.[4]

Subsumed under these criteria are matters of governance and administration; human, financial, and physical resources; educational programs and curricula; institutional services; student achievement; quality of services, of institutional life, and of contributions to the outside communities; and the planning process and plans for the future.

The self-study—a considerable document with accompanying appendices—is written and is studied by the panel of examiners and by the commission. When the on-site visit occurs, the examiners attempt through interviews and wide visitation and consultation to verify the contents of the self-study. The examiners then write a report to the commission indicating their collective judgment about whether, and to what degree, the criteria have been, and are being, met. After examining all the evidence, the commission decides (1) whether an institution should be granted initial or continued candidacy or accreditation; (2) whether its candidacy or accreditation should be accompanied by any stipulations; (3) whether any reports should be filed and/or focused evaluations should be conducted before the next comprehensive evaluation; and (4) when the next comprehensive evaluation should be conducted.[5]

Regional Associations and the Schools

Regional accrediting associations at the precollegiate level function in a manner similar to that described above. For example, a quality secondary school, according to the Commission on Schools, has effective board-superintendent relationships and a principal with autonomy and authority to provide leadership to accomplish improvement of instruction. It has teachers who are well qualified and a curriculum that imparts skills and knowledge. It maintains a diversified and balanced program of activities and is organized to encourage innovative ideas. The community in which the school is located provides adequate financial support to maintain excellence in staff, facilities, and materials. There is a feeling of mutual trust between the school and the community.[6]

A self-study, prepared by the staff of the school, is built around fifteen standards covering such topics as philosophy and objectives, organization, instructional program, staff, student activities, services, school improvement activities, media, financial support, facilities and equipment, evaluation, adult education, school-community relationships, residential provisions, and special standards. Twelve of the standards are "E" standards—that is, standards that are especially critical within a quality program of education.[7]

An on-site visit to the elementary or secondary school is conducted by a team of representatives from outside the district, who then write a report that is submitted to the school and to the state committee. At the annual meeting of the commission, the state committee makes a recommendation concerning accreditation and membership in the association, which is reviewed by the Central Reviewing Committee. Positive recommendations result in membership for the school and accreditation by the regional association.

Specialized Accreditation in Music

The National Association of Schools of Music (NASM), organized in 1924, is designated by the Council on Postsecondary Accreditation (COPA) and the United States Department of Education as the agency responsible for the accreditation of music curricula in higher education. NASM publishes a *Handbook,* a *Directory,* and a periodic *Report to Members;* provides statistical services; and holds an annual meeting. Accreditation reviews are the responsibility of the Commission on Accreditation, the Commission on Community/Junior College Accreditation, and the Commission on Non-Degree-Granting Accreditation.

Two procedures through which institutions must go in applying for initial membership or renewal of membership are the writing of an institutional self-study and submission to peer review. The peer evaluation provides professional, objective judgment from outside the institution and is accomplished through an on-site visitation, a formal visitors' report, and commission review.[8]

Members agree to adhere to the standards established by the association. These standards cover such items as objectives, admissions policies, record keeping, size and scope, governance, faculty, administration, facilities and equipment, library, financial policies, and community involvement and articulation with other schools. Specific standards are applied to curricula—expectations for the various undergraduate and graduate degrees offered by member institutions.

Members agree to abide the NASM Code of Ethics, a document that contains statements on matters of faculty appointments, financial aid, advertising, and the school's responsibility to the student. Article VIII of the code states, for example, that "after May 1, an offer for an appointment to take effect in the next academic year will not be made unless the administrative head of the offering college, school or institute, has previously determined that the date at which the appointment is to take effect is agreeable to the administrative head of the college, school, or institute that the individual will be leaving if the individual accepts the new appointment."[9]

NASM is divided into nine geographic regions. The chairman of each region sits on the board of directors, along with the nationally elected officers and the commission chairmen. An office, headed by an executive director, handles the day-to-day operations of the association in Reston, Va.

*   *   *

Although accreditation is viewed by some as intrusive and dicta-
torial, most people in education feel that the process is a helpful one.
At its best accreditation, both institutional and specialized, can raise
standards, improve quality, and assure constituents and the public
that a quality product is being offered.

Another point to be stressed is the *voluntary* nature of accreditation. Departments or schools of music do *not* have to belong to
NASM. They do so because they wish to take advantage of a needed
service. And further, they consider a "stamp of approval" advanta-
geous for students and for the institution. Likewise, institutions
choose to affiliate with regional accrediting associations because
membership represents having gone through an examination—
extensive and intensive—and approval for membership once again
represents a judgment by outside professionals that an institution
maintains standards of quality.

Interest in aligning one's department and institution with respected accrediting associations is on a barely perceptible rise. There
are more institutions that wish to align themselves in such ways than
those that do not. It would appear that accreditation will be with us
for the foreseeable future.

NOTES

1. *A Handbook of Accreditation*, (Chicago: Commission on Institutions of
   Higher Education, 1988–1989), p. 1.
2. *Ibid.*, p. 3.
3. *Ibid.*, p. 9.
4. *A Guide to Self-Study for Commission Evaluation*, (Chicago: Commission
   on Institutions of Higher Education, 1988–1989), p. 8.
5. *A Handbook of Accreditation*, p. 27.
6. *Standards for Secondary Schools* (Boulder, Colo.: Commission on Schools,
   North Central Association, 1985–87), p. 2.
7. *Ibid.*, p. 4.
8. *National Association of Schools of Music* (Reston, Va.: NASM, 1986), a
   brochure describing the functions of the association.
9. National Association of Schools of Music, *Handbook* (Reston, Va.: NASM,
   1987–1988), p. 23.

---------------------------------■---------------------------------

CERTIFICATION

Certification is the process by which students in undergraduate music-teacher education programs become licensed to teach the subject of music in elementary and secondary schools in the United States. There are other aspects to certification, to be sure, such as the certification of those involved in the administration and supervision of educational programs in the schools. These and matters, such as upgrading, renewing, and reciprocity, will be discussed in this section. The world of certification is changing rapidly, and what is observed to be an activity in one or two states today may well become a trend tomorrow. And, speaking of states, it should be noted that certification is a *state* function.

Since the public schools are controlled by the state and since the principal source of funding is the state legislature, the rules and regulations that describe and prescribe certification in a state are determined by its legislature. When that determination is made, the enforcement of the various rules and regulations is placed in the hands of a state agency—usually a department of education—headed by a state superintendent for public instruction or person with a similar title. Colleges and universities submit programs for approval by the appropriate state agency. Once approved, institutions of higher education are authorized to provide teacher preparation programs leading to licensure in the state. Normally, a certification officer is appointed by the institution. It is this person's responsibility to verify that the approved program requirements have been satisfied.

A typical program for a music student will include a block of credits in the major area (music), a block in general education, and a block in professional education, which will include student teaching.

Practices

The music component typically includes studies in basic musicianship, performance, and wide experience with instrumental, choral, and general music, including familiarity with, and competence in, keyboard skills. General education will include a variety of courses in the natural sciences, the social sciences, mathematics, languages, and the humanities and fine arts. Professional education courses may include reading methods, teaching exceptional children, computer literacy, and multicultural education, in addition to student teaching.

Several states provide for some kind of alternative certification (sometimes referred to as "emergency," "substandard," or "limited" certification). Such procedures are most popular in disciplines in which teacher shortages exist or in areas of the country where the teacher demand outstrips the supply. Such certification is usually short-term (one to three years) in nature and may be issued to an individual who holds a baccalaureate degree but has little or no work in professional education.

Legislators and governors are responding to demands from citizens for alternative certification in order to meet the need for an increasing number of teachers. There is great concern in professional education circles that this will lower standards, weaken the quality of the teacher force, and diminish the profession in the eyes of the public.

Depending upon the state, initial certification may be for anywhere from one to ten years in length, with a very few states offering life certification. The average length of initial certification is five years. In order to renew one's certificate, one must teach for a period of time and amass additional credits of collegiate course work. To move up to a more advanced certificate, teachers typically have to earn a master's degree, thirty semester hours beyond the baccalaureate degree, or have to complete a fifth year of study—this in addition to a stated length of time of actual teaching.

Supervision and Administration

Some states offer special certificates for those involved in the supervision and administration of music programs in the schools. The requirements for such certificates may include a master's degree, a certain number of years of successful teaching experience in the subject area, and graduate work in the areas of supervision, curriculum, and foundations (social, philosophical, psychological). In addition, a practicum may also be required. As with other certificates, these may be issued at different levels (e.g., provisional to professional, and basic to standard) to which persons may aspire and for which they may qualify with additional training and experience.

Reciprocity

For a number of years, agreements have been made between states that allow a certificate holder in one state to receive certification in the same field in the second state. Many states now are utilizing standards set by the National Council for the Accreditation of Teacher Education (NCATE) or by the National Association of State Directors of Teacher Education and Certification (NASDTEC) for purposes of interstate certification.

Several states have signed "interstate certificate agreement contracts," which may cover teachers (including vocational teachers), administrators, and/or school support personnel. Their number is growing. Some states have individual requirements that must be met before a certificate is issued (e.g., experience, age, fingerprints, citizenship, oath, health certificate, passing a test).

Trends

Perhaps the most widespread trend in the field of certification is the testing of candidates prior to the issuance of an initial certificate to teach. In addition, tests are often required prior to admission to teacher education or for promotion. Tests may include basic skills (reading, writing, mathematics, listening), subject matter (music), pedagogical skills (teaching methods, psychology and teaching, classroom management, evaluation techniques, ethics, and teaching of reading, among others), and general knowledge. While several states have developed their own tests, many are using the Pre-Professional Skills Test and/or the National Teacher Examination, developed by the Educational Testing Service.

In recent years, more than half the states have adopted the National Teachers Examination as a primary test to determine licensing for teachers. The examination consists of a core battery of questions designed to measure the candidate's communication skills and a second section dealing with the discipline or subject area. Where this test is used, teachers cannot get a license unless they pass the minimum standard. Practices vary from state to state; scores are kept confidential and may be revealed only when permission is granted by the prospective teacher. This examination is intended to serve only as a "gatekeeper" for entering the teaching profession. It is to be used for licensing purposes only and not for the purpose of selecting candidates.

Another trend is the enlargement of the professional education component in programs of teacher education. Common to such programs now are courses in the teaching of reading and the teaching of special education. Courses in multicultural education and human relations are also being seen with increasing frequency, although these may be found in general education as well.

Entry-year programs are being set up in an increasing number of states and are being used in conjunction with testing to determine whether initial certification will be conferred on the teacher education candidate.

With only a few states now requiring evidence of computer literacy, it is a bit early to describe this as a trend, although it may become one. Career ladders, too, are in evidence in a few states.

Whether this phenomenon will become more pervasive no one can foresee.

The Music Educators National Conference (MENC) has designed its Professional Certification Program to encourage high standards among music educators and to recognize the efforts of exemplary teachers. Two levels of certification are offered: the "registered professional music educator" designation is valid for three years; the "certified master music educator" is valid for five years and is awarded on the basis of peer evaluation of an applicant's videotape and completion of the first-level certificate. First-level certification is based on one's success in music teaching over at least an eight-year period, documentation of professional activities, continued growth as a teacher, and course work beyond the bachelor's degree. Whether other professional associations follow the lead of MENC in extending this kind of subject-specific certification remains to be seen.

The matter of certification of music teachers for the public schools is complex and ever-changing. The music supervisor or administrator in the schools and the music department chair on the college campus must remain abreast of the changes that occur and make the appropriate adjustments in curriculum, experiences, and expectations of both the teacher candidate and the practitioner. What appears today as an action taken by two or three state legislatures may tomorrow become a regional or even national trend.

The certification officer on the college campus is the one person to whom the department chair can turn for expert advice and counsel when questions about certification arise. He must remain informed not only with what is happening in that state but also with what is happening nationally, since those events will quite possibly affect graduates of that institution.

In addition to publications produced by state departments of education, the music administrator will want to consult the NASDTEC's *Manual on Certification and Preparation of Educational Personnel in the United States* and Robert L. Erbes's *Certification Practices and Trends in Music Teacher Education*.[1] Both of these sources were of assistance in preparing this section of the book.

NOTES

1. National Association of State Directors of Teacher Education and Certification, *Manual on Certification and Preparation of Educational Personnel in the United States* (Sacramento, Calif.: NASDTEC, 1988); Robert L. Erbes, *Certification Practices and Trends in Music Teacher Education* (Reston, Va.: Music Educators National Conference, 1988).

∎

NEGOTIATION

Thirty years ago, a faculty union was unthinkable. However, today on many college and university campuses and in communities large and small, unions and associations functioning as unions are the sole bargaining agents for teachers in contract negotiations. It is not the function of this text to discuss or take sides on the issue of whether a faculty should unionize but rather to assist music administrators in dealing with the negotiating process where these situations occur.

During negotiations specific issues such as class size, salaries and increments, promotions and tenure, faculty-improvement leave, faculty evaluation, chairperson evaluation, quantification of work loads, retirement, and, on college and university campuses, faculty responsibility in recruiting.[1] To this list could be added many other items.[2] Although all of these matters apply to the university level, most also have application to the schools. They all either directly or indirectly affect instruction; for example, salaries not only affect teachers' self-esteem but also attract competent faculty.

Although the music administrator is usually considered a part of the administration in these "confrontations," it is essential that in the negotiating process, music administrators and teachers cooperate and collaborate to protect the role of music in the classrooms. For example, if the maximum number for a class size is established in negotiations, the music administrator should alert the negotiators that the contract needs to specifically exempt from this clause classes devoted to ensemble performance (bands, orchestras, choirs, etc.). As obvious as this may seem, several years ago in Detroit following contract negotiations, a school principal interpreted the class-size clause literally to apply to *all* classes on school time, including ensembles, and until clarification and a formal exemption was secured from the union, he restricted all classes to an enrollment of thirty-five.

Susan Vaughan, a music education specialist for the Minnesota Department of Education, prepared revised guidelines for class size and pupil-teacher ratios for the state of Minnesota. This provided administrators with the specifics necessary to deal with the issue of class size in music.[3]

It is especially important to recognize that collective bargaining in education is not the same process as that found in a factory. In factory negotiations the issues are primarily related to the welfare of the workers. In academia the concerns are not only for the teachers and professors but also for the impact on students and learning. It is therefore incumbent on teachers and administrators to recognize each other's concerns, with the ultimate objective of seeing that the best learning environment under existing conditions is negotiated for all students as well as faculty.[4]

In the late 1960s this issue was so critical that the *Michigan Music Educator* (November-December 1970) published an article, "Contract for Professional Negotiations," addressing it. Although the ideas set forth therein could not possibly be binding, since each community handles its negotiations on an individual basis, the Michigan committee that prepared the guidelines thought it essential that *all* teachers of music "read, understand and *use* this document" to participate better in the negotiation process.[5]

Although earlier a reference was made to how salaries can affect instruction, music administrators should avoid any involvement in salary negotiations. Once the negotiating process is concluded and the contract signed, the music administration must work with the faculty and teachers, and nothing is more painful to a teacher than to think that one's immediate supervisor is responsible for a restriction or loss of expected salary; indeed, it undermines the relationship. The entire process is very delicate, and music administrators need to proceed cautiously, carefully thinking through the implications of each decision they support.

Unions and the Music Code of Ethics

On September 22, 1947, the Music Educators National Conference and the American Federation of Musicians entered into a continuing agreement that is reviewed regularly to accommodate it to changing conditions. The basis for this agreement between music educators and professional musicians is the shared commitment to the general concept of music as an essential factor in the social, cultural, and humanistic development of our nation. This unanimity of purpose is further exemplified by the fact that a great many music educators are, or have been, actively engaged as professional performing musicians and a great many professional musicians are, or have been, music educators.

Since both groups are in need of public attention in order to exist—in the case of one, for prestige and support, and the other, for employment and income—it is only natural that on occasion conflict arises in which the interests of the members of one group might be infringed on. Conflict results from a lack of forethought or a lack of understanding of standards mutually agreed upon.

In order to establish a clear understanding of the limitations of the fields of professional music and music education in the United States, a statement of policy adopted by the Music Educators National Conference and the American Federation of Musicians and approved by the American Association of School Administrators is recommended for the benefit of all concerned.

It is imperative that music administrators at both the university and school levels understand and respect the mutually agreed upon Code of Ethics in order to function properly in the world of music.

NOTES

1. E. D. Duryea, Robert S. Fisk, et al., *Faculty Unions and Collective Bargaining* (San Francisco: Jossey-Bass, 1973).
2. Youngstown State University and Youngstown State University Chapter of the Ohio Education Association, *Agreement 1982–1986* (Youngstown, Ohio: Youngstown State University, 1982).
3. Susan K. Vaughan, "Music Rule to Take Effect July 15, 1987!" *Gopher Music Notes* (Minnesota Music Educators Association), February 1987, p. 7.
4. "Collective Bargaining Issue," *Phi Delta Kappan* 63, no. 4 (December 1981), pp. 225–291.
5. G. Heydenberg, "Contract Language for Professional Negotiations," *Michigan Music Educator* (Michigan Music Education Association), November–December 1970, p. 7.
6. "Music Education," *International Musician*, New York: American Federation of Musicians (October 1975), p. 4.

SUPPLEMENTARY READINGS

Angell, George W., ed. *Faculty and Teaching Bargaining: The Impact of Unions on Education.* Lexington, Mass.: D. C. Heath, 1981.
Baldridge, J. Victor, and Kemerer, Frank R. *Unions on Campus.* San Francisco: Jossey-Bass, 1975.
Parker, Gail Thain. *The Writing on the Wall: Inside Higher Education in America.* New York: Simon and Schuster, 1980.
Youngstown State University and Youngstown State University Chapter of the Ohio Education Association. *Agreement 1982–1986.* Youngstown, Ohio: Youngstown State University, 1982.

RELIGIOUS MUSIC AND THE SCHOOLS

Religion and racial issues are difficult to deal with because one cannot arbitrarily establish rules to fit all situations. These problems are usually handled by "human relations" committees within a board of education or a comparable committee at the university, such as an affirmative action committee or the dean of faculties office. However, a music administrator must have a philosophy to assist and guide him in such situations. He should not be placed in a position where he is isolated and forced to make an arbitrary decision on a matter that affects many people.

Music administrators cannot permit themselves to be racially or religiously prejudiced. They must understand and value people for their differences. Music can enhance human dignity, and music administrators must be the champion of music's cause. Regardless of the quality of the music, if a performance infringes on an individual's personal beliefs, then the individual should be given first consideration. Music or a performance that is offensive or deprecating to a race or group of people should not be permitted. On the other hand, the individual responsible for decisions affecting music must be certain that where music enhances human dignity, without violating the previously stated objections, it has every right to be heard and performed.

The First Amendment of the United States Constitution states in part that "Congress shall make no law respecting an establishment of religion, or prohibiting the free exercise thereof." It is on this that much of the religious issue hinges, and it is a characteristic of our nation that makes it unique—freedom to worship according to one's belief without government interference or imposition. What further complicates the issue is that according to law, a teacher is considered a student's advocate. Under these circumstances, the teacher must conduct the lessons or presentations in such a way as not to discriminate against anyone for reasons of race, religion, sex, or country of origin.[1]

The Music Educators National Conference, in *Religious Music in the Schools*, points out:

> The First Amendment does not forbid all mention of religion in the public schools; it prohibits the advancement or inhibition of religion by the state. A second clause in the First Amendment prohibits infringement of religious beliefs. Nor are the public schools required to delete from the curriculum all materials that may offend any religious sensitivity. For instance, studying painting without those with scriptural themes, architecture without cathedrals, literature without mention of the Bible, or music without sacred music would be incomplete from any point of view.[2]

Although this issue has been brought before the lower courts, the performance and study of religious music in the public schools has not been brought before the Supreme Court. In South Dakota and Kentucky the stated position is that "Christmas carols are part of the nation's cultural heritage," according to a ruling by federal appeals courts. However, the South Dakota court cautioned all parties involved in the suit "that its decision would not apply in all cases" dealing with public instruction in religious songs and a biblical code of ethics.

At the same time, the judges said, "we recognize that this opinion ... will not resolve for all times, places or circumstances the question of when Christmas carols, or other music or drama having religious themes, can be sung or performed by students ... without offending the First Amendment."[3]

In some instances, parents wishing to follow the dictates of their beliefs and not take issue with the situation have requested that their children be excused during any exercise involving religion. E. A. Jackson Morris, in a series of three articles that appeared in the *Georgia Music News*, called to the reader's attention "the fact that individual students could absent themselves upon parental request made these religious exercises no less unconstitutional."[4]

Music cannot separate itself from religion, which is an integral part of its history. Until the latter part of the seventeenth century, music received its major financial support and inspiration from the church. However, religion should not be used to undermine the dignity of the people who make up the community. "It is the position of the Music Educators National Conference that the study of religious music is a vital and appropriate part of the total music experience in both performance and listening. To omit sacred music from the repertoire or study of music would present an incorrect and incomplete concept of the comprehensive nature of the art."[5]

The significant guideline in making decisions regarding this issue is that according to legal opinions to date, teaching *about* religion is acceptable and even desirable, but *teaching religion* in a public, governmental supported institution is unconstitutional.

NOTES

1. Chester M. Nolte, *How to Survive in Teaching: The Legal Dimension* (Chicago: Teach 'Em, 1978).
2. Music Educators National Conference Ad Hoc Committee, *Religious Music in the Schools* (Reston, Va.: MENC, 1987).
3. Associated Press Release, "Atheist, Civil Libertarians Lose Lawsuits" *Indianapolis Star*, April 24, 1980, p. 2.
4. MENC, *Religious Music in the Schools.*
5. E. A. Jackson Morris, "Religious Music and the Separation of Church and State," *Georgia Music News*, May 1981, p. 9.

SUPPLEMENTARY READINGS

Aquino, John. "Can We Still Sing Christmas Carols in Public School?", *Music Educators Journal* 62, no. 3 (November 1976), p. 70.

■

CONSTITUENT GROUPS

At the public school level the music administrator will work with parent-teacher associations and organizations and school foundations, as well as music booster groups of varying descriptions. Parent-teacher groups are often interested in having music be a part of their meetings, and very often they will provide not only a venue for performance but also financial support for particular projects associated with the music program. The effective administrator will utilize the various parent-teacher meetings to get across the message that music is *a part of* the total educational experience of the child, not *apart from* it.

School foundations are established with private contributions for the purpose of enhancing excellence in the community's school program. Since the funds are raised privately and administered by a body separate from the board of education, a foundation can solicit, consider, and provide support for all kinds of ideas—provided that the established criteria are met. Since the foundation's resources are separate from the board's and since the accounting system is relatively simple, it can respond quickly to proposals and projects that are presented to it.

Music booster groups are typically found in senior high schools, but not so frequently in elementary, middle, and junior high schools. They are often "band boosters," "choral boosters," or "orchestra boosters," and in some situations they are simply "music clubs" that exist to support all the musical organizations in the school.

Music clubs have the advantage of making every group feel that it is "cared for" and is important. Even though the needs of the band for tangible (i.e., monetary) support may be the greatest, the other organizations still have needs from time to time that cannot be met within the confines of the school budget. Rare is the school that can provide out of taxpayer funds for all of the equipment, uniforms, and travel expenses of its musical organizations. In fact, in some states the board of education may specifically *not* provide for those items.

The alert music administrator, directly or through his teachers, will work closely with the leadership of music booster organizations to see to it that an acceptable agenda is followed and that the philosophy of music teaching and learning that is operant in the district is kept in mind. Such booster groups are often composed of enthusiastic parents who want to do whatever they can to contribute to their child's musical education. There is an energy level, an enthusiasm, an excitement that must be harnessed and channeled in acceptable directions. It is unfortunate—unacceptable, actually—when a music club *runs* a music department. Yet it happens. The music administrator, through whatever means—diplomatic or otherwise—that are at his disposal, must not allow such a situation to develop or must correct it if it does. A booster organization, properly conceived and organized, can be a magnificent ally of the music director and can help make things happen that otherwise would be impossible.

The music administrator in higher education may work with alumni, "friends" groups, or other support organizations. Some administrators find the time spent with friends groups to be not worthwhile—too social and insubstantial—while others find them to be helpful and supportive. It may depend upon the purposes established for such a group, its vision, and its leadership. The music administrator can have an impact on all three.

Friends groups often raise money for scholarships and lectureships; they may assist with students' expenses in traveling to competitions or to deliver papers at professional meetings. Still others may contribute to school or department discretionary accounts—unrestricted money supervised by the music administrator.

Needless to say, the music chair or dean should have an ongoing relationship with alumni. Such people are usually proud of their education, want to be informed about what is happening on campus, and are willing to provide financial support for school or department projects as a way of helping those who come after them. Alumni can offer advice and counsel to the music administrator, can assist in identifying and recruiting talented young people for the institution, and can and will contribute dollars to help things happen. In order to do any of these things, however, they must have confidence in the leadership of the unit; they must believe that this administrator is moving the music unit in the right direction at the right speed. Effective and frequent communication with alumni is absolutely necessary if a sense of trust is to be established and maintained.

The music administrator should be prepared to deal with constituent groups of various kinds. They will take on different personalities, depending not only on their goals and objectives but often on the personality of the music teacher, director, or administrator who deals most closely with them. Such groups can be troublesome, testy, difficult, and headstrong, or they can be marvelous wells of support—both attitudinal and monetary. Our view is that such groups are here to stay in one form or another. The music administrator should help to chart the course, harness their energies, and provide direction consonant with the goals and objectives of the music unit in order for the most good to be realized. Ample amounts of leadership and diplomacy are required to make constituent groups into the excellent sources of support they can become.

SUPPLEMENTARY READING

Hoffer, Charles. "Who Controls the Genie?" *Music Educators Journal* 75, no. 4 (December 1988), pp. 75–76.

■

SEXUAL HARASSMENT

In recent years sexual harassment has emerged as a legal issue. Where there are complaints, the chief administrator is obligated to investigate these charges and to deal appropriately with the offending personnel. Whether it be a music teacher making innuendos to an individual or class, a professor offering grades for favors, or a supervisor harassing a colleague, these actions cannot be ignored or tolerated. Not only are such behaviors morally unacceptable, but they also interfere with learning and academic integrity.

Michigan State University states the case against sexual harassment as follows:

> Sexual harassment in the workplace and in the classroom cannot be tolerated in a university [or school] setting. Harassment devalues individuals and presents barriers to individual achievement and overall institutional productivity. Both outcomes are counter to basic academic [and even musical] values and counter to the best interest of the institution.[1]

Harvard University defines sexual harassment in the following manner:

> In the academic context, the term "sexual harassment" may be used to describe a wide range of behavior. The fundamental element is the inappropriate personal attention by an instructor or other officer who is in a position to determine a student's grade or otherwise affect the student's academic performance or professional future. Such behavior is unacceptable in a university because it is a form of unprofessional

behavior which seriously undermines the atmosphere of trust essential to the academic enterprise.[2]

The above statement applies to staff members or any other individuals in the educational matrix, regardless of their role.

The Association of American Colleges recently published a paper in which it recommended a number of ways to address the problem of sexual harassment. Boards of education, administrators, and boards of trustees may find that all of these items may not be appropriate for their institutions. However, selected elements from this list may help alleviate their particular situations. The suggestions for consideration are as follows:

Development of clear policy prohibiting sexual harassment. Such a policy might help eliminate some instances of sexual harassment.

Development of a grievance procedure to handle complaints. The procedure need not be identical to other grievance mechanisms if not appropriate. Institutions might find a two-step procedure helpful: a mechanism to resolve complaints informally, followed by a formal procedure if the first procedure has been unsuccessful. Institutions might also develop different procedures for students and for employees. Individuals who wish to pursue a grievance are likely to go to court if the institution has no procedure for them to use.

Development of union grievance procedures.

Public communication of the policy and procedures to students, staff and faculty.

Documentation of the problem by survey, hearings, meetings or other means. Bringing sexual harassment into the public arena will build support for institutional policies and procedures.

Development of a faculty code of conduct.

Inclusion of policy language in affirmative action plans and in union contracts such as agreeing "to afford protection to male and female employees alike against unfair abuse of sexual privacy."

Pamphlets advising women students and employees of their rights as well as advice on how to handle, and where possible avoid, sexual harassment. Such a pamphlet could be developed by a campus committee on the status of women or a women's center.

Pamphlets advising men students, staff and faculty about the nature of sexual harassment and its legal implications.

Inclusion of materials on sexual harassment in courses on human sexuality.

Inclusion of materials on sexual harassment in student handbooks.

Training of counselors and other student personnel to deal with sexual harassment issues raised by students.

Establishment of a 24-hour crisis hotline to provide counseling and referral services to students concerned with the problem of sexual harassment. This could be sponsored by a campus counseling center or women's group.

Campus-wide conference or speakout organized by students, staff and/ or faculty to sensitize the academic community to the issue of sexual harassment.[3]

Additionally, research is needed to analyze the causes, extent, and remedies concerning sexual harassment on campus.

The music administrator must be scrupulously fair and discreet in situations in which a charge of sexual harassment has been made. While an overwhelming number of these charges are made by women against men, the reverse may sometimes be the case, as in a midwestern university where a female faculty member made unwelcome sexual advances toward a male graduate student. The "charge" of sexual harassment must be substantiated before any formal accusations are made. However, under no circumstances should the music administrator arbitrarily dismiss an allegation of sexual harassment without ascertaining its validity. When a complaint is made, the music administrator must proceed with care—and with the advice, counsel, and approval of those who have the expertise and responsibility for such matters—to discover the facts of the case. Lives and careers are often at stake in such matters, so that the greatest discretion must be observed in bringing the situation to an agreeable and fair conclusion.

NOTES

1. Cecil Mackey, "The Dirty Little Fringe Benefit: Sexual Harassment and You," Division of Women's Programs, Department of Human Relations (Lansing, Mich.: Michigan State Department of Human Relations), August 1981, p. 1.

2. Project on the Status and Education of Women, "Harvard Issues Statement About Sexual Harassment and Related Issues," *Association of American Colleges*, January 1984.
3. Mackey, "The Dirty Little Fringe Benefit," p. 3.

SUPPLEMENTARY READINGS

Affirmative Action Office. *Sexual Harassment: A New Look at an Old Issue.* Terre Haute: Indiana State University, 1981.
Equal Employment Opportunity Commission. "Sexual Harassment: Suggested Policy and Procedures for Handling Complaints." *Academe*, March–April 1983.
Crocker, Phyllis L. "An Analysis of University Definitions of Sexual Harassment." *Signs* 8, no. 4 (Summer 1983).

■

STRESS AND BURNOUT

A matter of grave concern for music administrators is that of dealing with the problems of stress and burnout—problems that affect teachers for whom they are responsible, students who are seeking an entry into the music profession, and the administrator him/herself. It is the purpose of this section of the book to define what is meant by "stress," its causes and how it can be managed, in addition to seeing how stress relates to burnout. We will identify the kinds of persons who are susceptible to burnout, the symptoms, the stages and how one can develop coping mechanisms. And finally there will be some suggestions as to how one can examine oneself to check for tendencies for burnout and prescriptions for "wellness."

The Nature of Stress

Hans Selye, the Canadian endocrinologist, says that there is both positive stress ("eustress") and negative stress ("distress") and that a certain amount of both are needed to motivate action.[1]

Christina Maslach says that environments may be stressful to a person when they are noisy, smoke-filled, or lacking in proper ventilation or light.[2] If the strain falls within the coping limits of the individual, he will return to normal when the cause of stress is removed or when he is removed from the stressful environment. Maslach also points out that stress can be a challenge rather than a threat and can stimulate creativity and improve what would be normal or expected performance. How many times have we seen more than one runner run the very best race of their lives in the same race—with more than one person breaking a previous record? And how many times has a music group played or sung better than ever before in a contest setting because of the stress present on such an occasion?

But, while stress has its positive qualities, it is more often than not perceived as being negative. Stress *must* be handled properly. If is is not diffused, muted, controlled, or ameliorated, the following physiological changes may occur, according to Larry L. Collins:

1. The pituitary secretes adrenocorticotrophic hormone (ACTH) and other stress-related hormones.
2. The adrenal glands secrete epinephrine (adrenalin).
3. The liver secretes cholesterol.
4. The kidneys increase activity.
5. The blood vessels constrict in key muscle areas.
6. The respiration rate increases.
7. The heartbeat rate increases.
8. The blood pressure rises.
9. The pupils dilate.
10. The brain becomes increasingly alert.[3]

While no one of these—or even several in combination—is harmful in the short run, the prolongation of any can be problematic for the human organism.

Some researchers believe that the biological effects of stress are cumulative and, to a degree, irreversible and that chemical changes in the body resulting from long-term overstress will accelerate the aging process.

Part of defining stress is identifying just what are stressful conditions. Donna Raschke and her associates conducted such a study with elementary teachers and found that the things that caused the greatest stress among these teachers were lack of time to accomplish tasks, disruptive students, nonteaching duties, student apathy, dealing with multiability students, financial pressures, lack of parent support, lack of positive feedback from administrators, lack of input in curricular and administrative decisions, and lack of recognition.[4]

It should be noted that an event that causes stress in one person may not in another. So, while high noise levels, isolation, bereavement, and traumatic injury may cause great problems for one person, they may not affect another individual in any serious manner.

Job stress may include confusion about role (the worker is unclear about the job and the performance evaluation); role overload (the worker has too much to do and too little time to do it); role insufficiency (the worker does not have adequate supplies, equipment, or materials to do the job); nonstandard hours; responsibility for others (but often not the authority to go with the responsibility); assembly-line work (monotony); and limited participation in decision making.

Of special interest to music administrators should be the finding of Denise Eskridge that the highest levels of stress among teachers are related not to "things" or "teaching environment" but to relationships with supervisors, in this case the building principals.[5] The highest stress conditions were present because the principal did not defend or support the teacher, was overly critical, delegated bureaucratic duties to them, and seemed to care only about work production and not about personal matters, including socioemotional needs. A major concern of teachers and a significant cause of stress is a lack of respect for the person(s) empowered to evaluate them.

Management of Stress

We are told over and over again that stress need not be bad and, in fact, can be quite good, yet we know that unremediated stress can be harmful to the human organism in many ways. So our goal ought to be developing ways and means to manage stress. Selye suggests that one can pursue a syntoxic approach, pursue a catatoxic approach, or engage in flight.

Let us assume that two secretaries are working in the same office and Secretary A is bothered by Secretary B. A does not like the way B talks, chews gum, handles students and faculty, plays the radio, conducts business, or whatever. It becomes so bothersome (i.e., stressful) that *something* has to be done for the mental and physical well-being of A. She can ignore Secretary B (syntoxic) and simply come to terms with the problem and say, "I will just ignore her. I resolve to get along in a state of peaceful coexistence." That may not work, so a second approach is to fight (catatoxic). Secretary A complains, objects, criticizes, and maybe even yells a bit at Secretary B to voice her displeasure at B's behavior, making sure that the message of unhappiness and discontent with the situation is forcefully delivered. Failing that, the strategy may be to flee the scene—for frequent breaks if that will do the trick, or, if not, fleeing permanently to a new job!

In managing stress a person may take several courses of action suggested by Collins:

1. rest—it is extremely helpful to take breaks from work as well as to develop a consistent sleep schedule.
2. develop presentness—concentrate on one item at a time in the present; don't worry about the future nor regret the past.

3. establish relaxation routine—include at least thirty minutes a day for enjoyable activity. That may be reading, playing an instrument, singing, exercising, watching TV, listening to recordings or anything else that is relaxing and fun. The important thing is that activity should be for *you*.

4. change place—it is helpful to vary the scenery and widen the horizon by moving to a new location even for a few minutes—a library, chapel, book store, lounge, gallery—or wherever.

5. put laughter in your life—do something like go to a movie, a sporting event, or listen to a comedy record just for the chance to smile, giggle or laugh heartily.

6. develop non-work interests—the human contacts that are completely non-work can be most helpful as can activities that have nothing at all to do with "job."

7. exercise—physical exercise can hardly be overestimated as a part of any prescription for wellness. Not all exercise is appropriate for everyone of course, and certain activities can be harmful to certain people, but the *right* kind of exercise is indispensable for good physical and mental health.

8. relax—there are many kinds of relaxation procedures from which to choose but the following elements are common to many of them:
   a) sit quietly
   b) close your eyes
   c) relax all muscles—first by tightening and then loosening them
   d) breathe through the nose
   e) continue for 10–20 minutes
   f) let distracting thoughts occur[6]

In summary, it should be noted that *some* degree of stress is necessary for work productivity. The problem arises when stress is excessive or where work stress continues unremediated for a prolonged period. This can lead to exhaustion and to a susceptibility to mental and/or physical illness, thus opening the potential for *burnout*.

The Nature of Burnout

Before looking at the symptoms, conditions, and circumstances that allow burnout to happen, we should first define the term. Burnout is not the result of stress per se but rather the result of unremediated stress, of stress unresolved. It occurs when there is no support system for the person undergoing the stress. Eskridge relates burnout to stress when she says that burnout is the inability to cope with stress.[7] When one reaches the burnout stage it is harder to find the energy and ability to adjust to stress.

H. J. Freudenberger and G. Richelson define burnout as a "state of fatigue or frustration brought about by devotion to a cause, way of life or relationship that failed to produce the expected reward."[8] Maslach says that professionals "lose all concern, all emotional feeling for the persons they work with and come to treat them in detached and even dehumanized ways."[9]

R. L. Schwab and E. F. Iwanicki describe burnout as emotional exhaustion and fatigue, negative attitudes toward people with whom you work, a loss of feelings and accomplishment.[10] W. S. Paine simply says that burnout is when you are no longer effective and you no longer care.[11]

Those susceptible to burnout are apt to be persons in the helping professions (teachers, counselors, social workers, ministers) and "Type A" personalities (aggressive, hostile, ambitious, competitive, tense, impatient, unable to relax, oriented toward achievement, given to denying failure).

According to physicians and psychologists the symptoms of burnout may be physical, psychological, and/or psychosocial. Physical symptoms may include peptic ulcers, excess weight, high blood pressure, lack of appetite, impulsive eating, frequent heartburn, chronic diarrhea, chronic constipation, loss of sleep, fatigue, rheumatoid arthritis, thyroid disease, a rise in cholesterol level, chronic back pain, migraine headaches, muscle spasms, shortness of breath, nausea, inability to cry, sexual disorders, excessive nervous energy, body rashes, blurred vision, dizziness, arteriosclerosis, bronchial asthma, colitis, and gastrointestinal disturbances.

Psychological symptoms may include feelings of uneasiness, irritability toward family or associates at work, boredom, hopelessness, anxiety about money, inability to laugh, feeling of rejection, feelings of despair at failing as a parent, dread of the approaching weekend, reluctance to vacation, sense that problems cannot be discussed with others, inability to concentrate, inability to complete one task before beginning another, fear of heights, fear of thunderstorms and earthquakes, frustration, impatience, worry, anger, anxiety, decrease of self-esteem, feeling of worthlessness, feeling of being powerless and trapped, and abrupt mood swings.

Psychosocial symptoms may include the increased use of alcohol, drugs, and tobacco, weight gain or loss, pacing the floor, wringing the hands, a worried look, throwing or kicking objects, reckless behavior, changes in posture, hyperventilation, poor judgment, increased or reduced sexual activity, increased or reduced eating, cynicism, marital or family crisis, loneliness, discouragement.

Maslach describes the stages of burnout as being emotional exhaustion, depersonalization, and a lack of a sense of personal accomplishments.[12] In the first stage there is a feeling of being worn out, a loss of energy, fatigue, a loss of feeling or concern, and a loss of trust, interest, and spirit. The person feels drained by contact with others. In the second stage negative attitudes toward others are obvious. There is a loss of idealism, an irritability, a callous response toward others. Teachers, for example, no longer have positive feelings about students. They refer to them as animals. They dread contact and try to avoid going to class or rehearsal. The third stage (lack of a sense of personal accomplishment) involves a negative response to oneself and one's accomplishments. There is a low morale, depression, withdrawal, and reduced productivity or capability and an inability to cope. As a teacher, you enter the profession because you love music and kids, because you want to help children learn and grow. When you are in this third stage of burnout, you no longer feel you are accomplishing this or anything else, and you see nothing on which you can focus to receive rewards.

R. L. Veninga and J. P. Spradley express the stages of burnout as being honeymoon, fuel shortage, chronic symptoms, crisis, and finally "hitting the wall."[13]

J. Edelwich and A. Bradsky describe the sequence in still another way: enthusiasm, stagnation, frustration, apathy, and disability.[14]

Which teachers are apt to burn out and which are not? While there is no difference between male and female teachers in incidence of burnout, male teachers do score higher on the Maslach depersonalization scale. Teachers of emotionally disturbed or gifted children burn out more often than other special-education teachers. Secondary teachers burn out more frequently than do elementary teachers. White teachers burn out more frequently than do black. Music teachers have significantly higher burnout levels than do general classroom teachers, and among music teachers, public school band and orchestra directors have higher burnout levels than do music teachers in general and university music instructors. And finally, age is a significant predictor of burnout; that is, the *older* the teacher (the *greater* the experience), the *less* the tendency to burn out. As teachers get older, they develop more coping mechanisms to help them avoid burnout.

Studies have shown that the factors most closely allied to music teacher burnout are being single or divorced, being under age thirty-five, being male, having less than six years experience, living with children, lack of recognition by administration, unclear goals from administration, too much work and not enough time to do it, too many irrelevant classes outside music, and a poor work environment.

Patricia Brown found in her study of stress factors for teachers in Tennessee that the most stressful items were inadequate salary, the career-ladder program, unmotivated students, low status, and inadequate fringe benefits.[15] Coping mechanisms included religion, reading, diet and nutrition, deep breathing, muscle tension and relaxation, sports, aerobic exercise, crafts, and detachment. She found that the older teachers were better able to cope, for all stress variables produced more stress in the more inexperienced teachers.

The problems of burnout creep into the teaching career of the most successful music teachers and the most successful administrators. Music educators as a group become so involved in organizing and developing excellent programs that they frequently are not even conscious of the factors and incidents that begin to contribute to those incipient stages of burnout.

Douglas Nimmo, in a study of attrition of high school band directors, found 720 directors who left the music teaching profession in a five-year period.[16] The typical director in that group was male (87 percent), age 37, had taught 12.5 years, taught five periods per day, and directed a marching band that performed 9.3 times per year and a pep band that performed 15.4 times. He worked ten hours a day at school and then took work home. The factors for leaving the field of music teaching for this group were low salary, unappreciative administrators, too many school-related evening commitments, too many athletics-related commitments, not enough time with family, a feeling that "nobody cares," a desire to do something different, and a general feeling of emotional exhaustion and burnout.

Illustrative of the fact of emotional disturbance among teachers is a Mayo clinic study that found emotional illness in 9 percent of railroad engineers who came to the clinic for treatment, 17 percent of physicians, 19 percent of dentists, 30 percent of lawyers, but *55 percent of teachers.*

It may be useful to look at teachers who do *not* burn out. Basically they have adequate administrative, peer, and family support; are active in church, sports, and community work; are active in their profession; have an internal locus of control; report that their reward is in seeing students succeed; have an empathetic quality and lofty goals; have clear values and beliefs; have the capacity to deal with sameness; and have models to look up to.

It is estimated that the cost of teacher burnout in the United States is in excess of $3.5 billion. Burnout is infectious and insidious. When one person on a faculty becomes afflicted and incapacitated by burnout, it spreads to others who get caught in its influence.

There are those who say that "you can't burn out if you've never been lit," which is a way of saying that burnout afflicts only the *best* among us—the teachers who are idealistic and enthusiastic, who are excited by music teaching and the humanizing effects music has on people. It is those who try the hardest, work the most diligently, are the most creative, are not satisfied with results but always want them to be better who are most susceptible to burnout. That is the tragedy of it all and underscores why ways and means must be found to help those who may become afflicted by it.

Frequently, music teachers and administrators attempt to conceal from themselves those inherent factors that contribute to burn-out by describing themselves as "workaholics." If left unchecked, this attitude can contribute to stress buildup and lead to burnout. Being a workaholic in itself is not necessarily a negative thing if one learns to live with it. There are ways to compensate for this attitude. Those who fit this description may—and should—expand their interests. They should attend workshops and special classes of interest to extend their knowledge, especially in areas where they may feel deficient. These activities will help improve and build essential self-confidence.

A Case Study

Let us see what might happen to a young man who enters college to prepare for the field of music teaching and after graduation is hit with the stresses of the job and the attendant problems.

A young man enters college at eighteen with a full-tuition scholarship. He was in the honor society in high school and is consistently on the dean's list in college. He performs on honors recitals, wins concerto competitions, and is president of Phi Mu Alpha Sinfonia. He plays his instrument in band, orchestra, and jazz groups. He receives honor after honor and does a superior job of student teaching because he has already worked extensively and successfully with students in a church youth group and in band camps. His first job is in a small school where he is "Mr. Everything" in instrumental music. He starts all the beginners at the elementary level, directs two bands at the middle school, and directs bands at the high school, including a concert band, a stage band, a marching band, and a pep band. He does this for four years and then moves on to a larger school district where there are three teachers of instrumental music. He is the one in charge, however, and in addition to having many administrative duties and planning responsibilities, he teaches beginners at the elementary level; at the high school he directs the marching band, two concert bands, a stage band, and a pep band. He starts work with ensembles and sections at 7:30 every morning; with marching or pep band being the last period of the day, he is often at school until 5:15. During marching season there is one evening rehearsal per week; during basketball season there are two or three games per week to play for. Last year, the band marched in five parades, including one in the middle of the summer. There was a band camp that began the second week in August and a summer concert band and beginning lessons at the beginning of the summer that left our band director "free" (if you call it that) for about four weeks. Not mentioned are such things as marching band contests—all of which conveniently occur on Saturdays; there were five of these to help fill weekends during the fall. In the seven years since his graduation, this band director managed to earn a master's degree from a nearby university. This was done the hard way—since summers were already rather full with responsibilities in his school district. With courses, workshops, independent study, and extension experiences spread over seven years, there was little opportunity for synthesis of graduate information. In fact, on the first occasion of his taking the final master's oral exam, our director failed—a terrible blow to his ego and the first such academic failure of his life.

He proceeded through all the stages of stress and burnout. He was spending precious little time with his two small children, and his relationship with his wife was becoming perilous.

What happened?

Here are four courses taken by four individuals in his position:

1. Charles left the profession. He joined a fund-raising firm and now works with former band director colleagues on various projects to raise funds for trips, uniforms, equipment, and the like. You see him every year at the annual professional meeting.
2. Mark resigned his position and moved to a middle-school situation in a larger district where he is responsible for the instrumental music programs (including strings) in two schools.
3. Nathan resigned his position and went to graduate school to become certified as a principal. He subsequently accepted a position as an elementary principal. Some psychologists refer to this move as "quitting upward."
4. George stayed where he was, becoming less and less effective. The quality of the band suffered. The music was less exciting, the marching less precise. Students began dropping out, but George was determined to stick it out (after all, he had tenure) until retirement.

Some Remedies

Can anything be done? If so, what? Below are listed ten items—not presented in any priority order—that will, we feel, make the profession of music teaching at both the school and college levels more attractive to talented people, will reduce the incidence of burnout, and will serve to keep persons in the profession:

1. a decent salary
2. respect from students and community, and support from supervisors and principals
3. increased financial support for program
4. excellent retirement programs, including early-retirement opportunities

5. rewards for excellence
6. a work day and work year that are reasonable
7. working conditions that are comfortable and encourage one's best efforts
8. reductions of time spent in nonteaching duties
9. sabbatical-leave opportunities and other opportunities to grow and develop as professionals
10. a mentor program, which in public schools could be a supervised internship prior to certification and at the college level could entail the assignment of a mentor to work closely with a new colleague to guide him through the early days and months of faculty member status

These suggestions take cognizance of those factors which lead to stress and burnout problems. They also capitalize on what is known about that music faculty member who has no such problems. They emphasize respect, humanity, dignity of person and profession, rewards for doing an extraordinary job, and establishment of an atmosphere in which one can grow and develop as a musician, teacher, creative artist, and person. Administrators who read this book can help to make these things happen, can lobby for positive and supportive conditions for their colleagues with the upper administration, the school board, and the community. There are too many quality people being lost to teaching now, and there are ways and means of putting a stop to that loss or at least sharply reducing it. It must be done.

NOTES

1. Hans Selye, *Stress Without Distress* (New York: Lippincott and Crowell, 1974).
2. Christina Maslach, *Burnout: The Cost of Caring* (Englewood Cliffs, N.J.: Prentice-Hall, 1982).
3. Larry L. Collins, "Head of the Department: Short of Time and Under Stress," Paper delivered at the Center for Time and Stress Management, Rocky Mount, North Carolina.
4. Raschke, et al. "Teacher Stress: The Elementary Teacher's Perspective," *Elementary School Journal* 85, no. 4 (March 1985), pp. 559–564.
5. Denise Eskridge, "Variables of Teacher Stress: Symptoms, Causes, and Stress Management Techniques" (Unpublished research study, East Texas State University, 1984), pp. 17–25.
6. Collins, "Head of the Department."
7. Eskridge, "Variables of Teacher Stress."

8. H. J. Freudenberger, with G. Richelson, *Burnout: The High Cost of High Achievement* (Garden City, N.Y.: Anchor, 1980).
9. Maslach, *Burnout.*
10. R. L. Schwab and E. F. Iwanicki, "Who Are Our Burned-Out Teachers?" *Educational Research Quarterly* 7, no. 2 (1982), pp. 5–16.
11. Whiton Stewart Paine, ed., *Job Stress and Burnout* (Beverly Hills, Calif.: Sage, 1982).
12. Maslach, *Burnout.*
13. R. L. Veninga and J. P. Spradley, *The Work-Stress Connection: How to Cope with Job Burnout* (New York: Ballantine, 1981).
14. J. Edelwich, with A. Bradsky, *Burnout: Stages of Disillusionment in the Helping Professions* (New York: Human Sciences Press, 1980).
15. Patricia Brown, "An Investigation of Problems Which Cause Stress Among Music Teachers in Tennessee" (Ed. D. diss., University of Tennessee, 1987).
16. Douglas Nimmo, "Factors of Attrition Among High School Band Directors" (D.M.A. diss., Arizona State University, 1986).

SUPPLEMENTARY READINGS

Cooper, C. L., and Marshall, J. "Occupational Sources of Stress." *Journal of Occupational Psychology* 49 (1976), pp. 11–28.
French, J. R. D., and Kaplan, R. D. "Organizational Stress and Individual Strain," in A. J. Marrow, ed., *The Failure of Success.* New York: AMACOM, 1973.
Kahn, R. L. "Job Burnout Prevention and Remedies." *Public Welfare* 36, no. 2 (Spring 1978), pp. 61–63.
Kanner, A. D.; Kafry, D.; and Pines, A. "Lack of Positive Conditions as a Source of Stress." *Journal of Human Stress* 4, no. 4 (1975), pp. 33–39.
Maslach, C., and Pines, A. "Burnout, the Loss of Human Caring," in A. Pines and C. Maslach, eds., *Experiencing Social Psychology.* New York: Random House, 1984.
Pines, A. "On Burnout and the Buffering Effects of Social Support," in B. A. Farber, ed., *Stress and Burnout in the Human Professions.* Elmsford, N.Y.: Pergamon, 1983.
———, and Aronson, E. *Career Burnout: Causes and Cures.* New York: Free Press, 1988.
——— and Kafry, D. "Coping with Burnout," in J. Jones, ed., *The Burnout Syndrome.* Park Ridge, Ill.: London House, 1981.

STUDY QUESTIONS

1. What is accreditation? Why should music programs seek accreditation?
2. What are the accrediting agencies in music? What are their functions?
3. What is certification?
4. If one is certified to teach music in one state, can that individual move to another state and take the certification along? What are the patterns of certification nationwide?

5. What is the role of constituent groups for the music administrator? How do they differ in purpose and practice between precollegiate and collegiate levels?
6. Do constituent groups help or hinder the work of the music administrator and the music unit?
7. What is stress? What is burnout? How are they different?
8. How can one manage or control stress?
9. Who are the people in music most susceptible to burnout?
10. What is the music administrator's role in negotiations between the union and the school administration?
11. Discuss the use of religious music in a music program. What is acceptable and what is in violation of the constitution?
12. What procedures should be established to avoid litigation in cases of sexual harassment?

13

Issues and Challenges of Administration

*T*he increasing incidence of social disorder in our society is sufficient evidence of the social maladjustment of so many young people that exists in our schools. There is a need for some change. Administrators in education have traditionally been regarded as deterrents to change within the social structure. This, of course, is not true of all administrators. However, too many who have risen through the system came to represent its vested interests, were "successful" products of the system, and thereby defenders of the system. This too is changing. Qualifications for administrative posts in music administration have become more stringent as boards of education seek informed, enlightened people to fill those critical positions. Likewise, the qualifications for the music executive in colleges and universities have changed in recent years. It is expected now that such persons will be effective fund-raisers as well as educational and musical leaders. Furthermore, they must be abreast of the current technology as it impacts on assisting instruction and office procedures.

Administrators are expected to be sensitive, imaginative, and flexible. They need to be creative individuals who seek new solutions to problems. They are expected to be catalysts for change, for they are in the best position to influence change in their units.

Education in the field of music has not kept pace with most changes that have occurred in society. This was evidenced in the 1967 report of the Tanglewood Symposium on music education in the schools and its recommendations for action.[1] Ten years later this position was reaffirmed by the Ann Arbor Symposium.[2] These concerns include accommodating in the curriculum ethnic music, jazz, and music that is of interest to young people. In addition, there are issues that involve learning theories, psychology, ability to analyze music as well as perform it, and even contests versus festivals, where the emphasis is on the quality of a performance rather than a rating per se. These are issues that have been with us for far too many years and represent commitments that concerned music educators must face.

Research in administration has established that it takes a new idea or a change in direction approximately fifty years from the moment it is accepted and initiated in one school until it has fully permeated most of the school systems in our country. The mass media in our society may have reduced this figure somewhat. However, the implication is still frightening, especially when one realizes it is usually a direct result of inaction, apathy, or lack of concern on the part of an individual. The most obvious approach to improving the schools is through change—change in curriculum, change in human attitudes, and change in behavior in the classroom by the teacher and/or the student. There has not been sufficient evidence of this occurring to any great degree in music education, outside of the Contemporary Music Project (CMP) and its focus on comprehensive musicianship. Originally conceived as a project for placing composers in the public schools under a grant from the Ford Foundation and the Music Educators National Conference, the CMP not only influenced the way music was taught in many schools but also changed the attitude of many teachers and students who were exposed to these experiences, either through direct contact with composers or by performing their music. The change manifested itself in the increased support, comprehension, and performance of contemporary music. In its second phase, the project embarked upon a program of developing concepts and attitudes for teaching that promote comprehensive musicianship as the core of all instruction in music.[3]

Even the impact of the CMP seems to have disappeared from the educational scene. The most recent effort to improve instruction in music education is the Disciplined-Based Music Education (DBME) project, which is an outgrowth of the Discipline-Based Arts Education program, funded by the Getty Foundation. The four disciplines utilized in the approach to DBME are music performance, music criticism, music history, and music aesthetics. The University of Tennessee at Chattanooga received a grant from the Lyndhurst Foundation to hold a workshop in music at the Southeast Institute for Education under the direction of William Lee to prepare administrators and teachers to implement the program in Chattanooga in the fall of 1989 as a pilot project. It is much too early at this writing to determine the success of this venture.

Habits or ideas that have proven successful in past years often become so imbedded in behavioral patterns that they are accepted as a valid basis for teaching long after the initial purpose or function has ceased to exist. (Contests are still the major motivation factor in music performances.) This is a form of mental or educational atrophy. Evidence of it may be found in certain guides, textbooks, the subject matter being taught, and even the schedules being utilized. If symptoms of atrophy are there, the music administrator or his supervisory staff must read them properly and seek remedies that will release the frustrated energies confined by such restrictions.

It does not matter when this book will be read, for times are always changing. Unfortunately, what most educators fail to recognize is that the nature of change is itself changing and that it is occurring at a faster rate than ever before. An enlightened music administrator anticipates change; a complacent or frightened administrator will initiate change only when forced to do so or under the most dire circumstances. The key is knowing how to work with, and for, change. To do this, one must possess *administrative courage*. One must be able to identify stereotyped thought and practice and abandon them for the benefit of today's and tomorrow's learners. It is these qualities that enable an individual to act at the most propitious moment when motivated by need and conviction. Music administrators should not fear an occasional failure. Goethe once said that men will always be making mistakes as long as they are striving for something. The best way to avoid criticism is to avoid any responsibility or course of action. Unfortunately, too many administrators, both in and out of music, are satisfied with avoiding criticism.

ISSUES IN MUSIC EDUCATION

Although it is fairly well established that humanities and related or multiple-arts courses are desirable at virtually every level of the school experience, these programs are still regarded in many places as experimental. Music administrators should be holding dialogues with administrators in other related disciplines to determine how to implement these programs in their communities.

The concern for the 85 percent of the students in secondary schools not enrolled in music has taken on the character of a struggle between performance and nonperformance. As in so many debates, the basic issues have become obscured by rhetoric. One cannot have music without a performance. It is naive to assume as much. A listening lesson culminates in a performance either live or reproduced on a record, tape, or disc. The issue is that performance for the sake of performance is sterile and insufficient. Every performance should bring with it musical comprehension and musical understanding that will contribute to a more musically intelligent human being, one whose attitudes and involvement are reflected in musical behaviors—a comprehensive musician.

The issues affecting the vast number of students who reject music are why they do so and whether music education has rejected them. Too many classes in music are taught as though the "popular" or "student's" music that has ephemeral appeal to students were nonexistent. Teachers never discuss this music with their students, as though it were a taboo subject. Certainly it is worth making music programs more meaningful and even more relevant if we can acquire a commitment from this 85 percent that will involve them in music, whether of the past or present, by at least acknowledging the existence of their music by discussing it intelligently in a classroom. Probably more music is made in basements and garages than in schools. Teachers need to acknowledge the existence of such music.

Adult Education

Although some progress has been made in extending music education beyond the school years, much needs to be done to develop adult education programs that are extensions of the school music program. Senior citizens represent a growing segment of the nation's population, and there is a growing need to involve them in continuing experiences with music.

Education for the Handicapped

In spite of the fact that school music programs must, under Public Law 94-142 (1975), not only provide for handicapped students but also integrate them into regular class offerings whenever possible, programs for handicapped children still need more attention from the administrative leadership in music. There has been improvement as a result of the work of the organization Music Education for the Handicapped, but much still needs to be done to comply with the legal mandate.

Ethnic Music

Contrary to popular belief, music is *not* a universal language. It *is* a universal form of expression. In a world that is changing and shrinking, it becomes incumbent on us to learn the musical forms of expression of other cultures. It is no longer adequate in music education to limit students to one segment of the plurality of people that exist on this earth. Neither is this to be construed as advocating that music education minimize or ignore the plethora of great literature of the Western tradition. Music administrators have a tremendous task to educate, inform, and disseminate information in the area of ethnic music if they are to maintain a degree of balance and proportion in the total music picture. On the other hand, they cannot permit those experiences that acquaint students with the great moments that exist in Western music to disappear from the curriculum.

The appearance of electronic music and computer-organized music is another development of the latter half of the twentieth century that cannot be ignored. Students in today's schools will be the supporters of musical events in the twenty-first century. They must develop ears and understanding that enable them to express valid musical judgments of the music of their time. To do this, they must be exposed to experimental idioms, new styles, and new developments. It is the responsibility of music administrators to keep their staffs informed as these new idioms appear. They must devise ways and means of providing the necessary exposures.

Gabriel D. O'Fiesh points out that "music educators have not taken full advantage of the available media, of the available work that has been done in programming education."[4] There is still an untapped reservoir of individualized learning opportunities for students interested in music that music education is just beginning to explore. Materials and tools have not been sufficiently developed only because music educators have not demanded them or even seen the potential for individualized instruction in cassettes, portable cameras, computers, and synthesizers.

Unfortunately, music education as it exists in many of the schools of today is much more like the music education programs of 1935 than like the programs needed for 2005. In the schools of tomorrow, the tempo of change will accelerate even more rapidly. As this occurs, the role of the music administrator will assume increasing importance in determining the nature and direction of change. Administrators will need to determine what is educationally desirable and then attempt to make it administratively possible.

FUTURE OPERATIONAL PATTERNS FOR MUSIC ADMINISTRATION

The focus of any program should be the students. The source of power is the community, which realizes this power in an action program through its board of education (Figure 13–1). The superintendent and his administrative staff will develop programs with teachers and laypeople in the community that will be translated into desirable learning experiences for children. The patterns of operation, as indicated in Figure 13–1, will be circular and have channels in all directions rather than follow the traditional rigid line and staff. Interaction will be in all directions, with students and the concern for their growth and development acting as the hub of the wheel.

Tomorrow's music administrators will utilize even more-modern research and data to develop, carry out, and evaluate what is needed to improve instruction in the classroom. They will comprehend the role of the music educator not only as a musician-educator but as a socially sensitive individual. They will understand and appreciate diversity in people whether they are concerned with the inner city, a rural area, Appalachia or the Northwest. They will be leaders in curriculum development in every sense for every part of the community. They will possess skills that will enable them to work with those teachers and elements in the community that obstruct essential change, as well as releasing the energies of, and guiding, those who support it.

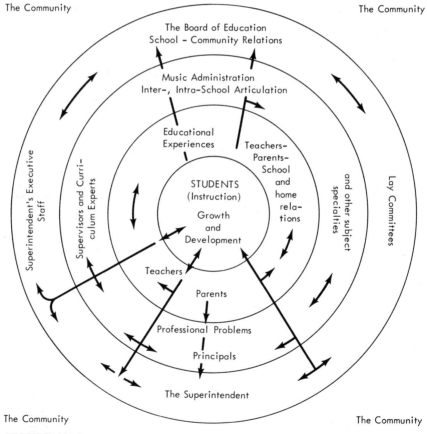

FIGURE 13–1

Future music administrators will possess a broad knowledge of the humanities that will enable them to deal with music in relation to other disciplines. They will involve themselves with all of the arts activities in the community so that music in the schools and on the campuses can assume its proper role in the lives of all people. In the college or university setting, the music executive will be a partner with music teachers, supervisors, and administrators in the public schools, will support what they do, will be physically present in the classrooms from time to time, and will offer continuing-education opportunities on the campus to assist music teachers in keeping current.

In the final analysis, music is an art and a discipline involving aesthetic judgment. It is a form of communication. Education is a science involving learning experiences based on developing an individual with certain behavioral goals. Thus, for tomorrow's schools we will need teachers who are artists, scientists, and humanists. The burden of securing them and encouraging their work will be borne by a music administration made up of individuals who are basically teachers. As administrators, they metamorphose into teachers' advisers and interpreters of concepts evolving from all the roles that affect the teacher, the student, and the community. They will be responsible for quality control in relation to the emerging concepts as they develop for tomorrow's society.

The challenge and obligation was laid before music educators by the Tanglewood Symposium. Although it was written in 1967, it is still a valid proposition:

> Educators must accept the responsibility for developing opportunities which meet man's individual needs and the needs of a society plagued by the consequences of changing values, alienation, hostility between generations, racial and international tensions, and the challenges of a new leisure.[5]

It is a large challenge facing the leaders of the music profession. It is one that must be accepted at all levels of the educational spectrum if musical art is to have the appropriate impact on humanity.

NOTES

1. Robert Choate, ed., *Music in American Society: Documentary Report of the Tanglewood Symposium* (Washington, D.C., Music Educators National Conference, 1968), chap. 9.
2. *National Symposium on the Application of Psychology to the Teaching and Learning of Music* (Ann Arbor Symposium), Reston, Va.: Music Educators National Conference, 1981.

3. Norman Dello Joio, *Comprehensive Musicianship: An Anthology of Evolving Thought* (Reston, Va.: Music Educators National Conference, 1971).
4. Gabriel, D. O'Fiesh, "Technology, the Road to Freedom," *Music Educators Journal* 156, no. 7 (March 1970), p. 45.
5. Robert Choate, *Music in American Society*, p. 139.

SUPPLEMENTARY READINGS

Manhattanville Music Curriculum Program. Elnora, N.Y.: Media Press, 1972.
Murphy, Judith. "Conflict, Consensus, and Communication: An Interpretive Report on the Ann Arbor Symposium on the Applications of Psychology to the Teaching and Learning of Music. *Music Educators Journal* 66, no. 7 (March 1980), pp. 47–79.
Music Educators National Conference. *Experiments in Musical Creativity.* Washington, D.C.: MENC, 1966.
———. "The Crisis in Music Education." *Music Educators Journal* 68, no. 3 (November 1981), p. 35.
Schaberg, Gail, ed. *Tips: Teaching Music to Special Learners.* Reston, Va.: Music Educators National Conference, 1988.

STUDY QUESTIONS

1. What are the challenges in music administration?
2. What are the opportunities in music administration?
3. What are the principal issues in the teaching of music at both the precollegiate and collegiate levels today?
4. How would you develop the case for the teaching of music in the schools and colleges of this country? Rationale?
5. What factors inhibit necessary "change" in music education courses and in the curriculum?
6. Describe the projected future method of operations in a school hierarchy. How does it differ from the traditional method of communication?

APPENDIXES

APPENDIX A. FACULTY EVALUATION FORMS

INDIANA STATE UNIVERSITY
EVALUATION OF TEACHING

Instructor _____   Course Number _____

Course Name _____   Class Size _____

Time of Day_____   Semester _____

Class Level _____   Cumulative GPA _____

Date _____

This course:

Major Area _____   Required _____

Minor Area _____   Elective _____

The goals and objectives of this course as developed by the instructor and/or students are:

Listed below are several qualities which describe aspects of instructor behavior. Using the rating scale below, rate your instructor on each of those items by circling that number that best indicates your assessment of his behavior.

	Excellent		*Good*		*Poor*		*No Opinion*
1. Organizes subject matter effectively	6	5	4	3	2	1	0
2. Is well prepared for class meetings	6	5	4	3	2	1	0
3. Stimulates and motivates the student	6	5	4	3	2	1	0
4. Varies the methods and procedures of the class	6	5	4	3	2	1	0

	Excellent	Good	Poor	No Opinion
5. Has a positive attitude toward the subject matter and to students	6 5	4 3	2 1	0
6. Has defined and stated goals and objectives clearly	6 5	4 3	2 1	0
7. Shows a willingness to help students, particularly outside of class	6 5	4 3	2 1	0
8. Shows a willingness to accept divergent viewpoints	6 5	4 3	2 1	0
9. Stresses important material	6 5	4 3	2 1	0
10. Gives tests which reflect the course content and experiences	6 5	4 3	2 1	0
11. Evaluates and grades students fairly	6 5	4 3	2 1	0
12. Permits and encourages students to express their opinions in class	6 5	4 3	2 1	0
13. Begins and ends class on time	6 5	4 3	2 1	0

14. What do you believe the instructor has done especially well in the teaching this course?

15. What suggestions would you make which might improve the conduct of this class?

16. Considering the previous 13 responses, the size of the class, its goals and objectives, how do you rate the overall effectiveness of this instructor?

Excellent	Good	Poor
6 5	4 3	2 1

17. Is there some important aspect of the teaching/learning process which is not adequately evaluated by this form? If so, please indicate and respond.

INDIANA STATE UNIVERSITY
CONDUCTOR EVALUATION

Date _____

Conductor _____   Ensemble _____

Listed below are several statements which describe conductor behavior. Using the scale provided, rate the conductor of this ensemble by circling the number that best indicates your assessment of his/her performance.

	Excellent	*Good*	*Poor*	*No Opinion*
The Conductor:				
1. Has a positive attitude toward music and this ensemble.	5 4	3	2 1	0
2. Begins and ends rehearsals on time.	5 4	3	2 1	0
3. Demands my best efforts.	5 4	3	2 1	0
4. Detects errors quickly and knows how to correct them.	5 4	3	2 1	0
5. Stimulates my enthusiasm for music.	5 4	3	2 1	0
6. Develops my sensitivity as an ensemble performer.	5 4	3	2 1	0
7. Chooses repertory that is interesting, worthwhile and challenging.	5 4	3	2 1	0
8. Is able to make the music come alive in performance.	5 4	3	2 1	0
9. Is well organized.	5 4	3	2 1	0
10. Gives instructions clearly.	5 4	3	2 1	0
11. Is expressive and compelling in gestures.	5 4	3	2 1	0
12. Stresses musical ideas.	5 4	3	2 1	0
13. Helps me understand musical structure.	5 4	3	2 1	0
14. Makes efficient use of rehearsal time.	5 4	3	2 1	0
15. Demonstrates procedures that I will use as a conductor-teacher.	5 4	3	2 1	0

16. What do you believe the conductor has done especially well with this ensemble?

17. What suggestions would you make that might improve this ensemble?

18. Considering your previous responses, how would you summarize the effectiveness of this conductor?

Excellent	*Good*	*Poor*
5 4	3	2 1

19. Further comments?

INDIANA STATE UNIVERSITY
DEPARTMENT OF MUSIC
EVALUATION FORM FOR PERFORMANCE
INSTRUCTION

Name of Teacher _____ Date of Evaluation _____
Class Standing _____ GPA (Optional) _____
Status: Major ____ Principal ____ Elective ____ Secondary _____

Rating Scale

POOR	FAIR	SATISFACTORY	GOOD	EXCELLENT	NO OPINION
1	2	3	4	5	(Leave Blank)

Rating

_____ 1. Instills in me a feeling of confidence

_____ 2. Encourages me to express my ideas

_____ 3. Helps me realize my musical potential

_____ 4. Shows an interest in me as an individual

_____ 5. Gives clear directions regarding *what* to practice

_____ 6. Gives clear directions regarding *how* to practice

_____ 7. Uses analysis as part of the approach to music

_____ 8. Remembers what music and exercises were assigned

_____ 9. Makes clear both semester and long-range goals

_____ 10. Gives clear and concise explanations

_____ 11. Uses methods of instructions which provide insights into teaching and performing

_____ 12. Diagnoses and explains technical problems and prescribes ways to correct them

_____ 13. Stresses expressive performance

_____ 14. Comprehends different musical styles and performance practices

_____ 15. Knows the repertoire

_____ 16. Knows reference materials and encourages me to use them

_____ 17. Includes a mixture of criticism and correction, compliments and praise

_____ 18. Knows current professional musical activities in the field

_____ 19. Encourages a sense of responsibility in me

_____ 20. Sets a high standard by performance on the instrument/voice

_____ 21. Considering your previous response, how would you rate the overall effectiveness of this instructor

Please turn this sheet over and write additional comments concerning your experience in this studio.

INDIANA UNIVERSITY
STUDENT EVALUATION OF INSTRUCTION

I. Evaluation of Instruction

Please carefully evaluate the effectiveness of the teacher of this course. Place an "x" in ONE of the blanks under each of the major categories. Comments may be extended to the other side of the sheet.

KNOWLEDGE OF SUBJECT MATTER   _Comment_
_____ Exceedingly well informed
_____ Adequately informed
_____ Not well informed
_____ Very poorly informed

ATTITUDE TOWARD SUBJECT   _Comment_
_____ Enthusiastic, enjoys teaching subject
_____ Rather interested
_____ Only routine interest displayed
_____ Uninterested

ABILITY TO EXPLAIN   _Comment_
_____ Explanations clear and to the point
_____ Explanations usually adequate
_____ Explanations often inadequate
_____ Explanations absent or totally inadequate

SPEAKING ABILITY   _Comment_
_____ Voice and demeanor excellent
_____ Adequate or average
_____ Poor speaking distracting
_____ Poor speaking a serious handicap

ATTITUDE TOWARD STUDENTS   *Comment*
_____ Sympathetic, helpful, concerned
_____ Usually helpful and sympathetic
_____ Avoids individual contact, routine attitude
_____ Distant, cold, aloof

PERSONALITY   *Comment*
_____ Attractive personality; I would like to know him better
_____ Satisfactory personality
_____ Not an outgoing personality
_____ Personality conflict

TOLERANCE TO DISAGREEMENT   *Comment*
_____ Encourages and values reasonable disagreement
_____ Accepts disagreement fairly well
_____ Discourages disagreement
_____ Dogmatic, intolerant of disagreement

COMPARED TO ALL COLLEGE INSTRUCTORS YOU HAVE HAD, HOW WOULD YOU RATE THIS INSTRUCTOR AS A TEACHER?
_____ Outstanding
_____ Better than average
_____ Average
_____ Below Average
_____ Poor

IF YOU COULD CHOOSE BETWEEN THIS INSTRUCTOR AND OTHERS IN A FURTHER COURSE, HOW WOULD YOU RATE YOUR PRESENT INSTRUCTOR?
_____ Would prefer him/her to most teachers I have had at I.U.
_____ Would be very pleased to have him/her again.
_____ Would be satisfied to have him/her again.
_____ Would rather not have him/her again.
_____ Would not have him/her again under any circumstances.

THE REVERSE SIDE OF THIS SHEET MAY BE USED FOR FURTHER GENERAL COMMENTS

Do not sign name. Please indicate class standing_____
Major subject_____
Approximate accumulative average_____

APPENDIX B. INDIANA STATE UNIVERSITY DEPARTMENT CHAIR EVALUATION FORM

This form is to be used for the evaluation of *administrative* function only and should be a response to the accompanying job description.

5 is Superior; 4 is Excellent; 3 is Good; 2 is Fair; 1 is Unsatisfactory; N.A. is "not applicable" or "no information available" to make a judgment.

THE CHAIRPERSON	*Circle your response*
1. is willing and capable of working with superiors for the benefit of his unit and its members.	5 4 3 2 1 N.A.
2. observes democratic procedures where appropriate.	5 4 3 2 1 N.A.
3. is efficient.	5 4 3 2 1 N.A.
4. sets a good example for his faculty.	5 4 3 2 1 N.A.
5. encourages new approaches, programs, and courses.	5 4 3 2 1 N.A.
6. demonstrates high professional standards.	5 4 3 2 1 N.A.
7. exerts leadership for achieving departmental objectives.	5 4 3 2 1 N.A.
8. has flexibility to meet changing situations.	5 4 3 2 1 N.A.
9. keeps abreast of current activities in the discipline.	5 4 3 2 1 N.A.
10. seeks out, listens to and utilizes feedback.	5 4 3 2 1 N.A.
11. solves problems well within the unit.	5 4 3 2 1 N.A.
12. is accessible to faculty and students.	5 4 3 2 1 N.A.
13. is a capable mediator.	5 4 3 2 1 N.A.
14. is prompt in meeting deadlines for reports and other information.	5 4 3 2 1 N.A.
15. considers all sides of an issue.	5 4 3 2 1 N.A.
16. makes decisions which, overall, are to the advantage of the entire unit.	5 4 3 2 1 N.A.
17. assigns jobs to faculty in the area of their expertise.	5 4 3 2 1 N.A.
18. plans carefully before any action is taken.	5 4 3 2 1 N.A.
19. is honest in dealing with people.	5 4 3 2 1 N.A.

20. communicates well verbally and in writing.　　　　　5　4　3　2　1　N.A.

21. informs students and faculty in the unit of matters affecting them.　　　5　4　3　2　1　N.A.

22. acts deliberately as opposed to precipitously or out of anger.　　　5　4　3　2　1　N.A.

Please add other comments which you think would be helpful.

■

APPENDIX C. JOB DESCRIPTIONS
DEPARTMENT OF MUSIC CHAIRMAN
JOB DESCRIPTION

1. Chair meetings
   A. Faculty
   B. Calendar Committee
   C. Administrative Advisory Committee
   D. Contemporary Music Festival Committee
2. Serve on and consult with departmental committees as needed and requested
3. Serve as regular member of Contemporary Music Festival Committee and Recruitment Committee
4. Maintain active correspondence with:
   A. Prospective students and their parents
   B. Deans
   C. Alumni
   D. Persons in the profession of music
5. Budget
   A. Consult with coordinators and others with budgetary responsibilities
   B. Develop, submit, defend and administer departmental budget ($145,000 in '86–'87 exclusive of salaries)
6. Personnel
   A. Appoint search committees and supervise/advise/recommend to Dean faculty members to be employed
   B. Evaluate faculty members in tenure track positions and recommend action to the Dean
   C. Evaluate and make recommendations for promotion candidates
   D. Assign faculty—upon the recommendation of the Administrative Assistant and the Coordinators—to class and other assignments within the Department
   E. Supervise the hiring and work of secretaries
7. Nominate faculty and students to college- and university-wide committees
8. Supervise publicity/promotion activities in the Department
9. Supervise inventory of equipment/supplies
10. Represent the Department of Music at college, university, community and state events as well as at professional meetings
11. Prepare reports for the college, university and professional associations
12. Fund Raising
    A. Write grant proposals

B. Seek ways and means for raising funds for scholarships/lectureships

C. Solicit and process gifts to the Department

13. Supervise publication of *Music at ISU* and *Music Notes.*

14. Monitor curricular proposals

15. Supervise physical plant and the need for repairs and maintenance

JOB DESCRIPTION
PARMA PUBLIC SCHOOLS
PARMA, OHIO

Director of Music Education　　　　　　　　　　*3-01-112.04*

Job Analysis

Under the direction of the Assistant Superintendent-Instruction and in cooperation with the Director of Secondary School Studies and Elementary Consultants, the Director of Music Education will provide for continuous study, development, implementation, and evaluation of the music curriculum in grades kindergarten through twelve.

Duties and Responsibilities

The Director of Music shall:

Serve as a consultant to the Assistant Superintendent-Instruction and other instructional personnel on matters pertaining to the curriculum and to the efficient functioning of the division of instruction.

Serve as coordinator for his department for any revision of the curriculum and registration guides and other curriculum publications.

Serve as an ex-officio member of appropriate curriculum and textbook study committees.

Observe and appraise teachers in his department, particularly new teachers and teachers of new programs, for the purpose of improving instruction. Such appraisal of teachers shall conform to school policy and, when appropriate, will be in consultation with the various building principals.

Conduct general supervision within the department to insure compliance with the established curriculum, department and Parma Public Schools policies and regulations.

Assist the Assistant Superintendent-Personnel, when requested, in the recruitment, selection, and assignment of staff within the department.

Advise the Assistant Superintendent-Personnel relative to promotion, transfer, or dismissal of personnel within the department.

Assist other staff in the curriculum department in the orientation of new teachers.

Maintain close liaison with the Department Chairmen in the secondary schools.

Serve as a liaison person when necessary between the department and the various building administrations and between the department and the central administration.

Schedule and conduct meetings with Department Chairmen and teachers for the purpose of curriculum review and revision and accomplishing necessary administrative details.

In cooperation with the Coordinator of Instructional Media, work toward achieving, on a system-wide basis, satisfactory levels of instructional materials and equipment.

Coordinate the selection, procurement, distribution, inventory, and evaluation of instructional materials related to the department.

Coordinate budget requests of all secondary buildings for his department and make budgetary recommendations on a system-wide basis.

Assist in the editing and publishing of bulletins, guides, courses of study, and pamphlets related to his department.

Assist in the development and direction of a continuous program of inservice education for department personnel.

Aid in the preparation and/or presentation of adequate reports and materials to provide the Superintendent, Assistant Superintendent-Instruction, and Board of Education with summary information concerning the instructional program.

Assist in the formulation of system-wide curriculum policies and procedures.

Personal Qualifications

The Director of Music Education should:

Be well informed on current national curricular developments and trends and be able to communicate this information to the staff.

Be able to promote inservice growth by encouraging staff in a variety of ways to advance their professional competence.

Exhibit a willingness to attend and participate in workshops, conventions, and conferences which have a value to the department and to the school system.

Possess qualities of leadership and have demonstrated his ability to organize and administer.

Have demonstrated an ability to develop a good working relationship with teachers, supervisors, and administrators.

Professional Background

The professional preparation and experience should include:

Having attained at least the master's degree or equivalent in the field of music education with related work in the area of supervision of instruction.

A minimum of six years of successful teaching experience, preferably at both the elementary and secondary levels.

Having exhibited superior ability in previous teaching and/or supervisory assignments.

Evidence of continuous professional growth.

Possession of a valid supervisory certificate for the State of Ohio.

■

APPENDIX D. JOB ANNOUNCEMENT

DETROIT PUBLIC SCHOOLS

TITLE OF POSITION: Supervisor of Vocal Music in Elementary and Junior High School (10 Months)

CLOSING DATE FOR APPLICATIONS:

PLEASE GIVE APPROPRIATE PUBLICITY TO THE FOLLOWING SUPERVISORY OPENING

ANNOUNCEMENT OF SUPERVISORY OPENING

TITLE OF POSITION	Supervisor of Vocal Music in Elementary and Junior High School (10 Months)
SALARY	Minimum—_____ Increment—_____ Maximum—_____ A candidate with preparation beyond the Master's degree will be eligible for a salary differential above this maximum: (1) Master's degree plus 30 hours—$700; (2) Earned Doctorate—$1,000.
QUALIFICATIONS	*Education.* Candidates for this position must be able to satisfy the legal requirements for teaching in the State of _____ and must possess a minimum of a Master's degree from an accredited institution. Graduate work beyond the Master's degree is desirable. Preparation should include systematic study and competence in the following areas:

1. Specialization in the field of music education.
2. Knowledge of child growth, supervision, curriculum development, and education research.
3. Knowledge of current curriculum trends and teaching methodology in music education.
4. Exhibited ability in written and oral communications.
5. Demonstrated outstanding musical competency.

Experience. The candidate must present evidence of successful experience in several of the following areas:

1. Teaching of music education subjects.
2. Some experience in coordination or supervision would be desirable.
3. A minimum of five years of elementary or junior high school music classroom experience.
4. Participation in curriculum committees, workshops, and/or general school committees.
5. Preparation of written materials, bulletins, and teacher guides.
6. Knowledge of methods of interpreting an instructional program to citizen and professional groups through oral, written, or visual materials.
7. Sound personal relationships, professional leadership, and productive scholarship.
8. Evidence of participation in community affairs and a variety of school experiences, one of which must have been in a school located in a low socio-economic area.

DUTIES AND RESPONSIBILITIES

Serving as a staff member of the Office for Improvement of Instruction, Department of Music Education, the Supervisor will have the following duties and responsibilities:

1. Supervising the teaching of music in elementary and junior high schools, giving help to teachers when and where needed.
2. Conducting in-service programs, meetings, institutes, and workshops to improve the instructional program.
3. Preparing instructional guides, courses of study, bulletins, and teacher's guides for music education.
4. Assisting in the preparation of TV programs dealing with music education.
5. Assisting in the selection of basic and supplementary books for music education; preparing specifications for the procurement of equipment, materials, and supplies; and assisting in the preparation of budget recommendations.

6. Interpreting the music education program to region superintendents, principals, staff members, and the general public.
7. Assisting with the continuing evaluation and research of the effectiveness of the music education program.
8. Keeping abreast of the current literature and research in the field; helping to improve and strengthen the music program through creative innovative programs.

METHOD OF
APPLICATION

Candidates meeting these qualifications and wishing to accept the duties and responsibilities outlined should file a letter of application to_____

_____ ,
indicating their desire for consideration. Application forms and other related information will be mailed to those who apply.

CLOSING DATE FOR
APPLICATIONS

Letters of application for the position of Supervisor of Vocal Music will be accepted in the Office of Personnel through_____.

■

JOB ANNOUNCEMENT

ANNOUNCEMENT OF FULL-TIME POSITION

MUSIC EDUCATION: CHORAL/GENERAL MUSIC

POSITION: Teaching choral/general music methods for majors and methods for non-music majors; supervising choral/general music student teachers. Depending upon School needs and the qualifications of the candidate, additional responsibilities may include coordinating the music education area, and field experience program; teaching undergraduate and graduate courses in the music education area; serving on graduate thesis committees; conducting choral ensemble(s); creating and teaching a course(s) in Kodaly, Orff-Schulwerk, Suzuki, and/or Dalcroze.

QUALIFICATIONS: Master's Degree required, completed doctorate (or degree nearing completion) preferred; candidate should be able to provide evidence of scholarly research skills; must have an established record of successful classroom/rehearsal teaching experience in elementary and/or secondary education; college teaching experience is desirable.

INTERVIEW: Finalists will teach open classes; give a presentation in an area of their specialty and/or conduct a rehearsal; and meet with faculty, students, and administration.

RANK/SALARY: Assistant Professor; Salary Competitive.

APPOINTMENT: Nine-month academic year. *Appointment to commence January, 1990.*

ADDITIONAL INFORMATION: Located thirty miles south of Cleveland, The University of Akron, a state-supported educational institution of 27,000 students, is situated in a metropolitan area of one-half million people which supports a metropolitan symphony orchestra and chorus, a youth orchestra, a professional chamber ballet company, an art museum, chamber ensembles, distinguished area artists, musical theatre, community theatres and other cultural organizations. The School of Music is located in a $20 million performing arts complex.

The School of Music, with over 300 majors, offers a Bachelor of Music degree with options in performance, accompanying, music education, theory/composition, jazz studies and history/literature. A Master of Music degree has options in performance, accompanying, music education, theory, composition and history/literature.

The School of Music is a member of the National Association of Schools of Music.

APPLICATION PROCEDURE: Applicants should include a letter of application; a resume; several current letters of recommendation and other supportive materials.

APPLICATION DEADLINE: March 1, 1989

CONTACT: The University of Akron is an Equal Education and Employment Institution

■

APPENDIX E. A CHECKLIST FOR THE EXAMINATION OF CURRICULUM GUIDES IN MUSIC

I. Guide Construction and Revision Criteria

	YES	NO
(1) There is evidence that the following people have been consulted in the formulation of the guide:		
a. classroom teachers	____	____
b. music teachers	____	____
c. music supervisors	____	____
d. professional musicians	____	____
e. parents	____	____
f. children	____	____
g. administrators	____	____
[h. curriculum specialists]	____	____
(2) Provisions are made for further revision, statements are given citing the need for further revision, or that the guide is tentative, or that there is a permanent curriculum committee at work.	____	____
(3) Opportunity is provided for teachers using the guide to register opinions and suggestions about the value of the guide. A statement may be given encouraging teachers to give their opinions regarding the worth of the guide. A questionnaire sheet may be included in order to elicit the opinion of teachers.	____	____
(4) The guide is five years old or less.	____	____
No date given____		

II. Format and Physical Features   Outs Good Fair Poor Omit

    (1) The table of contents is printed in a manner so as to provide for easy location of topics, subjects, and appendixes.   —— —— —— —— ——

    (2) The guide lends itself to quick reference due to the use of such devices as tabs or different colored papers.   —— —— —— —— ——

    (3) The guide is attractive in appearance.   —— —— —— —— ——

    (4) The binding is durable.   —— —— —— —— ——

    (5) The guide is easy to read. It is printed in large type. It uses easy to understand language; plenty of space is employed.   —— —— —— —— ——

III. Curriculum Planning Procedures

    (1) A philosophy of education is stated in a clear, concise manner and generally reflects the ideals of a democratic society.   —— —— —— —— ——

    (2) The broad goals of music education are stated in a manner that reflects the current thinking of the music education profession:

      a. The guide stresses the need for development of aesthetic discrimination.   —— —— —— —— ——

      b. The study of non-Western music is recognized as being an important objective.   —— —— —— —— ——

      c. Twentieth-century composers and their music are given consideration in the guides.   —— —— —— —— ——

(3) The immediate goals of music are stated in terms of observable behaviors.   ___ ___ ___ ___ ___

(4) Varied activities are included to promote musical learning.   ___ ___ ___ ___ ___

(5) Learning experiences are included that further stated aims of music education.   ___ ___ ___ ___ ___

(6) Characteristics and needs of children are listed appropriate to the grade level the guide deals with.   ___ ___ ___ ___ ___

(7) The basic referents of the child, society, and subject matter are equally considered throughout the guide, either implicitly or explicitly.   ___ ___ ___ ___ ___

(8) Evaluation is stressed as an important concept, and the guide suggests many appropriate ways of evaluating.   ___ ___ ___ ___ ___

IV. Materials, Equipment, and Aids for Guide Users

Number of Guides including the Following Materials

(1) A representative list of professional materials is to be found in the guide. For example:

a. professional books   ___

b. music books for children   ___

c. publishers/ manufacturers   ___

d. music lists   ___

e. films   ___

f. curriculum guides   ___

g. records   ___

h. resources of musics of other cultures   ___

	Outs	Good	Fair	Poor	Omit
(2) Sample lesson plans and units are included in the guide.	——	——	——	——	——
(3) In the guide, suggestions are given as to the time allotted for instruction.	——	——	——	——	——
(4) Space requirements for music instruction are stated.	——	——	——	——	——
(5) A basic equipment list is included in the guides.	——	——	——	——	——

Source: Philip McClintock, "An Examination of Curriculum Guides in Music with Reference to Principles of Curriculum Planning." (Ph.D. diss.) Reprinted by permission.

■

APPENDIX F. EVALUATION SHEET FOR MINORITY TREATMENT IN THE CURRICULA

Following is a list of criteria on which educators can evaluate most if not all curriculum materials. It was prepared jointly by the Office for Improvement of Instruction and the Division of School-Community Relations. (This topic was a chief concern of the October 4–6 Waldenwoods Workshop on "Racism in Textbooks.")

While not all 15 criteria will be applicable in every case, the questions raised by them do focus upon basic considerations in the materials that we use in the education of our children.

Do the curriculum materials—

1. Give evidence on the part of writers, artists, and editors of a sensitivity to prejudice, to stereotypes, and to the use of offensive materials?

2. Suggest, by omission or commission, or by over-emphasis or under-emphasis, that any racial, religious, or ethnic segment of our population is more or less worthy, more or less capable, more or less important in the mainstream of American life?

3. Provide abundant, but fair and well-balanced, recognition of male and female children and adults of Negro and other minority groups by placing them in positions of leadership and centrality?

4. Exhibit fine and worthy examples of mature American types from minority as well as majority groups in art and science, in history and literature, and in all other areas of life and culture?

5. Present a significant number of instances of fully integrated human groupings and settings to indicate equal status and non-segregated social relationships?

6. Make clearly apparent in illustrations the group representation of individuals—Caucasian, Afro-American, Indian, Chinese, Mexican-American, etc.—and not seek to avoid identification by such means as smudging some color over Caucasian facial features?

7. Delineate life in contemporary urban environments, as well as in rural or suburban environments, so that today's city child can also find significant identification for himself, his problems, and his potential for life, liberty, and the pursuit of happiness?

8. Portray racial, religious, and ethnic groups, with their similarities and differences, in such a way as to build positive images?

9. Emphasize the multi-cultural character of our nation as having unique and special value which we must esteem and treasure?

10. Assist students to recognize clearly and to accept the basic similarities among all members of the human race, and the unique-

ness and worth of every single individual, regardless of race, religion, or socio-economic background?

11. Help students appreciate the many important contributions to our civilization made by members of the various human groups, emphasizing that every human group has its list of achievers, thinkers, writers, artists, scientists, builders, and statesmen?

12. Supply an accurate and sound balance in the matter of historical perspective, making it perfectly clear that all racial, religious, and ethnic groups have mixed heritages, which can well serve as sources of both group pride and group humility?

13. Clarify or present factually the historical and contemporary forces and conditions which have operated in the past, and which continue to operate to the disadvantage of minority groups?

14. Analyze intergroup tension and conflict fairly, frankly, objectively, and with emphasis upon resolving our social problems in a spirit of fully implementing democratic values and goals in order to achieve the American dream for all Americans?

15. Seek to motivate students to examine their own attitudes and behaviors, and to comprehend their own duties and responsibilities as citizens in a pluralistic democracy—to demand freedom and justice and equal opportunity for every individual and for every group?

Instructions for Completion of Evaluation of Music Texts:

Most of the questions on the evaluation sheet are self-explanatory; however, some questions may be clarified by additional instructions. The following are offered as explanations of some of the instructions on the form.

#2. Include *only* those compositions which the *text* identifies as specifically part of the ethnic culture. Do not include those which you may know are part of the ethnic culture listed, but the text does not identify as such.

#3 & #4. Under sex, determine as closely as possible by the composer's/musician's/performer/s name, biographical notes, etc., whether the person is male or female and mark the appropriate category. If the sex is undeterminable by these methods, mark the "unknown" category. Under race, include only those composers/musicians/performers which the text identifies as belonging to a particular racial or ethnic group. If the text does not identify the composer/musician/performer as a member of a particular racial or ethnic group, indicate this by marking the "unknown" column.

#5. Determine by the size of the person in the illustration, the activity of the person, number of persons of each sex in the illustration, etc., whether a male or female is primarily featured and mark the appropriate category. If both are equally featured, mark the "both" category. Under race, use the above criteria to determine which race is primarily featured. If two or more races are equally featured, mark the "equally integrated" category. If the race is unidentifiable, mark this category.

#7, #8, #9. Indicate page numbers for each example cited. If there are examples in the text which you feel are pertinent to the evaluation, but are not discussed in the three questions, feel free to include these examples at the end of the evaluation form.

Source: "The Detroit Schools," October 29, 1968. Reprinted by permission.

■

APPENDIX G. EVALUATION SHEET FOR MUSIC TEXTS

Book Title _____   Grade Level _____
Publisher _____   Publication Date _____
Date of Review _____   Name of Reviewer _____
                                Position of Reviewer _____

1. Total number of songs/musical compositions _____
2. Indicate the total number of musical compositions which are specifically identified as part of the ethnic culture listed:
   Afro-American _____
   Latin American _____
3. Indicate the number of composers represented in the text in the following categories:
   Sex:
   Male _____
   Female _____
   Unknown _____
   Race:
   White _____
   Black _____
   Spanish-Surnamed American _____
   Other _____
   Unidentified _____
4. Indicate the number of musicians/performers represented in the texts in the following categories:
   Sex:
   Male _____
   Female _____
   Both _____
   Race:
   White _____
   Black _____
   Spanish-Surnamed American _____
   Other _____
   Unidentified _____
5. Indicate the number of illustrations featuring:
   Sex:
   Male _____
   Female _____
   Both _____
   Race:
   White _____
   Black _____
   Spanish-Surnamed American _____

Other _____

Equally Integrated _____

Unidentified _____

6. If biographical sketches of performers/musicians/composers are included in the text, indicate the number of the sketches which feature:

Sex:

Male _____

Female _____

Race:

White _____

Black _____

Spanish-Surnamed American _____

Other _____

Unidentified _____

7. Does the text portray Blacks, Mexican Americans, and women in such a way as to build positive images, or are the images portrayed stereotypically? Support your answer with specific examples. Discuss each group separately.

8. Do the illustrations in the text present a significant number of instances of fully integrated human groupings and settings to indicate equal status and non-segregated social relationships? Support your answer with specific examples and page numbers.

9. Does the text suggest by omission or commission, or by overemphasis or underemphasis, that any men or women, whites, blacks, or Mexican Americans are more or less worthy, or more or less important in the mainstream of American life? Support your answer with specific examples. Discuss each group separately.

■

APPENDIX H. SPECIFICATIONS FOR INSTRUMENT PURCHASES

The various instrument manufacturers cited here are used merely as examples of how one school system is exacting in determining its specifications. They do not represent any endorsement or recommendation of a particular product. Each school must determine for itself the type of instrument that it feels will satisfy the educational standard that it sets for itself.

Piccolo, C and D♭ (High School)

New, Boehm system with covered holes and closed G-sharp. Complete with standard plush-lined Keratol covered case (or equal), including swab. Case must be standard equipment as supplied by manufacturer for the instrument. Instrument and case to be delivered in perfect condition, with key action, intonation, and general playing response of the instrument *subject to the approval of the purchaser.* Instrument must be engraved with phrase "_____ BD. OF ED." on main body of instrument. Letters to be ⅛" to 3/16" high.

Brand	No.

Or Approved Equal

Piccolo, C (Junior High and Elementary)

New, student-line quality, closed G-sharp, nickel-silver alloy body, silver-plated. Complete with swab, tuning rod, and standard plush or velvet-lined Keratol covered case (or equal). Case must be standard equipment as supplied by manufacturer for the instrument. Instrument and case to be delivered in perfect condition, with key action, intonation, and general playing response of the instrument *subject to the approval of the purchaser.* Instrument must be engraved with phrase "_____ BD. OF ED." on the back of the body. Letters to be 3/16" to ¼" high.

Brand	No.

Brand	No.

Or Approved Equal

Flute (Junior High and Elementary)

New, student-line quality, nickel-silver alloy body, silver-plated. Covered holes, closed G-sharp. Complete with swab and standard plush-lined Keratol cover case (or equal). Case must be standard equipment as supplied by manufacturer for the instrument. Instrument and case to be delivered in perfect condition, with key action, intonation, and general playing response of the instrument *subject to the approval of the purchaser.* Instrument must be engraved with phrase "_____ BD. OF ED." on back of the body. Letters to be ³⁄₁₆" to ¼" high.

Brand	No.

Brand	No.

Or Approved Equal

Clarinet, B♭ (Wood) (High School)

New, wood, Boehm system, 17 keys, 6 rings, complete with ligature, cap, mouthpiece, three Ricco or Symmetricut reeds, #2 strength, lyre, and French-style case. 2 barrels: 1 standard and 1–4 mm shorter. Case must be standard equipment as supplied by manufacturer for the instrument. Instrument and case to be delivered in perfect condition, with key action, intonation, and general playing response of the mouthpiece and instrument *subject to the approval of the purchaser.* Instrument to be engraved with phrase "_____ BD. OF ED." on back of both joints. Letters to be ³⁄₁₆" to ¼" high.

Brand	No.

Brand	No.

Or Approved Equal

Clarinet, B♭ (Wood or Plastic) (Junior High)

New, student-line quality, 17 keys, 6 rings, complete with ligature, cap, Selmer HS Star mouthpiece, lyre, and French-style case. Case must be standard equipment as supplied by manufacturer for the instrument. Instrument and case to be delivered in perfect condition, with key action, intonation, and general playing response of the mouthpiece and instrument *subject to the approval of the purchaser.* Instrument must be engraved with phrase "_____ BD. OF ED." on back of both joints. Letters to be ³⁄₁₆" to ¼" high.

| _____ | _____ |
| Brand | No. |

| _____ | _____ |
| Brand | No. |

Or Approved Equal

Clarinet, B♭ (Junior High and Elementary)

New, student-line quality, metal, silver, nickel-silver, or nickel-plated finish, 17 keys, 6 rings, complete with ligature, cap, mouthpiece, lyre, and Keratol covered plywood, plush-lined case (or equal). Case must be standard equipment as supplied by manufacturer for the instrument. Instrument and case to be delivered in perfect condition, with key action, intonation, and general playing response of the mouthpiece and instrument *subject to the approval of the purchaser.* Instrument must be engraved with phrase "_____ BD. OF ED." on back of the body. Letters to be ³⁄₁₆" to ¼" high.

| _____ | _____ |
| Brand | No. |

| _____ | _____ |
| Brand | No. |

Or Approved Equal

Oboes (High School)

New, wood, full conservatory system, single-action octave keys (not automatic), covered holes, F-resonance key, complete with French-style plush-lined case including reed case, three Meeson reeds, medium strength, and one box of joint grease. Case must be standard equipment as supplied by manufacturer for the instrument. Instrument and general playing response of the instrument *subject to the approval of the purchaser.* Instrument to be engraved with phrase "_____ BD. OF ED." on back of both joints. Letters to be ³⁄₁₆" to ¼" high.

_____ _____

Brand   No.

_____ _____

Brand   No.

Or Approved Equal

Oboe *(Junior High)*

New, student-line quality, full conservatory system, open or closed tone holes, single-action octave key, F-resonance key. Must have low "B♭" key. Complete with French-style case including reed case, three Meeson reeds, joint grease, and cleaning feather. Case must be standard equipment as supplied by manufacturer for the instrument. Instrument and case to be delivered in perfect condition, with key action, intonation, and general playing response of the instrument *subject to the approval of the purchaser.* Instrument must be engraved with phrase "_____ BD. OF ED." on the back of the body. Letters to be ³⁄₁₆" to ¼" high.

_____ _____

Brand   No.

_____ _____

Brand   No.

Or Approved Equal

Bassoon *(High School)*

New, wood, full Heckel system with whisper key, F-sharp trill key, and the following roller keys: low F to A-flat, low D-sharp to C-sharp. Complete with three bocals (corked, not wound), reed case, three Meeson reeds, soft strength, joint grease, swab, and French fitted plush-lined leather, Keratol covered case (or equal), with compartments for bocals and accessories. Case must be standard equipment as supplied by manufacturer for the instrument. Instrument and case to be delivered in perfect condition, with key action, intonation, and general playing response of the instrument *subject to the approval of the purchaser.* Instrument must be engraved with phrase "_____ BD. OF ED." on boot joint. Letters to be ³⁄₁₆" to ¼" high.

Brand	No.

Brand	No.

Or Approved Equal

Bassoon (Junior High and Elementary)

New, student-line quality, full Heckel system with whisper key, F-sharp trill key, and the following roller keys: low F to A-flat, low D-sharp to C-sharp. Complete with three bocals (corked, not wound), reed case, three reeds, joint grease, swab, and French fitted plush-lined leather, Keratol covered case (or equal), with compartments for bocals and accessories. Case must be standard equipment as supplied by manufacturer for the instrument. Instrument and case to be delivered in perfect condition, with key action, intonation, and general playing response of the instrument *subject to the approval of the purchaser.* Instrument to be engraved with phrase " BD. OF ED." on both wing and tenon joints. Letters to be ³⁄₁₆" to ¼" high.

Brand	No.

Brand	No.

Or Approved Equal

Saxophone, E♭ Alto (High School)

New, satin finish, silver plate, complete with mouthpiece, cap, ligature, three Ricco or Symmetricut reeds, #2 strength, lyre, leather strap, and standard plush-lined Keratol covered case (or equal). Case must be standard equipment as supplied by manufacturer for the instrument. Instrument and case to be delivered in perfect condition, with key action, intonation, and general playing response of the instrument and mouthpiece *subject to the approval of the purchaser.* Instrument to be engraved with phrase "_____ BD. OF ED." on back of body. Letters to be ³⁄₁₆" to ¼" high.

_____ _____

    Brand   No.

_____ _____

    Brand   No.

Or Approved Equal

Saxophone, E♭ Alto (Junior High and Elementary)

New student-line quality, satin silver finish, silver bell, complete with mouthpiece, three reeds, cap, ligature, lyre, leather strap, and standard plush-lined Keratol covered case (or equal). Case must be standard equipment as supplied by manufacturer for the instrument. Instrument and case to be delivered in perfect condition, with key action, intonation, and general playing response of the instrument *subject to the approval of the purchaser.* Instrument to be engraved with phrase "_____ BD. OF ED." on the bell section. Letters to be ³⁄₁₆" to ¼" high.

_____ _____

    Brand   No.

_____ _____

    Brand   No.

Or Approved Equal

Trumpet, B♭ (High School)

New, satin silver, silver bell, complete with _____ mouthpiece, lyre, bottle of valve oil, and standard plush-lined Keratol covered case (or equal). Case must be standard equipment as supplied by manufacturer for the instrument. Instrument and case to be delivered in perfect condition, with valve action, intonation, and general playing response of the instrument *subject to the approval of the purchaser.* Instrument to be engraved with phrase "_____ BD. OF ED." on back of bell. Letters to be ³⁄₁₆" to ¼" high.

Brand   No.

Brand   No.

Or Approved Equal

Trumpet, B♭ (Junior High and Elementary)

New, student-line quality, satin silver, silver bell, complete with mouthpiece, lyre, bottle of valve oil, and standard plush-lined Keratol covered case (or equal). Case must be standard equipment as supplied by manufacturer for the instrument. Instrument and case to be delivered in perfect condition, with valve action, intonation, and general playing response of the instrument *subject to the approval of the purchaser.* Instrument to be engraved with phrase "_____ BD. OF ED." on back of bell. Letters to be 3/16" to 1/4" high.

Brand   No.

Brand   No.

Or Approved Equal

Cornet, B♭ (High School)

New, satin silver, silver bell, complete with _____ mouthpiece, lyre, bottle of valve oil, and standard plush-lined Keratol covered case (or equal). Case must be standard equipment as supplied by manufacturer for the instrument. Instrument and case to be delivered in perfect condition, with valve action, intonation, and general playing response of the instrument *subject to the approval of the purchaser.* Instrument to be engraved with phrase "_____ BD. OF ED." on back of bell. Letters to be 3/16" to 1/4" high.

Brand   No.

Brand   No.

Or Approved Equal

Cornet, B♭ (Junior High and Elementary)

New, student-line quality, satin silver plate, silver bell, complete with mouthpiece, lyre, bottle of valve oil, and standard plush-lined Keratol covered case (or equal). Case must be standard equipment as supplied by manufacturer for the instrument. Instrument and case to be delivered in perfect condition, with valve action, intonation, and general playing response of the instrument *subject to the approval of the purchaser.* Instrument to be engraved with phrase "_____ BD. OF ED." on bell. Letters to be ³⁄₁₆" to ¼" high.

| _____ | _____ |
| Brand | No. |

| _____ | _____ |
| Brand | No. |

Or Approved Equal

French Horn (Double) (High School)

New, nickel silver, complete with mouthpiece, lyre, and standard plush-lined Keratol covered case (or equal). Case must be standard equipment as supplied by manufacturer for the instrument. Instrument and case to be delivered in perfect condition, with valve action, intonation, and general playing response of the instrument *subject to the approval of the purchaser.* Instrument to be engraved with phrase "_____ BD. OF ED." on bell. Letters to be ³⁄₁₆" to ¼" high.

| _____ | _____ |
| Brand | No. |

| _____ | _____ |
| Brand | No. |

Or Approved Equal

French Horn in F (Junior High and Elementary)

New, student-line quality, gold, or clear lacquer, complete with mouthpiece, lyre, and standard plush-lined Keratol covered case (or equal). Case must be standard equipment as supplied by manufacturer for the instrument. Instrument and case to be delivered in perfect condition, with valve action, intonation, and general playing response of the instrument *subject to the approval of the purchaser.* Instrument to be engraved with phrase "_____ BD. OF ED." on bell. Letters to be ³⁄₁₆″ to ¼″ high.

Brand	No.

Brand	No.

Or Approved Equal

Trombone, Tenor (Medium Bore) (Junior High and Elementary)

New, student-line quality, satin silver finish, silver bell, complete with mouthpiece, lyre, bottle of oil, and standard plush-lined Keratol covered case (or equal). Case must be standard equipment as supplied by manufacturer for the instrument. Instrument and case to be delivered in perfect condition, with slide action, intonation, and general playing response of the instrument *subject to the approval of the purchaser.* Instrument to be engraved with phrase "_____ BD. OF ED." on bell. Letters to be ³⁄₁₆″ to ¼″ high.

Brand	No.

Brand	No.

Or Approved Equal

Trombone, Tenor (High School)

New, satin silver finish with silver bell, complete with _____ mouthpiece, lyre, bottle of slide oil, and standard plush-lined Keratol covered case (or equal). Case must be standard equipment as supplied by manufacturer for the instrument. Instrument and case to be delivered in perfect condition, with slide action, intonation, and general playing response of the instrument *subject to the approval of the purchaser.* Instrument to be engraved with phrase "_____ BD. OF ED." on back of bell. Letters to be ³⁄₁₆″ to ¼″ high.

Brand	No.

Brand	No.

Or Approved Equal

Baritone (High School)

New, euphonium-type single bell, satin silver finish, silver bell, complete with _____ mouthpiece, lyre, bottle of valve oil, and standard plush-lined Keratol covered case (or equal). Case must be standard equipment as supplied by manufacturer for the instrument. Instrument and case to be delivered in perfect condition, with valve action, intonation, and general playing response of the instrument *subject to the approval of the purchaser.*

Brand	No.

Brand	No.

Or Approved Equal

Baritone (Junior High and Elementary)

New, student-line quality, euphonium-type single bell, satin silver finish, silver bell, complete with mouthpiece, lyre, bottle of valve oil, and standard plush-lined Keratol covered case (or equal). Case must be standard equipment as supplied by manufacturer for the instrument. Instrument and case to be delivered in perfect condition, with valve action, intonation, and general playing response of the instrument *subject to the approval of the purchaser.* Instrument must be engraved with phrase "_____ BD. OF ED." on bell joint of instrument. Letters to be ³⁄₁₆″ to ¼″ high.

Brand	No.

Brand	No.

Or Approved Equal

Tuba BB♭ Upright (High School)

New, gold, or clear lacquer, complete with mouthpiece and lyre, and bottle of valve oil. Instrument to be delivered in perfect condition, with valve action, intonation, and general playing response of the instrument *subject to the approval of the purchaser.* Instrument to be engraved with phrase "_____ BD. OF ED." on main body of instrument. Letters to be ³⁄₁₆" to ¼" high.

Brand	No.

Brand	No.

Or Approved Equal

Tuba BB♭ Upright (Small Size) (Junior High and Elementary)

New, student-line quality, gold, or clear lacquer or silver finish, complete with mouthpiece and lyre. Instrument to be delivered in perfect condition, with valve action, intonation, and general playing response of the instrument *subject to the approval of the purchaser.* Instrument to be engraved with phrase "_____ BD. OF ED." on main body of instrument. Letters to be ³⁄₁₆" to ¼" high.

Brand	No.

Brand	No.

Or Approved Equal

Snare Drum, Orchestra (High School)

New, separate tensions, self-aligning tension rods, full-flanged counter hoops. All metal shell, chrome-plated. Wire snares, calfskin heads. Complete with macintosh zipper cover. Instrument to be delivered in perfect condition, and *subject to the approval of the purchaser.* Instrument to be engraved with phrase "_____ BD. OF ED." near vent hole. Letters to be ³⁄₁₆" to ¼" high.

Brand	No.

Brand	No.

Or Approved Equal

Snare Drum, Orchestra (5″ × 14″) (Junior High and Elementary)

New, student-line quality, separate tension, self-aligning tension rods, full-flanged counter hoops, collar screw must go through counter hoops, metal shell, nickel-plated hardware, wire snares, plastic heads. Complete with mackintosh zipper cover. To be delivered in perfect condition, and *subject to the approval of the purchaser.* Instrument to be engraved with phrase "_____ BD. OF ED." near vent hole. Letters to be ³⁄₁₆″ to ¼″ high.

Brand	No.

Brand	No.

Or Approved Equal

Bass Drum, Concert (High School)

New, size _____, separate tension, wood shell, white lacquer finish (or school color upon request), chrome plated hardware, calf skin heads. Complete with double end beater, web sling, and mackintosh waterproof zipper cover. To be delivered in perfect condition and *subject to the approval of the purchaser.* Instrument to be engraved with phrase "_____ BD. OF ED." near vent hole. Letters to be ³⁄₁₆″ to ¼″ high.

Brand	No.

Brand	No.

Or Approved Equal

Bass Drum, Concert (Junior High and Elementary)

New, student-line quality, size ____, separate tension, wood shell, white lacquer finish, chrome-plated hardware, plastic heads. Complete with double end beater, web sling, and mackintosh waterproof zipper cover. To be delivered in perfect condition and *subject to the approval of the purchaser*. Instrument to be engraved with phrase "____ BD. of ED." near vent hole. Letters to be ³⁄₁₆″ to ¼″ high.

Brand	No.

Brand	No.

Or Approved Equal

Timpani (Pedal-Tuned) (High School)

New, one pair (25″ and 28″ kettles) complete with two pairs standard professional felt mallets, 2 fiber head protectors, and short-skirt mackintosh cover for each timpani. All equipment to be delivered in perfect condition, with playing response of the instrument *subject to the approval of the purchaser*. Bowls to be engraved with phrase "____ BD. OF ED." Letters to be ³⁄₁₆″ to ¼″ high.

Brand	No.

Brand	No.

Or Approved Equal

Timpani (Machine-Tuned, 25″ and 28″) (Junior High)

New, machine-tuned kettles, heavy-grade copper fiberglass. Chrome-plated hardware and legs, telescoping. Complete with head covers and professional felt beaters. Equipment to be delivered in perfect condition, *subject to the approval of the purchaser*. Bowls to be engraved with phrase "____ BD. OF ED." Letters to be ³⁄₁₆″ to ¼″ high.

| _____ | _____ |
| Brand | No. |

| _____ | _____ |
| Brand | No. |

Or Approved Equal

Cymbals (High School)

Size _____ —High School   Weight: Medium
                                                    Medium-heavy
                                                    Heavy

New, one pair, genuine Avedis Zildjian matched cymbals, complete with leather strap and pad-type holders. To be delivered in perfect condition and *subject to the approval of the purchaser.*

Cymbals (Junior High)

Size_____

New, one pair, medium-heavy weight, genuine Avedis Zildjian matched cymbals, complete with strap and pad-type holders. To be delivered in perfect condition and *subject to the approval of the purchaser.*

See CYMBALS (High School) regarding straps.

Cymbals (Elementary)

Size_____

New, one pair, medium weight, Avedis Zildjian matched cymbals, complete with wood handle holder with adjustable strap. To be delivered in perfect condition and *subject to the approval of the purchaser.*

Violin Specifications (High School), 4/4 Size Only

Violin   To consist of: New violin. American-made thermo-
Outfits: plastic shaped plush-lined case. Fiberglass bow.
             Chinrest. Extra set of strings. Cake of rosin.
Violin: Made of properly loft-seasoned curly maple back and
             sides. Medium grain spruce top, Equipped with full
             genuine ebony fittings, correctly graduated finger-
             board, chinrest, _____ (type) pegs, glued-in

bass bar. Body to have four solid corner blocks. Instrument expertly adjusted. Fingerboard "dressed" in USA with proper curvature and string heights. Fingerboard nut of correct height and properly spaced. Soundpost fitted in the United States. Hand-rubbed oil-finished neck. No varnish on neck handle. Violin varnished with soft textured varnish. To be equipped with strings as listed below, with adjusters on E and A strings. One cake of rosin to be included. All instruments with label inside showing model number, serial number, date of adjustment in USA, certifying adjustment to MENC specifications. Instrument must be engraved with the phrase "＿＿ BD. OF ED."on scroll. Letters to be ³⁄₁₆" to ¼" high.

Acceptable Brands:

＿＿＿＿＿＿	＿＿＿＿
Brand	No.

＿＿＿＿＿＿	＿＿＿＿
Brand	No.

Violin Specifications (Junior High and Elementary), 1/2, 3/4, 4/4 sizes

Violin Outfits:
To consist of: New violin. American-made thermoplastic shaped plush-lined case. Fiberglass bow. Chinrest. Extra set of strings. Cake of rosin.

Violin:
Made of properly loft-seasoned curly maple back and sides. Medium grain spruce top. Equipped with full genuine ebony fittings, correctly graduated fingerboard, chinrest, ＿＿ (type) pegs, glued-in bass bar. Body to have four solid corner blocks. Instrument expertly adjusted. Fingerboard "dressed" in USA with proper curvature and string heights. Fingerboard nut of correct height and properly spaced. Soundpost fitted in the United States. Hand-rubbed oil-finished neck. No varnish on neck handle. Violin varnished with soft textured varnish. To be equipped with strings as listed below, with adjusters on E and A strings. One cake of ＿＿ rosin to be included. All instruments with label inside showing model number, serial number, date of adjustment in USA, certi-

fying adjustment to MENC specifications. Instrument must be engraved with the phrase "_____ BD. OF ED."on scroll. Letters to be $\frac{3}{16}$" to $\frac{1}{4}$" high.

Acceptable Brands

Brand	No.

Brand	No.

Chinrest: _____ model, deep cup, rubbed.

Bow: Fiberglass bow with correct resilience, firmness, and proper weight and balance. Guaranteed not to warp. Stick should have metal reinforcing core. Genuine wire winding soldered at both ends with genuine leather thumb grip. Screw to turn freely. Bow must be dusted and rosined, ready to play.

Acceptable Brands:

Brand	No.

Case: Strong, durable thermoplastic vacuum form-fitted, with snug-fitting aluminum valance. Two bow pockets and at least one enclosed compartment. Equipped with nickel long-last latches—sturdy nickel bumbers, three heavy-type hinges. Heat-resisting, waterproof. Plush-lined interior. Bow clips may not be plastic. Case must be engraved with phrase "_____ BD. OF ED."

Acceptable Brands:

Brand	No.

Brand	No.

Or Approved Equal

Strings: E— _____ _____
                          Brand   No.

         A— _____ _____
                          Brand   No.

         D— _____ _____
                          Brand   No.

         G— _____ _____
                          Brand   No.

Instrument and bow must be expertly shop adjusted and assembled ready to play with bridge set up.

Viola Specifications (High School)

Viola Outfit:
To consist of: New viola made of properly loft-seasoned curly maple back and sides. Medium grain spruce top. American-made thermoplastic shaped plush-lined case. Fiberglass bow. Chinrest. Cake of rosin.

Viola:
New, imported German model, made to correct size measurements. Equipped with genuine high-grade ebony fittings. Fingerboard correctly graduated according to MENC specifications with proper curvature and string height. Fingerboard nut of correct height and properly spaced. Four solid corner blocks. Lower and upper rib edges fully lined. Glued-in bass bar. New soundpost fitted in USA. Equipped with _____ pegs. Hand-rubbed oil-finished neck. No varnish on neck handle. Viola varnished with soft textured varnish. To be equipped with chinrest of proper size. To be equipped with strings as listed below. All instruments with label inside showing model number, serial number, date of adjustment in USA, certifying adjustment to MENC specifications. Stradivarius imported model. Instrument must be engraved with the phrase "_____ BD. OF ED."on the scroll. Letters to be ³⁄₁₆″ to ¼″ high.

Acceptable Brands:
High School—15½″, 16″, 16½″ (to be specified)

_____ _____
Brand   No.

_____ _____
Brand   No.

Bow: Fiberglass bow with correct resilience, firmness, and proper weight and balance. Guaranteed not to warp. Stick should have metal reinforcing core. Genuine wire winging soldered at both ends with genuine leather thumb grip. Screw to turn freely. Bow must be dusted and rosined, ready to play. Natural hair for High School–line outfits.

Acceptable Brands:

_____   _____

    Brand   No.

Case: Strong durable thermoplastic vacuum form-fitted, with snug-fitting aluminum valance. Two bow pockets and at least one enclosed compartment. Equipped with nickel long-lasting latches—sturdy nickel bumbers, three heavy-type hinges. Heat-resisting, waterproof. Plush-lined interior.

Acceptable Brands:

_____   _____

    Brand   No.

or equal

        or

Three-ply veneer Keratol or equivalent cover. Silk plush-lined. Two bow pockets with ribbons, at least one accessory pocket. No plastic bow clips. Three sturdy hinges. Nickel bumpers and heavy-duty locks and hardware. Case must be engraved with phrase "_____ BD. OF ED."

Acceptable Brands:

_____   _____

    Brand   No.

_____   _____

    Brand   No.

Strings:

E— _____ _____
       Brand   No.

A— _____ _____
       Brand   No.

D— _____ _____
       Brand   No.

G— _____ _____
       Brand   No.

Adjusters on A and D strings. Instrument and bow must be expertly shop-adjusted and -assembled ready to play with bridge set up.

Viola Specifications (Junior High and Elementary)

Viola Outfit:

To consist of: New viola made of properly loft-seasoned curly maple back and sides. Medium grain spruce top. American-made thermoplastic shaped plush-lined case. Fiberglass bow. Chinrest. Cake of _____ rosin.

Viola:

New imported German model made to correct size measurements. Equipped with genuine high-grade ebony fittings. Fingerboard correctly graduated according to MENC specifications with proper curvature and string height. Fingerboard nut of correct height and properly spaced. Four solid corner blocks. Lower and upper rib edges fully lined. Glued-in bass bar. New soundpost fitted in USA. Equipped with _____ pegs. Hand-rubbed oil-finished neck. No varnish on neck handle. Viola varnished with soft textured varnish. To be equipped with chinrest of proper size. To be equipped with strings as listed below. All instruments with label inside showing model number, serial number, date of adjustment in USA, certifying adjustment to MENC specifications. Stradivarius imported model. Instrument must be engraved with the phrase "_____ BD. OF ED." on the scroll. Letters to be ³⁄₁₆" to ¼" high.
Acceptable Brands:

13"— _____ _____
        Brand   No.

14"— _____ _____
        Brand   No.

15"— _____ _____
        Brand   No.

Bow:

Fiberglass bow with correct resilience, firmness, and proper weight and balance. Guaranteed not to warp. Stick should have metal reinforcing core. Genuine wire winding soldered at both ends with genuine leather thumb grip. Screw to turn freely. Bow must be dusted and rosined, ready to play.

Acceptable Brands:

_____ _____
　　　Brand　　　　No.

Case:

Strong, durable thermoplastic vacuum form-fitted, with snug-fitting aluminum valance. Two bow pockets and at least one enclosed compartment. Equipped with nickel long-lasting latches, sturdy nickel bumpers, three heavy-type hinges. Heat-resisting, waterproof. Plush-lined interior.

Acceptable Brands:

_____ _____
　　　Brand　　　　No.

or

Three-ply veneer Keratol or equivalent cover. Flannel-lined. Two bow pockets with ribbons, at least one accessory pocket. No plastic bow clips. Three sturdy hinges. Nickel bumbers and heavy-duty locks and hardware. Case must be engraved with phrase "_____ BD. OF ED."

Acceptable Brands:

15"— _____ _____
　　　　　Brand　　　　No.

_____ _____
　　　Brand　　　　No.

14"— _____ _____
　　　　　Brand　　　　No.

_____ _____
　　　Brand　　　　No.

13"— _____ _____
　　　　　Brand　　　　No.

_____ _____
　　　Brand　　　　No.

_____ _____
　　　Brand　　　　No.

Strings: 13"— _____   _____
                          Brand   No.

             14"— _____   _____
                          Brand   No.

             15"— _____   _____
                          Brand   No.

             A— _____   _____
                          Brand   No.

             D— _____   _____
                          Brand   No.

             G— _____   _____
                          Brand   No.

             C— _____   _____
                          Brand   No.

Adjusters on all four strings. Instrument and bow must be expertly shop-adjusted and -assembled ready to play with bridge set up.

Cello Specifications (High School Line), 4/4 Size Only

Cello Outfit: To consist of: Instrument, bow, bag, and Rock-stop endpin rest. Cake of _____ rosin, mute, tuner.

Cello: Imported Stradivarius model. Two-piece properly loft-seasoned curly maple back. Medium-grain spruce top. Genuine ebony fittings of high grade. Fingerboard "dressed" and correctly graduated according to MENC specifications, with proper curvature and string height. Fingerboard nut of correct height and properly spaced. Four solid corner blocks. Glued-in bass bar. New soundpost fitted in USA. Lower and upper rib edges fully lined. Equipped with _____ pegs. With adjustable endpin, nickel-plated steel rod and rubber tip. Endpin rest. Hand-rubbed oil-finished neck. No varnish on neck handle. Soft textured varnish. To be equipped with strings listed below. Instrument must be engraved with phrase "_____ BD. OF ED."on scroll. Letters to be ³⁄₁₆" to ¼" high.

Acceptable Brands:

_____	_____
Brand	No.

or Accepted Equal

Bow:
Fiberglass with correct resilience and proper weight, firmness and balance. Guaranteed not to warp. Equipped with genuine wire winding soldered at both ends and with genuine leather thumb grip. Or: High-grade pernumbuco bow with fully lined ebony frog and genuine wire winding.

Acceptable Brands:

_____	_____
Brand	No.

_____	_____
Brand	No.

Bow to be dusted and rosined, ready to play.

Bag:
Extra heavy canvas, bound edges, reinforced neck area. Zipper fasteners and protector. Bow pocket, string and music pocket. Study handle.

Acceptable Brands:

_____	_____
Brand	No.

or Approved Equal

Strings:

A— _____ _____
        Brand   No.

D— _____ _____
        Brand   No.

G— _____ _____
        Brand   No.

C— _____ _____
        Brand   No.

Adjusters for A and D strings. Instrument, bow, and bag to be expertly shop-adjusted and -assembled ready to play with bridge set up.

Cello Specifications (Junior High and Elementary), 1/2, 3/4, 4/4 Sizes

Cello Outfit:
To consist of: Instrument, bow, bag, and Rockstop endpin rest. Cake of _____ rosin, mute, tuner.

Cello:
New, imported, German- or French-made with genuine ebony purfling, fingerboard, and fittings. Fingerboard "dressed" and correctly graduated according to MENC specifications with proper curvature and string height. Fingerboard nut of correct height and properly spaced. Four solid corner blocks. Glued-in bass bar. New sound post fitted in USA. Equipped with _____ pegs. Adjustable endpin, nickel-plated steel rod and rubber tip. End pin rest. Hand-rubbed oil-finished neck, no varnish on neck handle. Soft textured varnish. To be equipped with strings listed below. Instrument must be engraved with phrase "_____ BD. OF ED." on scroll. Letters to be 3/16" to 1/4" high.

Acceptable Brands:

_____	_____
Brand	No.

Bow:
Fiberglass with correct resilience, proper weight, firmness, and balance. Guaranteed not to warp. Equipped with genuine wire winding soldered at both ends and with genuine leather thumb grip.

Acceptable Brands:

_____	_____
Brand	No.

or Approved Equal

Bow must be dusted, rosined, and ready to play.

Bag:
Extra heavy canvas, bound edges, reinforced neck area. Zipper fasteners and heavy protector. Bow pocket, string and music pocket. Sturdy handle. Flannel lined.

Acceptable Brands:

Brand	No.

Brand	No.

or Approved Equal

Strings: A— _____ _____
      Brand   No.

    D— _____ _____
      Brand   No.

    G— _____ _____
      Brand   No.

    C— _____ _____
      Brand   No.

Adjusters for A and D strings.
Instrument, bow, and bag to be expertly shop-adjusted and -assembled ready to play with bridge set up.

String Bass (High School, Junior High and Elementary), 3/4 and 1/2 Sizes

String Bass Outfit:
Fiberglass (standard 3/4 or 1/2 size), to consist of instrument, bow, bag, and rosin.

Instrument:
American-made fiberglass bass in brown violin finish. Scientifically fused construction, guaranteed against cracking or splitting. Adjustable endpin. Model: _____, or acceptable equal. Instrument to be engraved with phrase "_____ BD. OF ED."on scroll. Letters to be $\frac{3}{16}$" to $\frac{1}{4}$" high.

Bow:
Fiberglass with correct resilience and proper weight and firmness, guaranteed *not* to warp. Equipped with genuine wire winding soldered at both ends and genuine leather thumb grip. Or: high grade brazilwood with genuine ebony frog, nickel-silver trimmings. Equipped with genuine wire winding soldered at both ends and genuine leather thumb grip. Prerosined. Bow screw must turn freely. Natural hair, must be dusted and rosined ready to play. Model: Fiberglass: _____ (Buttler Model), _____ (French model), _____ (French or German), or accepted equal.

Bag:
High-grade canvas with zipper fastener and reinforced edges. _____, or accepted equal.

Strings: Four flat chromium wire strings (G, D, A, and E), wound on steel.

A— _____ _____
       Brand   No.

D— _____ _____
       Brand   No.

G— _____ _____
       Brand   No.

E— _____ _____
       Brand   No.

Rosin: Minimum 1¼ cubic inches in telescoping cardboard box.
All instruments with label inside showing model number, serial number, and date of adjustment in USA, certifying adjustment to MENC specifications. All instruments assembled, ready to play, bridge set up, instrument pretuned.

String Bass (Junior High and Elementary) 1/2, 3/4 Sizes.

See specifications for String Bass (High School).

Specification for Pianos (Console Style)

These specifications are intended to cover all labor, materials, and transportation necessary to furnish, deliver, unpack, and set up in locations as directed.

1. Overall Size

Height to be at least 44 inches.
Keyboard shall have full seven and one-third octaves (88 keys).

2. Key Bed

The piano key bed shall be of "paneled" construction, made of kiln-dried lumber and measuring at least 1⁹⁄₁₆ inches thick. Underside of key bed shall be at least 24 inches from the floor to allow proper knee room for pianist.

3. *Action*

Action to be positive and responsive to power and lightness of touch. No plastic parts are to be used. Entire action to be moth-proofed.

_____ or other approved.
   Brand
(Bidder to state name of manufacturer).

4. *Keys*

All "natural" keys shall be made of either pine or basswood, with ivory or white plastic tops and ends. If ivory, then nothing less than No. 3 grade shall be used. "Sharp" keys shall be either black plastic or ebonized hard maple.

5. *Pedals*

Solid brass. Two or three; if three, one to be a bass sustaining pedal. Height at top of pedals (area of contact) to be not more than 2¾ inches from the floor, adjusted or installed to compensate for any added height resulting from the use of large-sized casters.

6. *Case and Finish*

Case to be made of suitable hardwood, preferably oak.
Music rack: Full-length, permanently fixed at the proper angle for ease of reading.
Top: Single-piece top to be constructed with a fixture at each end to prevent opening at more than a 90 degree angle.
Finish: Blond color. Not less than two coats of good grade of lacquer or varnish, in addition to the stain and filler, and rubbed to a dull satin luster.
Sample: Showing color and quality of finish to be submitted by the successful bidder and approved before proceeding with contract.

7. *Casters*

Heavy-duty, free-running, double-wheel casters of hard rubber (or other approved). To be of double-ball-bearing swivel type (plate with spindle) construction. Bidder to state name of manufacturer.
_____ or other approved.
   Brand

8. *Bass Strings*

Bass strings to be copper-wound.

9. *Bench*

Piano bench to match piano in style and finish to be furnished and included in price submitted.

10. *Back and Pin Plank*

The piano back shall be made of at least five hardwood posts, securely anchored to the plate.
The pin plank shall be laminated with at least four sections of hard maple. It may or may not be exposed.

11. *Tuning Pins*

Piano tuning pins shall be threaded and properly sized, made of blued steel. Pickled or brass pins will not be accepted.

12. *Hammers*

Weight shall be in keeping with the scale design, but not less than 12-pound felt made of 100% top-grade wool to be used. Felt to be chemically treated to resist moths.

13. *Plate and Scale*

Plate to be what is known as full-cast plate made of gray iron with either a bronze or silver finish.
Scale to be scientifically balanced so as to produce consistently resonant and clear tone quality in all registers of the instrument.

14. *Sound Board*

The sound board to be made of close-grained, hard-texture, quartersawed mountain spruce, properly ribbed and crowned.

15. *Voicing and Tuning*

All pianos to be voiced "medium brilliant" subject to the approval of the purchaser prior to delivery.

Each piano to be tuned by the vendor's own tuner within one week after delivery, plus three additional tunings to be given at approximately 75-day intervals. Vendor to tune the pianos during school hours and to furnish the Purchasing Department with a copy of a signed service report showing the date of tuning and approval.

All such "voicing" and "tunings" to be included in the price submitted by the vendor.

16. *Locking Device*

A locking device should be installed on each piano which would lock both the top lid of the piano cabinet and the fall board in one operation. A piano lock must protect not only the piano keyboard but also the sounding board, strings, hammers, and the like found inside the piano so that the inner workings of the various parts will be protected from vandals.

17. *Tone Quality*

The piano shall possess throughout the entire range of the keyboard (scale) a musical tone of sufficient depth and power to warrant the written approval of the Music Education Department and the Piano Evaluation Committee of the Public Schools. NO PIANO SHALL BE ACCEPTED WHICH FAILS TO QUALIFY FOR THIS WRITTEN APPROVAL, EVEN THOUGH SUCH PIANO COMPLIES WITH ALL OTHER REQUIREMENTS AND MAY BE ENTERED AS THE LOWEST BID.

18. *Guarantee*

Each piano to be guaranteed as to workmanship and parts for one full year from date of delivery.

Pianos to be delivered in perfect condition, with all foregoing factors subject to the approval of the purchaser.

19. *Delivery Date*

To be indicated on bid blank in terms of the numbers of days after receipt of order.

20. Pedal linkage, rods, studs, and brackets shall be strongly built and so designed that the sustaining-pedal damper-lifter rod arm is not subjected to excessive torque to cause breakage. The total pedal linkage design shall be one that has been successfully used in _____ and has not resulted in broken damper-lifter rod arms and studs.

21. Pianos quoted to be [list acceptable instruments] or other approved.

22. VENDOR MUST SHOW IN WRITING IN SPACE PROVIDED ANY DEVIATIONS OF PRODUCT QUOTED FROM LISTED SPECIFICATIONS, AND FAILURE TO SO INDICATE IN WRITING MAY DISQUALIFY SAID VENDOR FROM FURTHER INVITATIONS TO BID. EXISTING DEVIATIONS FROM LISTED SPECIFICATIONS NOT SHOWN BY VENDOR IN WRITING ON THE BID FORM MUST BE CORRECTED AT THE VENDOR'S EXPENSE AND THE ITEM QUOTED MUST BE MADE TO COMPLY WHEN DELIVERED IN EVERY RESPECT TO THE LISTED SPECIFICATIONS.
DEVIATIONS:_____
_____
_____
_____
_____

Note: For grand pianos, be specific as to size and make.

APPENDIX I. PUBLIC RELATIONS HEADINGS

A Publication of the Dekalb County Instrumental Music Department   Vol. 1 No. 3

Hoyt F. LeCroy, Ph.D.
Coordinator of Instrumental Music

the explorer

featuring IDEAS for

The Study of Music in Grades Four, Five and Six through LISTENING to music, PERFORMING music, and COMPOSING music.

ARIZONA DEPARTMENT OF EDUCATION

Published by ARIZONA MUSIC EDUCATORS ASSOCIATION

music
for primary children

Published by : Arizona State Department of Public Instruction
Arizona Music Educators Association
APRIL, 1970   VOL. V, NO. 8

■

APPENDIX J. OUTSIDE ENGAGEMENT FORM

SUBJECT: Request for Outside Music Engagement and Confirmation
From:
To:
For:
Date:
We have received a request for music from:
For:
Date:
Time and Place:
Group and type of music required:
If you can accept, will you kindly make necessary arrangements
(transportation, etc.) directly with:

Note: Keep this half of the form. It is your confirmation, if the assignment is accepted.

(Please fill in and return promptly to the Music Education Department, division for Improvement of Instruction.)

We WILL ACCEPT this invitation. _____

We are UNABLE to accept this invitation. _____

The engagement requested by _____
                                    (Name of Organization)

will be furnished music by _____
                          (Type of Group)   (Number)

from _____ on_____
              (School)   (Date)

_____   _____
       (Director)   (Department Head)

                              _____
                                  (Principal)

                                        (Date)

Name and Address

Dear _____:

   This is to inform you that your request for music from the _____ Schools has been confirmed. Entertainment will be provided by:

School:

Type of Music:

Director:

Organization:

Date:

I would like to inform you that as a matter of long-established policy, your organization is expected to pay the costs involved in transporting the members of the performing group. [Director's name] has been asked to contact you concerning the various details pertaining to this engagement. If you do not hear from _____ within a few days, please feel free to call _____ at the school

                                         Very truly yours,

∎

APPENDIX K. SEXUAL HARASSMENT

Harassment on the basis of sex is a violation of Title VII. Indiana University does not tolerate sexual harassment of students or employees and responds to every complaint, providing proper remediation when harassment is determined.

Provisions

Employees and students have the right to raise the issue of harassment, and they are protected by faculty and staff personnel policies and student codes. Sexual harassment can be a grievous action having serious and far-reaching effects on the careers and lives of individuals. False accusations can have similar impact. Thus, the charge of sexual harassment is not to be taken lightly by a charging party, a respondent, or any other member of the university community.

Prevention is the best tool for the elimination of sexual harassment. Each dean, director, department chairperson, and/or administrative officer is responsible within his/her area of jurisdiction for the implementation, dissemination, and explanation of this policy. It is the obligation of each faculty, staff, and student member of the university to adhere to this policy.

Definition

Unwelcome sexual advances—requests for sexual favors and other verbal or physical conduct of a sexual nature—constitute sexual harassment when:

1. Submission to such conduct is made either explicitly or implicitly a term or condition of an individual's employment or education or
2. Submission to or rejection of such conduct by an individual is used as the basis for employment or academic decisions affecting such individual or
3. Such conduct has the effect of unreasonably interfering with an individual's work or academic performance or creating an intimidating, hostile, or offensive working or learning environment.

AFFIRMATIVE ACTION

Indiana University pledges itself to continue its commitment to the achievement of equal opportunity within the University and throughout American society as a whole. In employing and advancing the careers of academic appointees and staff, in admitting students, and in planning academic programs, it is not only morally but also educationally sound that decisions should focus upon the qualifications of the individual rather than upon such arbitrary considerations as race, ethnic or national origin, sex, marital status, religion or age (within the legitimate limits imposed by university regulations). Affirmative action, positive and extraordinary action, shall be undertaken to overcome the discriminatory effects of traditional policies and procedures.

(Board of Trustees, June 29, 1974)

THE HANDICAPPED

Indiana University historically has been committed to the principles of affirmative action which guarantee fair and equitable treatment of all persons, including the mentally and physically handicapped. The University provides equal employment opportunities to all employees and applicants for employment who are qualified. Handicapped persons shall be considered for employment, advancement, salary, and benefits on the basis of qualifications and capability to perform in a particular job assignment. Indiana University is committed to make a reasonable accommodation to the physical or mental limitation of an employee or applicant except where accommodation would impose an undue hardship on the University.

(Excerpt from Affirmative Action Plan for the
Handicapped, Board of Trustees, Jan. 17, 1976)

VETERANS

The University guarantees that qualified disabled veterans and veterans of the Vietnam Era shall not be refused educational opportunity, employment, or advancement for reasons unrelated to specific job performances.

(Excerpt from Affirmative Action Plan Supplement,
University Faculty Council, February 13, 1979;
Board of Trustees, March 3, 1979),

Source: The Academic Handbook (Bloomington, Ind. Dean of the Faculties, Indiana University, 1988), p. 17.

━━━━━━━━━━━━━━━━━━━━━━━━■━━━━━━━━━━━━━━━━━━━━━

APPENDIX L. THE MUSIC CODE OF ETHICS
AN AGREEMENT DEFINING THE JURISDICTIONS
OF PROFESSIONAL MUSICIANS AND SCHOOL
MUSICIANS

American Federation of Musicians
of the United States and Canada, AFL-CIO
Music Educators National Conference
American Association of School Administrators

Music educators and professional musicians alike are committed to the general acceptance of music as an essential factor in the social and cultural growth of our country. The music educators contribute to this end by fostering the study of music among the children, and by developing a greater interest in music.

This unanimity of purpose is further exemplified by the fact that a great many professional musicians are music educators, and a great many music educators are, or have been, actively engaged in the field of professional performance.

The members of high school instrumental groups—orchestras and bands of all types, including stage bands—look to the professional organization for example and inspiration. The standards of quality acquired during the education of these students is of great importance when they become active patrons of music in later life. Through their influence on sponsors, employers and program makers in demanding adequate musical performances, they have a beneficial effect upon the prestige and economic status of the professional musicians.

Since it is in the interest of the music educator to attract public attention to his attainments, not only for the main purpose of promoting the values of music education but also to enhance his position and subsequently his income, and since it is in the interest of the professional musician to create more opportunities for employment at increased remuneration, it is only natural that upon certain occasions some incidents might occur in which the interests of the members of one or the other group might be infringed upon, either from lack of forethought or lack of ethical standards among individuals.

In order to establish a clear understanding as to the limitations of the fields of professional music and music education in the United States, the following statement of policy, adopted by the Music Educators National Conference and the American Federation of Musicians, and approved by the American Association of School Administrators, is recommended to those serving in their respective fields:

I. Music Education

The field of music education, including the teaching of music and such demonstrations of music education as do not directly conflict with the interests of the professional musician, is the province of the music educator. It is the primary purpose of all the parties signatory hereto that the professional musician shall have the fullest protection in his efforts to earn his living from the playing and rendition of music; to that end it is recognized and accepted that all music to be performed under the "Code of Ethics" herein set forth is and shall be performed in connection with non-profit, non-commercial and non-competitive enterprises. Under the heading of "Music Education" should be included the following:

1. School Functions initiated by the schools as a part of a school program, whether in a school building or other building.

2. Community Functions organized in the interest of the schools strictly for educational purposes, such as those that might be originated by the Parent-Teacher Association.

3. School Exhibits prepared as part of the school district's courtesies for educational organizations or educational conventions being entertained in the district.

4. Educational Broadcasts which have the purpose of demonstrating or illustrating pupils' achievements in music study, or which represent the culmination of a period of study and rehearsal. Included in this category are local, state, regional and national school music festivals and competitions held under the auspices of schools, colleges and/or educational organizations on a non-profit basis and broadcast to acquaint the public with the results of music instruction in the schools.

5. Civic Occasions of local, state or national patriotic interest, of sufficient breadth to enlist the sympathies and cooperation of all persons, such as those held by the American Legion and Veterans of Foreign Wars in connection with their Memorial Day services in the cemeteries. It is understood that affairs of this kind may be participated in only when such participation does not in the least usurp the right and privileges of local professional musicians.

6. Benefit Performances for local charities, such as the Welfare Federations, Red Cross, hospitals, etc., when and where local professional musicians would likewise donate their services.

7. *Educational or Civic Services* that might beforehand be mutually agreed upon by the school authorities and official representatives of the local professional musicians.

8. *Student or Amateur Recordings* for study purposes made in the classroom or in connection with contests, festival or conference performances by students shall be limited to exclusive use by the students and their teachers, and not offered for general sale to the public through commercial outlets. This definition pertains only to the purpose and utilization of student or amateur recordings and not to matters concerned with copyright regulations. Compliance with copyright requirements applying to recordings of compositions not in the public domain is the responsibility of the school, college or educational organization under whose auspices the recording is made.

II. Entertainment

The field of entertainment is the province of the professional musician. Under this heading are the following:

1. *Civic parades* (where professional marching bands exist), ceremonies, expositions, community concerts and community-center activities; regattas, non-scholastic contests, festivals, athletic games, activities or celebrations and the like; national, state and county fairs (See I, Paragraphs 2 and 5 for further definition).

2. *Functions for the furtherance,* directly or indirectly, of any public or private enterprise; functions by chambers of commerce, boards of trade, and commercial clubs or associations.

3. *Any occasion that is partisan* or sectarian in character or purpose.

4. *Functions of clubs,* societies and civic or fraternal organizations.

Statements that funds are not available for the employment of professional musicians, or that if the talents of amateur musical organizations cannot be had, other musicians cannot or will not be employed, or that the amateur musicians are to play without remuneration of any kind, are all immaterial.

This code, first entered into on September 22, 1947, is a continuing agreement which shall be reviewed regularly to make it responsive to changing conditions.

Revised, March 1977. Hal. C. Davis, President, American Federation of Musicians; Robert H. Klotman, President, Music Educators National Conference; Dana Whitmer, President, American Association of School Administrators.

∎

APPENDIX M. MUSIC RULE TO TAKE EFFECT JULY 15, 1987

By Dr. Susan K. Vaughan
Music Education Specialist
Minnesota Department of Education

An Interpretation of the Music Rule

At the elementary level, the new rule provides an amendment to the current 30-to-1 classroom pupil-teacher ratio in grades K-6 or K-8. The recommended pupil-teacher ratio of 240 to 1 for teachers of music is based on the average number of students a teacher is assigned over a five-day teaching period. For example, if 400 students have music instruction 3 times per week (five days), a total of 1200 students receive instruction from that music teacher during that week. 1200 students divided by the 5 days equates to the average of 240 pupils per day per week

240 pupils per day per week is considered to be a reasonable and equitable teaching assignment by the Minnesota Music Educators Association, the Minnesota Elementary Music Educators Association, the Minnesota Department of Education, and other music organizations of the Allied Music Organization.

The new rule *requires* that a written school board policy be developed by any district that exceeds these ratios. These policies must be submitted to the State Board of Education by August 1 of each year and they must explain why the ratio is being exceeded. Although the original proposed wording of the rule included language that described the membership of the local school board committee, this portion of the proposed rule could not be retained for statutory reasons. When the development of such policies becomes essential, music educators are encouraged to advocate for representative viewpoints among committee members.

At the secondary level, the maximum pupil-teacher ratio has been 160 to 1 for all classes *except* for physical education classes and classes with performing music groups. The maximum pupil-teacher ratio in physical education was recently defined as 40 to 1.

The recommended average number of pupils per day per week for performing music groups has been defined in the new rule as 180. This number is considered to be both reasonable and equitable in retaining a balance between individualized instruction and large ensemble rehearsals.

Consistency is established at the elementary and secondary levels of the rule. At the elementary and secondary levels, the new rule *requires* that a written school board policy be developed by local school boards. And the new rule requires that the policy be submitted to the State Board of Education explaining why this ratio is being exceeded.

Contract Language for Professional Negotiations (Michigan)

The following Article was drafted by the Michigan Music Educators Association and the Michigan Education Association. It represents an answer to needs relative to music education programs and working conditions as expressed by music teachers. It is difficult to prepare guidelines which would apply to every situation. Use and adapt this to fit your conditions.

Article
Special Program Conditions

A. Vocal and Instrumental music shall remain as an integral part of the total school curriculum throughout the duration of this agreement. Budgetary and personnel expenditures in the area of music shall not be decreased below the level of expenditure reflecting a budgetary percent during the _____ school year.

B. Secondary class size shall be determined by the nature and scope of the activity reflecting the following maximum and/or minimum norms.

1. Bands   _____ pupils (maximum)
2. Choirs   _____ pupils (maximum)
3. Orchestra   _____ pupils (maximum)
4. General Music   (Shall conform to academic class load maximums.)
5. Beginning Instruments   _____ pupils (maximum)
6. Theory   _____ pupils (maximum)
7. Voice Class   _____ pupils (maximum)
8. Music Literature   _____ pupils (maximum)
9. Ensembles   _____ pupils (maximum)

C. The Elementary Vocal Music Program (K-6) shall meet in a normal classroom situation and be conducted by music specialists no less than two (2) separate days each week for periods of time no less than twenty-five minutes each. Music class size maximums shall not exceed the number of pupils assigned each elementary classroom.

The District shall provide time to take care of exceptionally talented pupils, i.e., Select Choir, opportunity for General Chorus, i.e., one chorus per grade level.

D. The Elementary Instrumental Music Program shall be conducted by instrumental specialists and will require the meeting of classes for periods of time no less than forty (40) minutes each. There will be maximums of _____ pupils in elementary instrumental classes and _____ pupils in elementary strings classes.

E. Where music instruction and responsibility which must of necessity fall outside the regular school day is an added assignment and/or expectation and is not covered in Salary Schedule "B" attached, the following teaching load adjustments shall be in effect:

F. Further concerns in the area of music that become evident during the duration of this agreement will be referred, with accompanying rationale, to the "Instructional Policies Council" for consideration, study, and subsequent recommendation for implementation following the expiration of this agreement

---

Source: Susan K. Vaughan, *Gopher Notes*, February 1987. Reprinted by permission.

INDEX